DISABILITY RESEARCH TODAY

Grouped around four central themes – illness and impairment, disabling processes, care and control, and communication and representations – this collection offers a fresh perspective on disability research, showing how theory and data can be brought together in new and exciting ways.

Disability Research Today starts by showing how engaging with issues around illness and impairment is vital to a multidisciplinary understanding of disability as a social process. The second section explores factors that affect disabled people, such as homelessness, violence and unemployment. The third section turns to social care, and how disabled people are prevented from living with independence and dignity. Finally, the last section examines how different imagery and technology impacts our understandings of disability and deafness.

Showcasing empirical work from a range of countries, including Japan, Norway, Italy, Australia, India, the UK, Turkey, Finland and Iceland, this collection shows how disability studies can be simultaneously sophisticated, accessible and policy-relevant. *Disability Research Today* is suitable for students and researchers in disability studies, sociology, social policy, social work, nursing and health studies.

Tom Shakespeare is Senior Lecturer in Medical Sociology at the Medical School of the University of East Anglia, UK. Previously he worked for the World Health Organization, where he was an author and editor of the *World Report on Disability* (WHO, 2011), and *International Perspectives on Spinal Cord Injury* (WHO, 2013). His books include *The Sexual Politics of Disability* (Cassell, 1996) and *Disability Rights and Wrongs* (Routledge 2006, 2013). He has been involved in the disability movement since 1986.

D0322260

DISABILITY RESEARCH TODAY

International perspectives

Edited by Tom Shakespeare

Routledge
Taylor & Francis Group

LONDON AND NEW YORK

First published 2015
by Routledge
2 Park Square, Milton Park, Abingdon, Oxon OX14 4RN

and by Routledge
711 Third Avenue, New York, NY 10017

Routledge is an imprint of the Taylor & Francis Group, an informa business

British Library Cataloguing-in-Publication Data
A catalogue record for this book is available from the British Library

Library of Congress Cataloging in Publication Data
Disability research today : international perspectives / edited by
Tom Shakespeare.
    p. ; cm.
Includes bibliographical references and index.
I. Shakespeare, Tom, 1966– , editor.
[DNLM: 1. Disabled Persons. 2. Social Behavior.
3. Social Environment. 4. Social Perception. HV 1568]
HV1568
362.4–dc23   2014038935

ISBN: 978-0-415-74843-8 (hbk)
ISBN: 978-0-415-74844-5 (pbk)
ISBN: 978-1-315-79657-4 (ebk)

Typeset in Bembo
by HWA Text and Data Management, London

Printed and bound in Great Britain by
TJ International Ltd, Padstow, Cornwall

To Alice

CONTENTS

FIGURES

TABLES

CONTRIBUTORS

Dikmen Bezmez is Assistant Professor of Sociology at Koç University, Istanbul. She has published work on accessibility politics in Istanbul and citizenship and disability organization in Turkey. Her present interests lie in politics of rehabilitation and care. She is co-editor of the only Disability Studies reader in Turkish, *Sakatlık Çalışmaları: Sosyal Bilimlerden Bakmak* (2011).

Kristín Björnsdóttir is an Assistant Professor of Disability Studies at the School of Education, University of Iceland. She received her doctorate in Disability Studies from the University of Iceland in 2009. Kristín's early career was centred around the education and support of disabled children and youth. Since 2003 she has been a lecturer and a researcher at the Iceland University of Education and University of Iceland. Her research interests include the feminist theory of intersectionality, inclusive education and social justice.

Fabio Corbisiero is Senior Lecturer at the Department of Social Sciences of the University of Naples Federico II. His main topic is urban sociology, with a focus on people with disabilities, the LGBT community and immigrants. He has been a Visiting Scholar at CUNY, New York (2008–2009) and a Visiting Professor at KTH Stockholm (2011) and at the Social Science Research Centre, University College Dublin (2013). His latest book is *Over the Rainbow Cities: LGBT Inclusiveness in Contemporary Europe and Italy* (McGraw-Hill, New York).

Michela Cortini is Assistant Professor of Organizational Psychology at the Department of Psychological Sciences, Humanities and Territory, University Gabriele d'Annunzio at Chieti-Pescara. She is responsible for career guidance and disability services in the Faculty of Psychology. Since 2009 she has been a member of the Executive Committee of the Italian Association of Psychology (Division of Work and Organizational Psychology). Her main research interests include organizational communication, career psychology, and mixed methods for applied psychology.

Jo Ferrie is Lecturer in Social Research Methods in the School of Social and Political Sciences at the University of Glasgow. Previously, she was based at the Strathclyde Centre for Disability Research at the University of Glasgow. After doctoral research exploring the impact of the Disability Discrimination Act on Scottish schools, she worked on over a dozen research projects examining the barriers faced by disabled people. She is co-convenor of the Equality and Diversity cluster of the Glasgow Human Rights Network and a member of the Scottish Human Rights Commission's Research Advisory Group.

Fabio Ferrucci is Professor of Sociology of Cultural Processes in the Department of Humanities, Social and Educational Sciences of the University of Molise. He was the Scientific Coordinator of UE EQUAL Program – ARTEMIS Project on work integration of disabled people (2001–2005) and of the Project "ICF and services personalization in higher education" financed by the Italian Ministry of Education and Universities (2010–2012). In 2013 he was appointed Delegate of the Rector for student services and Disability Services at the same university. His publications include the book *La disabilità come relazione sociale. Gli approcci sociologici tra natura e cultura* (Rubbettino, 2004).

Nandini Ghosh is Assistant Professor of Sociology at the Institute of Development Studies Kolkata. She teaches gender, marginalization and social movements in the M.Phil in Development Studies course at IDSK and applied sociology and sociology of marginalized communities in the Master's in Sociology course at Jadavpur University. Her research interests include gender and disability studies, disability and development and marginalization.

Jan Grue is a Postdoctoral Fellow in Sociology at the University of Oslo, and an editor of the *Scandinavian Journal of Disability Research*. His research interests are in disability studies, chronic illness, discourse analysis, rhetoric, and forms of representation. His publications include *Disability and Discourse Analysis* (Ashgate, 2015).

Halvor Hanisch holds a PhD in Sociology, as well as an MA in Comparative literature, and is currently a Postdoctoral Research Fellow at Oslo University Hospital, Norway. His research explores the different shapes and dimensions of disabling processes, including: (1) qualitative work in sociology, emphasizing the relationship between disability and different social arenas, such as private spaces, public spaces and workplaces, as well as the importance of families and other close relations; (2) quantitative research, in particular on the relationship between disability, psycho-emotional well-being and violence; (3) interpretations of representations of disability, from nineteenth-century landscape paintings and Ibsen's plays to public information material aimed at people on sick leave.

Hilde Haualand is a Social Anthropologist, who has focused most of her research on disability and Deaf related social and cultural themes. She has published in a variety of anthropology and Disability Studies journals. She currently works at the Fafo Institute for Labour and Social Research, Oslo, where she has undertaken research on marginalized groups and participation in work and social life, communication technology, disabled people in prison and LGBT persons with disabilities.

Kohji Ishihara is an Associate Professor at the Graduate School of Arts and Sciences at the University of Tokyo. His areas of research include Phenomenology, Philosophy of Psychiatry, and Philosophy of Disability. His recent publications include K. Ishihara (ed.), *The Study of Tohjisha Kenkyu*, Tokyo: Igakushoin, 2013 (Japanese), and K. Ishihara and M. Inahara (eds.), UTCP Uehiro Booklet, No.2. *Philosophy of Disability and Coexistence: Body, Narrative, and Community*, 2013 (Japanese with English abstracts).

Stephen Macdonald is a Senior Lecturer in Criminology at the University of Sunderland, where he is Programme Leader for the BSc (Hons) in Criminology. He teaches undergraduate modules in criminology and disability studies and has published widely in these areas. In recent research, he has investigated pathways into criminality for young adults with learning difficulties; examined biographical narratives of institutionalisation in the UK's 'care' system and is currently researching disability hate crimes in the Northeast of England.

James Rice is an Assistant Professor at the University of Iceland in Disability Studies and Anthropology. He received his doctorate in anthropology from Memorial University of Newfoundland, Canada, in 2007. He has since completed postdoctoral fellowships at NOVA (Norwegian Social Research) and the University of Iceland, both of which were held at the Centre for Disability Studies, University of Iceland. These projects focused on the intersection of disability with policy and everyday life in the context of the changing social welfare state.

Lucy Series is a Research Associate at Cardiff Law School. She is currently working on a research project about the Court of Protection, funded by the Nuffield Foundation. Her research interests include legal capacity, deprivation of liberty and disability rights. Prior to becoming a socio-legal researcher, she studied Psychology and Philosophy and worked in a variety of roles in health and social care settings. Lucy writes a blog about legal capacity and disability rights issues called *The Small Places*.

Tom Shakespeare is Senior Lecturer in Medical Sociology in the Medical School at the University of East Anglia. Previously he worked for the World Health Organization, where he was an author and editor of the *World Report on Disability* (WHO, 2011), and *International Perspectives on Spinal Cord Injury* (WHO, 2013). His books include *The Sexual Politics of Disability* (Cassell, 1996) and *Disability Rights and Wrongs* (Routledge 2006, 2013). He has been involved in the disability movement since 1986.

Howard Sklar is a University Lecturer in the Department of Modern Languages (English Philology Unit) at the University of Helsinki, Finland. Prior to his present assignment, Sklar worked as an Academy of Finland postdoctoral researcher. For that research project, he examined some of the ethical implications of the ways that narratives represent people with intellectual disabilities. He has published articles in *Poetics Today*, *Storyworlds*, *Partial Answers*, and the *Journal of Literary and Cultural Disability Studies*, as well as *The Art of Sympathy in Fiction: Forms of Ethical and Emotional Persuasion* (John Benjamins, 2013).

Eiríkur Smith is a doctoral candidate in Disability Studies in the Faculty of Social and Human Sciences at the University of Iceland. He has many years of experience working in disability services and has been a disability activist and advocate. His background is in Philosophy and Disability Studies. He has worked on various research projects including studies on childhood, disability and identity, critical analysis of service policies, and disability in Icelandic history. His doctoral research focuses on everyday lives in group homes.

Iva Strnadová is Senior Lecturer in Special Education at the University of New South Wales in Sydney, Australia. She is also an Honorary Senior Lecturer at the University of Sydney, Faculty of Education and Social Work, Australia. Her research aims to contribute to better understanding and the improvement of life experiences of people with disabilities. Iva's research interests include ageing with intellectual disabilities, women with intellectual disabilities, lifespan transitions of people with disabilities, well-being of people with developmental disabilities (intellectual disabilities and autism) and their families over the life span, and mobile learning for people with developmental disabilities.

Nick Watson is Professor of Disability Studies and Director of the Strathclyde Centre for Disability Research at the University of Glasgow. He has researched and written on a range of disability issues including disability theory, disability and childhood, ageing with an impairment, disability and identity, and disability policy. He is co-editor of the *Routledge Handbook of Disability Studies*.

Sibel Yardımcı is Associate Professor in Sociology at Mimar Sinan University of Fine Arts, Istanbul. She previously worked on globalization, cities, urban culture and citizenship, and nationalism. Her current interests lie in biopolitics, queer studies and disability. She has published on disability in national edited collections, journals and newspapers, as well as co-authoring an article in *Disability and Society*. She was co-editor of the Turkish Disability Studies Reader *Sakatlık Çalışmaları: Sosyal Bilimlerden Bakmak* (2011).

INTRODUCTION

Disability is both a fascinating intellectual conundrum and an urgent political issue. Despite progress with disability research, there remain considerable gaps in our knowledge and understanding of disability, and there are major problems in the ways in which society responds to the challenge of disability. This became particularly evident while we were editing the *World Report on Disability* (WHO, 2011). Disability studies can help fill knowledge gaps, and can help support policy change. To do so effectively, the discipline has to steer a sometimes tricky course. If it is too political, it loses objectivity and nuance; if it is too academic, it loses relevance and accessibility. Towards the end of the first decade of disability studies, I edited a disability reader in an attempt to define the new discipline (Shakespeare, 1998). Now, I have put together what is effectively another reader, because I wanted to provide my answer to a fundamental question: what are we doing, when we do disability studies?

To spell out a personal response to that challenge, and thinking about the UK context in particular, I want first to suggest that research in disability studies is not activism by other means. Often, as in my own life, people begin from their personal or political positions, and then move into academia to try and make sense of their experiences or increase their political impact. But academic work is not just about political expediency; it is about trying to get as close to lived reality as possible. It may be impossible for researchers ever to achieve an exact truth, but that does not mean we should abandon the pursuit of accuracy and objectivity. This explains why I am also frustrated by relativist approaches inspired by post-structuralism and post-modernism, which seem to eschew the pursuit of truth.

I think research is about finding out what we do not know, and being prepared to rethink taken-for-granted assumptions. When I read research, I want to be surprised! I don't want to read research reports which simply confirm existing prejudices, or promote ideologies. Both disability studies and progress in disability policy depend on sound empirical research and valid normative argument, not slogans, assertions or anecdotes. The hope is that many of the findings will then support political activism to improve the lives and living conditions of disabled people. Strong disability studies research should lead to better disability politics.

What about the topics for disability studies research? It sounds rather simplistic, but I suggest that disability studies enquiries can either start from the individual, or from the society: bottom up, or top down. So first, disability studies can be about understanding the experiences and views of disabled people. This might include questions such as:

- what it is like to have a particular impairment, and how it interacts with environmental factors;
- what people with different impairments think and say about their lives;
- what impact disability has on family life, on self-esteem, on participation and so on.

Second, disability studies explore society's responses to the challenges of impairment and inclusion. What does it mean to be a disabled person in a particular society? For me, the priority is to focus on environmental factors which disable or enable. This could include medical, psychological, educational, social, legal, economic, political issues, as well as the exploration of cultural representations and discourses. And, prescriptive though I undoubtedly am, I am sure that I have overlooked much valuable work which is not covered within my personal rubric, for which I apologise.

The current collection reflects both my personal and philosophical approach to disability research. Personal, because I have had the great good fortune to be invited to speak in many countries. Outside Britain, North America and the Nordic countries, disability studies is often in its infancy, and I have sometimes been asked to support the development of the discipline, for example in countries such as Australia, the Netherlands, Finland, France, Italy and Turkey. As a result of these visits, I have had the great pleasure of meeting scholars, young and old, who have become fascinated by disability and who are developing new research projects, together with activists and advocates who want to collaborate with academics. These fruitful contacts explain why this book draws on research from a broader selection of settings than is usual. I hope that the results will broaden our understandings of what disability entails, and the responses to it.

The collection is philosophical, because the selection of chapters reflects my intellectual biases and my preferences for what disability studies should be. In previous work (Shakespeare, 2013), I distinguished three dominant approaches in disability studies. The first approach could be called materialist, epitomised by the work of Mike Oliver and Colin Barnes. This work has the virtues of being politically engaged and not overly theoretical, but the vices of being reductionist and overly simplistic, in my opinion. The second approach could be called constructionist, epitomised by the work of Dan Goodley or Margrit Shildrick, an approach which is often described as Critical Disability Studies, although I would include here many American scholars, who often describe their approach as cultural disability studies. This work has the virtues of being more sophisticated and diverse, but often has the vices of being overly theoretical and lacking in political utility (Vehmas and Watson, 2014). Third, I described a broadly Critical Realist approach, as followed by Nick Watson, myself and others. The authors in the current collection represent diverse epistemological positions, but I have been biased towards those espousing the third approach.

I feel that the firm distinction between 'medical model' and 'social model' perspectives, often drawn in UK disability studies of the materialist type, is too crude. As I have written elsewhere (Shakespeare, 2013), I understand disability to be a complex, diverse and above all multi-factorial phenomenon. Medical, psychological, social, cultural and political levels of explanation are all relevant. The majority of these chapters do not mention the terms 'medical model' or 'social model', but instead adopt this more nuanced understanding. However, this does not mean that the work is apolitical. Although all of these authors are aspiring to produce high quality academic scholarship, they are doing so from an engaged position, with the ultimate goal of helping improve the lives of disabled people.

Almost all these chapters draw on empirical research, rather than theory alone, and this was a deliberate move. There has been an explosion of publications in disability studies, but it is regrettable that the balance has been distorted in favour of theoretical work. In my view, theory is not an end in itself, but should be a means to a greater end, which is understanding. I would rather start by trying to find out things about the lives of disabled people and the disabling barriers that they face, and then draw on theory, where required, to explain the patterns and relationships which are uncovered. As with the idea of Ockham's razor, this approach has the virtue of parsimony. As Einstein said, 'Make things as simple as possible. But not simpler'. Another important outcome is that the results are likely to be more accessible to non-academic readers.

The book covers broad ground, because disability itself is very diverse. I was conscious that the disability category is generally taken to include people with sensory conditions like hearing and sight loss, as well as people with chronic illness and physical impairments, people with intellectual impairments, and people with mental health conditions, and I wanted to try and include research covering this range of experience. Again, the lives of disabled people encompass health, education and employment, social care, as well as wider participation in society and culture. Of course, with only fourteen chapters and 100,000 words to play with, it is impossible to cover all the topics, but I have tried to include work discussing some of the most important issues. Above all, it is work that is of particular interest to me personally – for example, I think the question of violence against disabled people urgently requires both analysis and action.

The volume opens with three chapters which engage with the experience of illness and impairment. Bezmez and Yardımcı report on their fieldwork in a Turkish rehabilitation hospital, work I was delighted to include because since spending time in rehabilitation myself I have realised how important and neglected a topic this is. Ferrie and Watson draw on research with people with motor neurone disease, a condition which has not previously been discussed within disability studies. It might be thought that the topic belongs in medical sociology. Yet it seems to me clear that people with MND are disabled, and that we need to hear all voices, and learn from the complex ways that health conditions and barriers intersect in specific instances. As with the first chapter, their work foregrounds the role of the family, another issue that requires deeper discussion. Finally, Ishihara's chapter shows how user involvement in mental health can entail users studying their own mental health conditions, with therapeutic benefits. I was particularly interested in the way that this Japanese innovation steers a middle course between psychiatry and the radical anti-psychiatry movement that often opposes it.

This first cluster is followed by four chapters which discuss the processes of disablement and enablement, using a range of methodologies. One could perhaps say that these were papers about 'disabling barriers', but this would not capture the complexity. Corbisiero uses social network analysis to explore how the ICF conceptualisation of disability has been operationalised in job placement strategies for disabled people in Italy. Ghosh shares her qualitative research with disabled women in India, highlighting the role that violence plays in their lives. Hanisch then helps us re-conceptualise violence as an over-arching factor in our understanding of disability. Finally, Macdonald offers an analysis of quantitative data to draw out some of the factors underlying the over-representation of people with dyslexia within the UK homeless population.

In the third section, I group together a set of chapters which explore common themes of care and control. Series offers a detailed legal analysis of mental capacity as it relates to sexuality. Strnadová explores how older women with learning difficulties in Czech Republic and Australia struggle for control over their lives through qualitative interviews. Smith and colleagues take us to Iceland, and offer two case studies which evidence the barriers which disabled people face in accessing the new system of direct payments for personal assistants.

The final section explores communication and representation. Ferrucci and Cortini explore metaphors deployed in discussions of disabled people's participation in Higher Education in Italy. Haualand's chapter on video interpreting reflects her anthropological training, uncovering the subtleties in how technologies enable or constrain Deaf people in different countries. Grue questions some positive images of disability, through analysis of popular TV shows. Finally, Sklar offers a fascinating discussion of representations of learning difficulties in fiction.

This collection epitomises the diversity of disciplines, methodologies and topics which are typical of contemporary disability studies. To me, it does not greatly matter whether a disability studies researcher is disabled or non-disabled. I do want to see disabled people progress in the academy, and develop careers in different fields, including disability research, and more should be done to support this and to remove barriers. And I do want to see disability researchers listen carefully to what disabled people say about their lives, and consult and involve service users in their studies. When those without impairments theorise in ways that can potentially minimise the physicality of disability, then I have concerns. But I still think that good disability research has been and can be done by both disabled and non-disabled people, as with the contributors to this volume. To me, it was not important to ask everyone about their impairments, because my priority has been to select good contributors and then work with them to achieve the best chapter possible.

I hope this book will inspire students and researchers who are interested in doing disability research, by showing the wealth of approaches they can adopt. By showcasing original research, I hope that the book will contribute to placing disability studies on a stronger empirical footing. And very importantly, I hope that policy-makers will reflect on what can be done to reduce violence; to promote participation in higher education; to get disabled people into universities and jobs; and above all, to increase control and quality of life for disabled people who depend on social care.

I am very grateful to all the colleagues who have invited me to speak across the world and to their institutions for funding my visits; to the contributors who agreed to participate in this project; to Routledge for enabling me to bring together another edited collection. I am particularly grateful to Lucy Jones, one of Britain's leading painters, for allowing us to use one of her artworks. Finally, thanks are due to Alice, for her continuing love and support.

References

Shakespeare, T. (ed.) (1998) *The Disability Reader: social science perspectives*, London, Continuum.

Shakespeare, T. (2013) *Disability Rights and Wrongs Revisited*, London, Routledge.

Vehmas, S. and Watson, N. (2014) Moral wrongs, disadvantages, and disability: a critique of Critical Disability Studies, *Disability and Society* 29:4, 638–650, DOI: 10.1080/09687599.2013.831751.

WHO (2011) *World Report on Disability*, Geneva, World Health Organization.

PART I
Illness and impairment

1

SOCIAL EXPERIENCES OF PHYSICAL REHABILITATION

The role of the family

Dikmen Bezmez and Sibel Yardımcı

Introduction

This chapter is part of a larger ethnographic study conducted in one of the leading Turkish rehabilitation hospitals in Istanbul during 2013 to explore social constructions of disability and the experiences of disabled people themselves with these constructions. The fieldwork highlighted the role of the family in rehabilitation and in the social construction of disability during rehabilitation, which is the main focus of this chapter.

Semi-structured interviews were conducted with 42 people including seven doctors, two nurses, two physiotherapists, one social worker, one non-medical personnel, 20 patients staying in the hospital, and nine former patients who now live in their homes: seven of these 29 disabled people were women. The interviewees were all more than 20 years old and had acquired physical disabilities through traumatic injury or illnesses. For the sake of anonymity, we use numbers for participants, together with the letters D for the doctors, PT for physiotherapists, N for nurses, SW for social workers and P for current and former patients.

The literature on the family and disability often concentrates on the difficulties families have to cope with when raising disabled children (Dowling and Dolan 2001; Al-Krewani *et al.* 2011; Stevens 2010; Lowell and Mason 2012; Ryan and Runswick-Cole 2008) and their coping mechanisms (Rao 2001; Blum 2007; Avery 1999). Discussions of the family as an agent actively participating in the social construction of disability during rehabilitation are rare. Yet in Turkey, the health care system generally and physical rehabilitation specifically are inherently based on the assumption that the patient/disabled person enters the system with a carer (*refakatçi*), who is often a family member. The presence of the *refakatçi* is such a given that in several interviews the medical personnel (interviews with

D1, D2, PT1, PT2) mentioned the family as one of the prime determinants of 'success' in rehabilitation. Family members' taken-for-granted responsibilities include continuing the exercises learnt from the physical therapist, supplying medication, promoting hygiene, and psychological support. Rehabilitation, as a concept and as a process, assumes the presence of the family to such an extent that any consideration of social construction of disability needs to put the family's role centre stage. This chapter will do just that, by engaging with questions such as: What is the role that families play in the social construction of disability during rehabilitation? How do disabled people experience such constructions? Do they internalize/negotiate/resist? How does family presence affect their lives in the long run, years after the initial rehabilitation?

This chapter combines a multiplicity of theoretical approaches to disability. Disability studies began with the shift from a medical model to a social model, based on the dichotomy between (social) disability and (physical) impairment. Next, this dichotomy was rejected and impairment itself was conceived as a socially constructed category (Tremain 2005; Davis 2006). Finally, it was argued that the social constructionist approach had been ignoring the reality of the body (Siebers 2006), the importance of subjective experience of living with a disability and the agency of disabled people (Hughes 2005). Consequently, emphasis was drawn on the concepts such as embodiment and everyday life (Moser 2005; Watson 2002; Zitzelsberger 2005) and phenomenological approaches (Hughes 2005): all of these studies put the subjective lived experience of disability centre stage. Finally, many argued for a multiplicity approach, combining analyses of social structures with processes of social construction and the everyday experience of living with disability (Thomas 2007; Turner 1995; Siebers 2008; Gareth 2005; Shakespeare 2006; Papadimitriou 2008; Zitzelsberger 2005). This chapter applies a similar approach by analysing both processes of social construction of disability and disabled people's experiences with such constructions: we refrain from arguing that families are either 'good' or 'bad'. Different disability constructions can come to the fore at different stages of rehabilitation and such constructions are not always mutually exclusive: they can take place concomitantly. The chapter opens with a review of the literature on social construction of disability and embodiment in rehabilitation, as well as family and disability. Next, we elaborate on the discourses summarized above using numerous examples from the field, before drawing some conclusions.

Rehabilitation, family and embodiment

An overview of the disability studies literature on encounters with health and rehabilitation services highlights three main categories of disability construction: the disabled body is constructed as dependent, docile and subservient (Thomas 2001; Sullivan 2005); as invested with the possibility of a 'second chance' to 'fit back' into society (Barnes and Mercer 2003: 82) and as a 'self-reliant client' (Abberley 2004), in the sense that it should take responsibility in its 'treatment'.

The literature also highlights the roles that disabling ideologies play in facilita such constructions (Swain and French 2008) such as the 'personal tragedy approach (Hughes 1999), the conception of the disabled body as some sort of an 'abnormality' in need of 'fixation' (Thomas 2001) and as an 'economic burden' (Berger 2005).

Although there are few discussions of the role of the family in rehabilitation, there is work on the relationship between the family member and the disabled person. For example, there is work that explores how mothers become representatives of disabling ideologies: in a social context where disability is often devalued, mothers might seek to increase their own and their disabled child's social value by positioning themselves as 'good mothers', who are 'remarkable' caretakers (Traustadottir 1991; Todd and Jones 2003; McKeever and Miller 2004; Knight 2013; McLaughlin and Goodley 2008). Similarly, Blum refers to work which argues that 'to defend their valor, mothers reinforce the 'natural' gendering of care' (Litt 2004; Malacrida 2003; Singh 2004; Blum 2007). This can lead to overprotection and a reinforcement of relationships of dependence. Second, parents, absorbing medical language due to their frequent encounters with health professionals, could internalize and promote a medical approach to disability at home (Avery 1999), where concepts of 'normalcy' (Avery 1999; Darling 2003) or 'dependency' (Veck 2002) might dominate their approach to their children. Another axis in this literature highlights the 'mother-blaming' tendency in some of the arguments above and draws attention to some of the structural factors that could underlie such relationships.[1] Here, factors such as the role of the 'heightened public stinginess' in exacerbating ideas of 'economic burden' (Blum 2007: 203) and thus the social devaluation of the disabled body, the isolation and discriminatory attitudes that mothers experience along with their disabled children (Blum 2007; Ryan and Runswick-Cole 2008: 202) are highlighted and a need for caution in approaches to mothering a disabled child is underlined.

The embodiment literature explores the mechanisms through which disabled people try to resituate themselves in their social setting: first, disabled people re-evaluate and renegotiate their interests and abilities in the past in their effort of embodiment (Papadimitriou 2008: 699). They 'redefine, re-examine or modify past experiences, abilities, lifestyles and habits in their efforts towards re-embodiment' (ibid: 691). Second, there is also a constant negotiation with the outside world, in the sense that the social forces within which the disabled person finds herself/himself determine the process of embodiment significantly (Thomas 1999: 48; Watson 2002: 519). Papadimitriou calls this a 'situated accomplishment' (ibid.: 697, 699). Whether workplaces, public spaces are accessible (ibid.: 701), whether the status of being a 'wheelchair user' is socially devaluing (ibid.: 699), whether one is exposed to disability activism (Thomas 1999: 53) will all have an effect on the embodiment process.

Others have looked at the outcome of the embodiment process, where normality appears as a key dimension: Moser (2005) explains this through

who emphasized 'that he is a competent, normal subject'
talks about a 'disembodied' (2002: 515) disabled identity,
airment, but so that any difference between disabled/non-
l as an outcome of 'discrimination and prejudice' rather
d.: 514). Similarly, Swain and Cameron explain how some
mpairments try to pass as non-disabled (1999: 76) and thus
social identity' (ibid: 75) in order to avoid the perceived
stigma.

Another such framework through which the embodied experience of
disability is explained relates to the concept of 'fate' (Moser 2005: 678–681).
Through Siv's example, Moser explains how Siv 'enacts disability ... as a fate to be
accepted and lived with' (2005: 679) and continues with a discussion on the kind
of subject this acceptance of disability can lead to – e.g. this position's potential
relation with the concept of 'normality' and the way it works in the orderings
of everyday practice. A different form of acceptance is found when Watson
(2002) refers to a process of 'the reconstruction of normality in constructions
of self-identity' (ibid.: 519). Accordingly disabled people 'challenge the social
construction of what it is to be normal' (ibid.: 519) and in people's everyday
experience of embodiment, they perceive themselves as both different and
normal, because 'this difference has little or no consequence' (ibid.: 520).

Alternatively, Watson refers to some disabled people – all women (ibid.: 522) –
who describe themselves in negative terms. Watson describes a process where self-
identity is being damaged, because people 'attribute blame to the self for things
that are the responsibility of others...' (ibid.: 523), like the tendency to blame
one's disability in the case of an inaccessible building instead of the architect.
Watson quotes an informant saying: 'I think that I look terrible ...' (ibid.: 522) and
another stating: 'Well, you are so much trouble to people' (ibid.: 523).

Finally, there is the category called 'passion' by Moser (2005, 681), where
the author refers to those embodiment processes, in which disabled people are
described as 'being immersed in intimate interaction ..., of being passionately
taken and carried away by it and the bodily kick and transformation that comes
with it' (ibid.: 682). Moser exemplifies this experience by Vidar, one of her
informants, who is an active performer of downhill wheelchair racing. She
refers to both a kind of 'agency and control' delegated to the body (ibid.: 682)
and yet also a process of being taken away by passion.

Situating the family in the context of rehabilitation:
the Turkish example

In Turkey, we found that the family is not only the last resort to which a person
turns when s/he discovers s/he has become disabled, but also a major stakeholder
in rehabilitation processes, and quite generally, the determining actor of her/his
remaining lifetime. This is clearly expressed in one interviewee's statement that
'when I first had the accident, what I was most scared of was the thought that

my wife might leave me' (P1), and another's description of how life unf
after disablement:

> If the general public is not conscious and supportive, the family is an
> incredible support. Its love, respect and support mean everything to you.
> You live through and get over this tragedy with them [...]. You help
> them overcome this trauma, and they help you. Without this [help] life
> would be intolerable. I know many cases, where people said they did not
> love their families, they did want to continue without them, and life has
> become very very difficult.
>
> (P2)

Especially due to lack of investment in this hospital and the lack of medical
personnel (especially physiotherapists) and cleaning staff, *refakatçis* have to
undertake a range of responsibilities, from helping in physiotherapy exercises
through cleaning rooms to giving psychological support. Except a few cases where
paid *refakatçis* are present, spouses (P1, P3, P4, P5, P6, P7), siblings (P8, P9, P10,
P11), mothers (P2, P12, P13, P14), children (P15, P16), nephews (P18), or a
combination of those (P19) constitute the primary support for a person who has
become disabled. Many interviewees made clear that 'if they had made such an
improvement, this was due to their spouse's help' (for example, P19). The role
of the family does not end at the hospital however, and the majority of disabled
people continue to live with their families, with a very limited social life, leading
an interviewee to say, 'there is no one left in my life except my wife' (P5). For
example, in Turkey, it is the whole family who are assessed for welfare benefits, not
the individual (Yılmaz 2011). As a result, the family becomes a key determinant
of how a disabled person experiences embodiment during and after rehabilitation.

Rehabilitation: a shared experience

The support of family members as *refakatçis* is so widespread and the organization
of hospital life and treatment procedure are so firmly based on the family that
rehabilitation may be described as an experience shared by the patient and
the family. There are major gender differences: if a wife becomes disabled,
in 70–80 per cent of the cases, the husband does not perform the care-giving
tasks, but often either arranges a paid attendant or leaves his wife. Conversely,
a wife rearranges her life in accordance with her disabled husband's needs. If
the newly disabled person is a child, then it is usually the mother who assumes
the duties (SW1).

As one interviewee states, 'his spouse has been through everything with him'
(P6), and another describes, 'you live there with your *refakatçi*' (P2). Finally a
third one says, 'rehabilitation is mutual, between you and your *refakatçi*' (P8). It
may be interesting to note how families' interventions are not informal, casual
or coincidental but have become, maybe over the years, a principal dimension

pital. Comments from a doctor and then a nurse may help

d her/his friends and relatives are instructed and trained
jectives are set, walking exercises assigned. In addition,
ay spend her/his time, what s/he can do in daily life – such
ssed.

(D3)

You cannot only think about the patient, you should also think about the family. The family does not know what to do with the patient. We provide help as much as we can, and discharge the patient only after having the family's awareness raised.

(N1)

Awareness-raising is especially important, since the negative and exclusionary attitudes surrounding the issue of disability in Turkey seem to affect the family as much as the patient. The fact that almost everyone we interviewed insistently referred to a 'patient' may be taken as a sign of this. The disabled person is a patient, and remains so until one day s/he starts walking. Until then her/his life is paused; life decisions are suspended and taken by the family. This is not easy however. It means that the family will not only become stigmatized itself, but also undertake the education of a child with disability who will probably be rejected by many schools, or economically support an adult with a disability who will be denied any proper job; and in both cases, assume physical and psychological care. A quotation from the mother of a disabled child in an online forum on a popular disability web site for disabled people,[2] exemplifies how families feel smashed under this burden:

I have a daughter with disability, she is 14 years old. We discovered the condition when she was 1. For 13 years, I have had a child, who is not growing up. She is depending on me in all sorts of way. She cannot talk – I talk for both of us. She cannot walk – it is me, who proudly stand behind her wheelchair. There are so many examples to give. You would guess, it is my responsibility, as a mother to provide her self-care. I hope I would not be misunderstood, I am not complaining … I am only begging God not to let her survive me. If I had known she would be disabled, considering what I am going through now, yes I would have ended my pregnancy.

(Belgin, 26.03. 2013)

As this quotation highlights, disability is a condition whose hardships are shared as much by the family as the person herself/himself, in a social-political-legal context where the economic, psychological and social support of disabled people fall almost entirely on the shoulders of the families.

This situation is made worse by the fact that the physical conditions of the hospital are very poor. Most of the patients stay in three or six-bedded rooms, and their *refakatçis* share the same room, with a chair-bed for each *refakatçi*, meaning that up to 12 people have to spend day and night within this very limited space. Since daily life is organized as in an ordinary hospital, meals are served very early and *refakatçis* are expected to conform to early waking and sleeping hours. Aside from a garden, the hospital offers very little in terms of leisure activities, which is a real problem for *refakatçis*, especially young ones, who spend months there. Besides, as an interviewee explains patients may tend to treat *refakatçis* badly, sometimes lash out, yell at them 'because they are dependent on them. As to them, they are always gentle, never respond, or shout back, because they love us. We are relatives at the end' (P8), but the period is long, and 'both parties get tired of each other' (P2). As a physiotherapist complains, '*refakatçis* are sometimes harder to deal with. They are aggressive, reluctant to communicate, and have very high expectations. Always the same question: 'When s/he is going to walk?'' (PT2). This is why the psychologist we interviewed explained that she tried to consult both the patients and the *refakatçis*, who are also affected by depression, or do not know how to deal with this new situation (PS1). This psychological help seems especially important as all parties we talked to, from doctors, through nurses, to patients, insisted that the support of the family was the key factor in a successful rehabilitation:

> It is very important for us to understand each other both with the patient and her/his close family and friends. The latter is the key, because the patient is psychologically feeble. People close to her/him would know the patient much better than us, understand her/his reactions, and should therefore cooperate with us. If they join the patient in her/his denial, it is even harder for us.
>
> (D2)

> You know how education is like a trivet: the school, teachers and the family. It is the same here. Doctors are like teachers, but your family is also like the school here – all should come together [for a good education or successful rehabilitation].
>
> (P19)

Multiple responsibilities of Refakatçis and family members

As we have tried to summarize, the roles played by the *refakatçis* in the hospital, and the family afterwards, are multiple and diverse. Some of these roles are literally 'medical', others have more psychological or social qualities, or consist of complementing or supplementing the basic services (such as hygiene) provided by the hospital. Accordingly, they may be discussed under three headings:

Refakatçis as therapists, physiotherapists and nurses: It is more than common to see *refakatçis* and other family members help patients do physiotherapy exercises. The former are actually trained and instructed on how to do this, as physiotherapists are few and thus only capable of assisting the patients in a limited period of time (N1, N2). Some of these exercises have the objective of strengthening the muscles; others are designed to prevent other complications, such as helping promote digestion, or helping maintain flexibility. *Refakatçis* are also taught how to insert catheters and how to place the patient in the bed so that s/he does not have bedsores (N2). Finally aphasia rehabilitation is also carried out by the family.

As almost all interviewees attest, these duties are immediately or eventually assumed by *refakatçis*, most often by mothers (P12, P14) or spouses (P1, P3, P13). It is interesting to note how consistently *refakatçis* describe the physiotherapy from a first-person plural perspective, pointing not only to the sharing of experience but sometimes to a blurring of the line which separates the patient from the family: 'Two months have passed since the operation, we are doing our exercises, waiting' says a spouse, whose husband admits that 'his wife is his biggest chance' (P3). She says that she is completely 'indexed' to her husband (P3's spouse). This dedication and effort is so remarkable that it leads quite often to specialization from the part of the *refakatçis* – as in the cases of a mother who states that 'what she does is ten times better than private physiotherapy centers' (P13's mother), and a patient whose father-in-law, himself looking after his own father, has become over time more skilled than physiotherapists (P1).

Refakatçis as a source of psychological support and main agents of socialization: The second main role that families play in the rehabilitation process is more of a psychological quality. First of all, the family is almost always a last resort when everything seems destroyed, a close and valuable support to cling to for a person who finds herself/himself disabled. As an interviewee states, 'I clung to my brothers and sisters, [like] others do to their children' (P8). Second, family members also constitute the concrete and effective link to life for a person affected by disability. Again as P8 attests, 'when my sister was going away, I immediately started to wait for her to come back, as I was incapable of doing whatsoever by myself. I felt abandoned'. Third, *refakatçis* are also important as they start the socialization of a newcomer. By talking to doctors, nurses, physiotherapists and other patients and *refakatçis*, they start to build an intra-hospital network of acquaintances and friends, which they support and sustain through mutual help, casual chats and long afternoons spent in the garden, or in the hall, over cups of coffee and tea. Most see other patients 'as their own brothers' (P11's sister), love them, and take care of them if necessary (P2). After all, this is a friendship, which develops among people who 'share intimate moments and a similar fate (P2)'.

Refakatçis as providers of daily necessities: Finally families and other *refakatçis* are determining figures in the daily life in the hospital, as they provide most of the daily necessities. They gather information about various types of medicine, provide them when necessary; bring, cook, order and sometimes share food;

clean the rooms, beds and toilets; help patients wash their hands, brush their teeth and hair, or have a bath. Most of these services are in fact provided by the hospital, but this provision remains at a basic level, and most families who spend enormous times in the hospital assume a complementary/supplementary role either voluntarily, or by sheer necessity. As such, they try to make the hospital, which has now become a temporary home, more agreeable both for themselves and their patients.

The key role that the family starts to play in the hospital continues afterwards, with very little alteration. The majority of disabled people in Turkey remain dependent on their family economically and otherwise. Families keep giving and taking care, keeping track of medicines, bladder and bowel problems, helping the disabled person move within the house, or through terribly inaccessible cities (sometimes carrying her/him up and down stairs to a fifth-floor flat, in a building without a lift), and thus producing and reproducing this dependence whether involuntarily, or by necessity. As a result, their homes become for disabled people, and in more severe cases for their carers, a sort of confinement, one refrains from returning:

> One who is discharged from GATA [another rehabilitation hospital] wants to come here, once discharged from here s/he would go to the new rehabilitation centre in Nevşehir. No one wants to go home.
>
> (D4)

This reluctance is not only due to an unfading hope of walking again, but also to the fact that the home has become a sort of prison. 'The ones who can make room in their life for this new condition can adapt to it, others have only a computer – if they do … or a window to connect to life' (SW1). As another interviewee describes, 'you feel good at hospital, because you do not feel disabled. At home, especially because your family is hardly prepared, you are straightaway taken to bed. You are confined at home and free at the hospital' (P20). This of course triggers a new fear. Almost everyone in the hospital starts to consider her/his future (P20) and the conditions of her/his survival become a poignant issue:

> We cannot expect our parents to be here, with us, to take care of us for our whole life. So the more I do now, the better it is for me. I have a brother; we will send him to Scotland for higher education. Possibly he will be taking care of me in the future.
>
> (P13)

Of course there are exceptions. One of our interviewees claimed:

> Being at home is different. I eat at [the] dinner table, not in bed. The loved ones are all around me. I move more frequently. Here you receive

physiotherapy but at the end you are lonely. It is different at home. You miss home.

(P19)

Yet this statement is rather an exception. Most of the time, patients claim to be happier in the hospital than in their homes.

Social constructions of disability by the family

As we have described, the relationship between a disabled person and her/his family quickly becomes one of mutual dependence, most often with bitter overtones. A doctor who compares this situation to 'the West', states that,

> There, people live by themselves, not in a clan as it is here. Their wives or husbands do not turn into caregivers; if they stay with them, it is as partners, maintaining their love and sex lives. In our society the family becomes the [primary] caregiver, and if relationships were not very brilliant before – which is the case most often, it becomes hellish and people run away. More decent men look after their wives but do get a second one; women run away if possible, if not, they stay with husbands, but possibly create themselves other rooms of maneuver.

(D4)

This is the context where a person reconstructs her/his identity around a newly acquired disability. It seems that this endeavour is affected and shaped by four interrelated processes that do not necessarily exclude each other. These are (1) the loss of a separate individuality, the (2) infantilization and (3) devaluation of the disabled person, (4) families' constant referring to her/him as a tireless 'crusader' (Darling 2003) pushing to carry on.

Loss of separate individuality: The rupture that marks one's life upon disablement comes most of the time with a gradual and eventual loss of a separate individuality. As an interviewee puts plainly,

> Do you think that one who becomes disabled and comes to the hospital may establish a life for herself/himself? It is the family who does this in Turkey. A disabled person dies, when her/his family dies, due to lack of proper care. I've seen that many times in the media. Such a person is, for our society, someone who should stay at home and keep living with the few coppers the state gives her/him. Our choices are made by our families, who most probably decide where we should live ...

(P21)

This 'we' is not only composed of disabled people, but also includes the family members who assume the responsibility of living with the person in question. As it was also exemplified above, this process eventually leads to a blurring of the boundaries between the disabled person and her/his most close *refakatçi*(s). The first-person plural narrative of most *refakatçi*s (P3's spouse, P13's mother) attests to this development, which in reality goes against the grain: whereas rehabilitation has the primary objective of making the disabled person independent (D5), the procedure and conditions here make and keep her/him almost completely dependent on others. This also results in the loss of intimate spaces and moments:

> One day I asked myself: Is this disability? Will I not be able to stay alone? I won't be able to day dream; I won't ever have a girlfriend anymore?
>
> (P20)

In another interview, it felt like the mother of the interviewee, who was the prime caregiver of her quadriplegic son of 26 years, was not even considering leaving us alone with her son and she was often responding to the questions before her son did (P13's mother).

Infantilization: This loss of individuality goes hand in hand with the infantilization of the disabled person. This is a general inclination, shared by almost everyone from doctors to families and society in general, and promoted both by a medical approach to disability, and widespread understandings about disability as loss of sexual function, incapacity to work, and incompetence in almost everything.

> I do describe the procedure to the family. [I say] your patient is like a child, like a baby. S/he would first move within the bed, then start sitting, eventually, when her/his muscles grow stronger, stand on the parallel bars, but cannot walk, and then only maybe later walk.
>
> (D5)

> They [spouses] behave as if they are their mothers, and this pleases them. Families treat them as kids, as if they have a mental problem.
>
> (D4)

This process of infantilization becomes also visible in some mothers' efforts to position themselves as 'good mothers' and 'remarkable caregivers' as this was mentioned in our literature review. In this regard, P13's mother presented herself as one such caregiver, only to be approved by her son.

Devaluation: As exemplified in many cases, disability comes also with a sort of devaluation of the person attended by it. As in the case of the husband-*refakatçi* who intimidated his wife with an innuendo about getting divorced (P22's husband), disablement means for almost everyone a loss of status, but especially for women. This again stems from the belief that disability means loss of sexual function, incapacity to work, and incompetence in almost everything. This rather extended quote from a *refakatçi* is a clear evidence of this:

[the patient] has thought he could live like a normal person, as if he could walk – he had a partner, he started seeing her as if he was healthy. But he had to admit that he was not ... They [patients] cannot think – as we do – hundred percent capacity, but they are not aware of that either. Normally if I tell ... [the patient] this, he would react badly, but this is how it is. That's why we should treat them normally, but also make them are aware of their illnesses.

(P23's *refakatçi*, friend)

Keeping the struggle alive: A fourth attitude that disabled people face is families' tendency to approach the rehabilitation process and its aftermath as a continuous, possibly never-ending, struggle. This tendency does not necessarily exclude the former three, but on the contrary complements them in terms of the underlying assumption that disability means a kind of deficiency that should be either overcome or compensated. This struggle thus can only end when the state of 'normality' is reached. Till then, the disabled person is pushed to be a 'warrior', exercising continuously, backed by modern and alternative medicine (a diet rich in walnuts, or wrapping a donkey's intestines around the feet (P2)). It is believed that s/he could walk if firm and determined enough, or that one day, technological developments would make this possible. Almost every patient and attendant echoed the following quote:

What matters is that you are determined in your mind. Even if the doctor had stated that I was not going to walk again, I would have continued to exercise.

(P14, who came paralysed to the hospital and could walk again at the end of the rehabilitation process)

Considering the three main categories of disability construction referred to above, it is easy to detect that families' disability constructions in Turkey happen to draw upon the first two approaches, promoting first, the disabled body as dependent, docile and subservient, and second, somehow invested with the possibility of a second chance. Whereas the infantilization and devaluation of the disabled person assumes the dependence of his/her body, the crusader approach is the expression of a deeper belief that the person in question may have indeed a second chance of getting back to normal life. The third construction referred to above – namely the disabled person as a self-reliant client, is translated here into the crusader approach, where the patient is perceived as someone who could walk only if s/he wanted to and worked hard enough.

As it was hinted above, these four attitudes are received, appropriated and adopted by disabled people themselves, in various ways sometimes changing over time. Again, these responses are not excluding each other, and most often, it is a combination that a disabled person puts into effect in shaping and reshaping her/his new life and process of embodiment.

Processes of embodiment

Disabled people's embodiment processes and experiences with such constructions can be summarized under four headings:

Internalization of disabling ideologies

One may easily detect that the most common tendency is to internalize the
disabling ideologies of 'personal tragedy', 'abnormality', and 'economic burden'.

> You piss your pants. Who else would take care of you except your family?
> Who would accept you like this?
>
> (P12)

This seems to be a mirror image of the processes of infantilization and
devaluation that we tried to explain above, but it is also partially related to the
fact that most disabled people remain economically dependent on their families,
because they are not offered proper jobs that may help them establish a separate
life. As a result, many interviewees believed a disabled body to be incapable, or
a disabled life not worth living (P3, P6, P14, P20).[3]

> It is not that I am revolting [against God's wish], but it is better to die than
> to live like this.
>
> (P6)

Embracing the crusader approach

A second response that can be considered in this context is the internalization of
the 'crusader' image. In a sense, this is also the internalization of the disabling
ideology, coupled with a counter-undertaking: whereas in the first case, disabled
people are more or less withdrawn from public life and inured to that, in the
second, they keep working hard with the hope of walking again – as once again,
a life worth living is one where walking is possible.

> Patients think that exercising is to stimulate nerves, whereas it is more
> to protect the other organs, prevent calcification etc. [...] Medically
> you know that only one of 99 [patients] would be walking but it is your
> irrational part that steps in, you think that it is going to be you. Because
> our whole perception is based on able-bodiedness.
>
> (P20)

This is especially true for newly disabled people, who do not want to be
discharged from the hospital. If they are, they try other rehabilitation hospitals
or centres. Some continue to believe that they would walk even after years, and
resist adapting their homes, and lives to this new situation (like P24, who after

ten years of disability has not had a lift installed in her house). It is as if their lives have paused, until they walk again. Till then they keep exercising with the help of their families, not only to prevent other complications, but to keep their bodies ready for any technological/medical development that would make this possible.

Embracing living with disability

Exceptions to these two strategies are rare, but worth noting. They are either due to a necessity (such as the loss of carers – such as in the case of P21), or to an opportunity for emancipation (such as coming across a disability NGO – such as in the cases of P8 and P20). In both cases, a break is necessary so that the person in question can distance themselves away from this disabling ideology. As P21 notes,

> 'My son is disabled now; he won't be able to do anything henceforth'. This was how my mother thought. She was not very educated. She used to say so, when people were coming at our place. Imagine how a patient hearing this would feel. 'My son cannot be married, I cannot have any grand-child' and alike. Or 'if he gets married, his children may be disabled as well'. All sorts of taboos … I was smashed under this viewpoint for four years. When the 'viewpoint' died, I came into view. I started going out, to be more independent, earn money, go out with girls.

This embracing of living with disability can take different forms:

1   For some this could mean the embracing of disability identity (P2, P21). For instance when asked about how he would define himself, one of the first terms that P2 identified with was his nickname 'the sitting bull' referring to himself as a wheelchair user and as one of the leaders of the disability community. This embracing of the disability identity can also materialize itself in the form of accepting it as a 'fate', as we mentioned in our literature review. We believe that P2's stance represents almost exactly the way Moser talks about Siv's approach to disability (2005), where disability is enacted as something to be accepted and to be lived with.

2   For some this acceptance does not come with peace:

> One cannot be in peace with disability. One can only live with it … If there is a pimple in the middle of your forehead, would you say 'This is beautiful'? No, but you would live with it. The best you can do is to prevent it from enchaining you … Some parts of my soul are cancerous because of disability. Yet, I prevented it from turning malignant. I wrapped it with fresh new tissues. I cannot ignore it, nor can I like it.
>
> (P20)

3   Finally for others this could mean the embracing of disability with passion, as mentioned in our review of the literature. This seems to be the case with P21, whom almost every patient in the hospital admires, because he rides the motorcycle, even though he is paralysed. P21 is also a political activist on the streets confronting the police in social demonstrations.

Negotiating with the family

This breaking away from the disabling ideology is not so clear cut in all cases. Many people enter into a sort of negotiation with their families. As it is in P20's case – whose complaint about the loss of his privacy was presented above, or in that of P25:

> My family is very emotional, too much protective. They would not let me do anything, even if I actually could do it. When I first wanted to help them in the kitchen, they used to tell me 'you get a rest, what you can do in two hours, we could do it in five minutes'.
>
> (P25)

P25 has found her way out of this situation with the cooperation of her psychologist, as P20 had asked for the help of his doctors. Both P25's psychologist and P20's doctor persuaded their respective families that they can and have to stay, live, work by themselves. A similar point was made by the social worker (SW1) we interviewed, when she said that in many cases she has to back up the patient in the latter's negotiation with relatives, and tells the family that their child 'has to' go out, for example.

As P20 and P25, many others continue to live with their families, and they certainly draw many benefits from that. However they do not internalize the disabling ideologies straightaway but negotiate them, and develop a different relationship to disability, which is not completely dependent on the family, but neither completely independent of it. As it was stated above, the help of the family is very important in a context where official regulations and the public support are weak (P2); and supportive spouses, attentive fathers-in-law (P1) are key to happiness for disabled people. In addition families and *refakatçis* are the major actors who trigger socialization in the hospital, by looking after each other's patients (P11), sharing problems and help, and creating opportunities to chat in the garden (almost all interviewees). We were told about love affairs between patients and *refakatçis* (P2, P20, P12), or that *refakatçis* were made to dance for the patients (P20). It is especially due to this role the family plays in socialization that most people come to terms with their disabilities, and learn to be humorous about them.

On the other hand, the huge role families assume in the life of disabled people also creates a sort of 'laziness' in the latter (P2), making it harder to negotiate for the right to individuality and has therefore some restrictive effects. Finally, this leads some people to stay with their families but 'resist' them, sometimes secretly, as part of daily life – as in the case of P4, who despite his diabetes, steals sweets from his wife's handbag.

Conclusion

In this chapter, drawing upon the Turkish context where the family has a central role in the rehabilitation processes, we tried to reveal the ways families construct disability and their disabled relatives respond to such constructions. Our main argument is that this nexus between the family and the disabled person is key to understanding the embodiment of disability in this context.

This finding seems to be an important contribution to the existing literature, which covers a range of related issues but neglects the interaction in-between. Accordingly, the role of rehabilitation processes in the construction of disability, the relationships between families and disabled children, and the conditions and forms of embodiment are separately discussed. This deficiency seems to stem from the fact that the existing literature most of the time draws upon 'Western' cases, where the health system in general, and rehabilitation processes more specifically are not based on the family.

In cases where the family is a key stakeholder of rehabilitation processes and remains the most important support of a disabled person afterwards, its approach to disability becomes a very important determinant of how disability is experienced. Our research has revealed that in the Turkish context families produce and reproduce the most common disabling ideologies, reconstructing disability as tragedy and abnormality, or in the best-case scenario, as a fate that has to be undergone. This in turn contributes to the construction of the disabled person as dependent to the family, largely infantilized and sometimes devalued. In such cases, which are the rule rather than the exception, the huge economic, psychological, social and often medical support of the latter, which is by far the main source of joy and persistence for disabled people, turns into a carceral undertaking.

Disabled people respond to this inclination in various ways – some internalize these disabling ideologies straightaway, approving their own dependence; others take this as a continuous struggle for normality; again some others embrace this new condition to different degrees or enter into various daily negotiations with their families. Most remain with them however, not situating themselves as separate individuals.

Considering that within the disability literature, discussions on non-Western settings refer more often to the family (e.g. Al-Krewani *et al.* 2011; Rao 2001), one can conclude that the case described here is not unique to Turkey. It may therefore be beneficial to conduct further research in other countries, on the role of the family in rehabilitation processes, and its effects on the construction of disability.

Notes

1 These two arguments do not necessarily exclude each other. It is the same literature that refers both to mothers' potential to reflect disabling ideologies and calls for caution regarding tendencies of mother-blaming.
2 http://www.engelliler.biz/forum/sakatlik-calismalari-inisiyatifi/109530-sakat-bebek-dogurmak-sakatlik-kurtaj-ve-gen-teknolojileri-uzerine-dikmen-bezmez.html.
3 P14 and P20 seriously considered suicide when they became disabled. Both dropped the idea: P14 because he could walk again and P20 after he was introduced to disability activism. P3 decided to undergo a very risky operation, because he 'preferred dying to living with paralysis'.

References

Abberley, P. (2004) A critique of professional support and intervention, in J. Swain, S. French, C. Barnes and C. Thomas (eds), *Disabling Barriers – Enabling Environments*. London: Sage.

Al-Krewani, A., Graham, J. R. and Al Gharaibeh, F. (2011) The impact of intellectual disability, caregiver burden, family functioning, marital quality and sense of coherence, *Disability & Society*, 26 (2): 139–150.

Avery, D. M. (1999) Talking 'tragedy': identity issues in the parental story of disability, in M. Corker and S. French (eds), *Disability Discourse*. Philadelphia, PA: Open University Press.

Barnes, C. and Mercer, G. (2003) *Disability*. Cambridge: Polity Press.

Berger, J. (2005) Uncommon schools: institutionalizing deafness in early-nineteenth century America, in S. Tremain, (ed.), *Foucault and the Government of Disability*. Ann Arbor, MI: University of Michigan Press.

Blum, L. M. (2007) Mother-blame in the Prozac nation: raising kids with invisible disabilities, *Gender & Society*, 21 (2) : 202–226.

Darling, R. B.(2003) Toward a model of changing disability identities: a proposed typology and research agenda, *Disability & Society*, 18, 7: 881–895.

Davis, L. J. (2006) Constructing normalcy: the bell curve, the novel, and the invention of the disabled body in the nineteenth century, in L. J. Davis (ed.), *The Disability Studies Reader*. New York: Routledge.

Dowling, M. and Dolan, L. (2001) Families with children with disabilities: inequalities and the social model, *Disability & Society*, 16 (1): 21–35.

Hughes, B. (1999) The constitution of impairment: modernity and the aesthetic of oppression, *Disability & Society*, 14, 2: 155–172.

Hughes, B. (2005) What can a Foucauldian analysis contribute to disability theory?, in S. Tremain (ed.), *Foucault and the Government of Disability*. Ann Arbor, MI: University of Michigan Press.

Knight, K. (2013) The changing face of the 'good mother': trends in research into families with a child with intellectual disability and some concerns, *Disability & Society*, 28, 5: 660–673.

Litt, J. (2004) Women's carework in low-income households, *Gender & Society*, 18: 625–644.

Lowell, A. and Mason, T. (2012) Caring for a child with a learning disability born into the family unit: women's recollections over time, *Scandinavian Journal of Disability Research*, 14, 1: 15–29.

Malacrida, C. (2003) *Cold Comfort*. Toronto: University of Toronto Press.

McKeever, P. and Miller, K. L. (2004) Mothering children who have disabilities: a Bourdieusian interpretation of maternal practices, *Social Science and Medicine*, 59: 1171–1191.

McLaughlin, J. and Goodley, D. (2008) Seeking and rejecting certainty: exposing the sophisticated lifeworlds of parents of disabled babies, *Sociology*, 42 (2): 317–335.

Moser, I. (2005) On becoming disabled and articulating alternatives, *Cultural Studies*, 19, 6, 667–700.

Papadimitriou, C. (2008) 'It was hard but you did it': the co-production of work in a clinical setting among spinal cord injured adults and their physical therapists, *Disability & Society*, 30 (5): 365–374.

Rao, S. (2001) 'A little inconvenience': perspectives of Bengali families of children with disabilities on labelling and inclusion, *Disability & Society*, 16 (4): 531–548.

Ryan, S. and Runswick-Cole, K. (2008) Repositioning mothers: mothers, disabled children and Disability Studies, *Disability & Society*, 23, 3: 199–210.

Shakespeare, T. (2006) *Disability Rights and Wrongs*. London: Routledge.

Siebers, T. (2006) Disability in theory: from social constructionism to the new realism of the body, in L. J. Davis (ed.), *The Disability Studies Reader*. New York: Routledge.

Siebers, T. (2008) *Disability Theory*. Ann Arbor, MI: University of Michigan Press.

Singh, I. (2004) Doing their jobs: mothering with Ritalin in a culture of mother-blame, *Social Science & Medicine*, 59: 1193–1205.

Stevens, C.S. (2010) Disability, caregiving and interpellation: migrant, non-migrant families of children with disabilities in urban Australia, *Disability & Society*, 25 (7): 783–796.

Sullivan, M. (2005) Subjected bodies: paraplegia, rehabilitation, and the politics of movement, in S. Tremain (ed.), *Foucault and the Government of Disability*. Ann Arbor, MI: University of Michigan Press.

Swain, J. and Cameron, C. (1999) Unless otherwise stated: discourses of labelling and identity in coming out, in M. Corker and S. French (eds), *Disability Discourse*. Philadelphia: Open University Press.

Swain J. and French S. (eds.) (2008) *Disability on Equal Terms*. London: Sage.

Thomas, C. (1999) Narrative identity and the disabled self, in M. Corker and S. French (eds), *Disability Discourse*. Philadelphia: Open University Press.

Thomas, C. (2001) Medicine, gender, and disability: disabled women's health care encounters, *Health Care for Women International*, 22 (3): 245–262.

Thomas, C. (2007) *Sociologies of Disability and Illness*. Basingstoke: Palgrave.

Todd, S. and Jones, S. (2003) 'Mum's the word!': maternal accounts of dealings with the professional world, *Journal of Applied Research in Intellectual Disabilities*, 16: 229–244.

Traustadottir, R. (1991) Mothers, who care: gender, disability and family life, *Journal of Family Issues*, 12 (2): 211–228.

Tremain, S. (2005) *Foucault and the Government of Disability*. Ann Arbor, MI: University of Michigan Press.

Turner, B. (1995) *Medical Power and Social Knowledge*. London: Sage Publications.

Veck, W. (2002) Completing the story: connecting relational and psychological processes of exclusion, *Disability & Society*, 17 (5): 529–540.

Watson, N. (2002) 'Well, I know this is going to sound very strange to you, but I don't see myself as a disabled person': identity and disability, *Disability & Society*, 17, 5: 509–527.

Williams, G. (2005 [1998]) The sociology of disability: towards a materialist phenomenology, in T. Shakespeare (ed.), *The Disability Reader: Social Science Perspectives*. London: Continuum Books.

Yılmaz, V. (2011) *The Political Economy of Disability in Turkey: Disability and Social Policy Reform in Turkey*. Saarbrücken: LAP Lambert.

Zitzelsberger, H. (2005) (In)visibility: accounts of embodiment of women with physical disabilities and differences, *Disability & Society*, 20 (4): 389–403.

2

LEARNING FROM *TOJISHA KENKYU*

Mental health "patients" studying their difficulties with their peers[1]

Kohji Ishihara

Introduction

This chapter introduces *tojisha kenkyu* and discusses its significance in the context of disability studies. The term *tojisha kenkyu* (当事者研究) consists of two Japanese words: *tojisha* and *kenkyu*. *Tojisha(s)* refers to "interested person(s)," disabled persons themselves, or patients (service users) themselves. *Kenkyu* means "study," "research," or "investigation." Therefore, *tojisha kenkyu* literally translates as "study by interested persons themselves." In practice, it refers to a unique activity of self-study by persons with mental health problems or other problems in which they study their difficulty ("symptoms" and everyday worries) with their peers and often with the help of professional supporters.

Tojisha kenkyu developed against the background of self-help/peer-support activities and *tojisha undo* (the disability movement in Japan). However, *tojisha kenkyu* differs from self-help/peer-support activities in that its processes and results are often open to the public. *Tojisha kenkyu* is also different from *tojisha undo*. The motto of *tojisha undo* is "we know what we need; we decide what service should be provided," while *tojisha kenkyu* assumes that patients do not know themselves well and need to study themselves. The most important feature of *tojisha kenkyu* is that the *kenkyu*-attitude could make patients capable of addressing their own problems.

In what follows, I will briefly introduce the Japanese disability movement and the history of the term *tojisha*. Then, I will introduce Bethel House activities and the development of *tojisha kenkyu* in Japan. Next, the functions of *tojisha kenkyu* will be compared to those of the consumer/survivor movement in psychiatry. Finally, I will discuss the question of who speaks for whom, before concluding.

The Japanese disability movement and its terminology

In Japan, the disability movement (*shogaisha undo*) began to emerge around 1970 when two famous events occurred (Nakanishi and Ueno 2003: 25–7). The first was a protest against the public petition to reduce the sentence of a mother who had killed her two-year-old daughter with cerebral palsy. The public petition advocated taking into account the extenuating circumstances of the mother – namely, the fact that institutional care was not sufficient and that she was forced to take care of her daughter on her own. Koichi Yokotsuka and his colleagues at the Kanagawa prefecture federation of the *aoi shiba no kai* (Blue Lawn Grass Club), an association of people with cerebral palsy in Japan, protested against the public petition, because it implied that it was understandable that a mother, under certain circumstances, has no choice but to kill her disabled child (Yokotsuka 2007; Tateiwa 1990).

The second event was the *fuchu ryoiku* center (Fuchu Care and Education Center) conflict. The *fuchu ryoiku* center was established by the Tokyo Municipal Government in 1968 and provided 400 beds for people with severe mental and physical disabilities. The institutionalization of disabled people was thought to be a pressing issue; indeed, a case in which a medical doctor murdered his disabled son was assumed to have been caused indirectly by the lack of institutions (Asahi Shimbun 1968; Yomiuri Shimbun 1967, 1968). In 1970, some residents of the center began to protest against maltreatment and the oppressive administration of the staff of the center (Tateiwa 1990). Moreover, in 1971, the center made plans to move people with severe disabilities to private institutions and turn itself exclusively into a center providing therapy to people with profound disabilities. Some people with severe disabilities protested against both these developments, claiming the center as their living space (ibid.).

Throughout the 1970s and 1980s, the development of the disability movement in Japan was mainly spearheaded by people with cerebral palsy. Yokotsuka and his colleagues protested against the proposal to amend the Eugenic Protection Act to allow the intentional abortion of disabled fetuses (Yokotsuka 2007). In 1986, the first Center for Independent Living (CIL) was established in Tokyo; in the 1980s and 1990s, CILs spread throughout Japan (Tateiwa 1990; Nakanishi 2014).

Turning to terminology, in Japan, the disability movement was referred to as the *shogaisha undo* (disabled persons + movement). In the *shogaisha undo*, the term *tojisha* has come to be used by people with disabilities to refer to themselves. Originally, *tojisha* seems to have been coined as a translation of a legal term: *tojisha* can refer to the "party" or "interested persons" in a lawsuit.[2] It is still used in this sense, as well as to refer to stakeholders engaged in economic or political conflicts or negotiations. It was not until the mid-1980s, when the CIL was established in Japan, that the term *tojisha* began to be widely used to refer to the users of services for disabled people.[3]

Throughout the 1980s and 1990s, the term *tojisha* gradually came to be preferred when referring to disabled people. The terms *tojisha shutai* (*tojisha*-centered or *tojisha*-initiative) and *tojisha shuken* (*tojisha* sovereignty) have been used to represent the philosophy of the disability movement (Watanabe 1985; Nakanishi 1993; Tateiwa 1995: 417). These terms are representative of the philosophy of the CIL, which argues that disabled people should be service providers as well as users and should manage their own services. In 1986, Ichiji Makiguchi, an advocate for the disability movement in Japan, wrote an article entitled "The *Tojisha* Movement and Volunteers," in which he used the term *tojisha* to refer to "the aggrieved party of a social issue." He insists that the *tojisha* movement has always articulated accusations from the side of *shogaishas* – people who have been oppressed (Makiguchi 1986: 292–3).

In 2003, Nakanishi and Ueno published a booklet entitled *Tojisha Shuken* (*Tojisha* Sovereignty[4]) which contributed to the "boom of *tojisha*" in the context of the disability movement (Ueno 2013: 25). Retrospectively, Ueno noticed that the term *tojisha* refers to the socially vulnerable – people who have been deprived of the capacity to be parties represented by the social majority (Ueno 2013: 32). "*Tojisha* Sovereignty" was deliberately declared in order to enable the socially vulnerable to reclaim their agency.

Bethel House and *Tojisha kenkyu*

Tojisha kenkyu began in February 2001 at Bethel House (*Bethel no Ie*) in Urakawa, Hokkaido, two years before the publication of Nakanishi and Ueno's *Tojisha Shuken*. The origin of Bethel House, a local center for the activities of psychiatric patients and ex-patients that is supported by Mr. Mukaiyachi and the people of Urakawa, dates back to 1978, when Ikuyoshi Mukaiyachi began employment as a social worker at the Urakawa Red Cross Hospital. He soon started supporting the activities of the ex-patients' self-help group, called the *donguri no kai* (acorn shell group) (Ishihara 2013b: 13). Some members of this group came to live in the old building of the Urakawa church, which was named "Bethel House" in 1984, after the Bible and the Bethel Foundation (see *Bodelschwinghsche Stiftungen Bethel*) in Germany (Mukaiyachi 2013b: 4).[5] Later, Bethel House became the name that refers to the community of patients who have mental illnesses and their carers in Urakawa. Members of Bethel House have engaged in unique activities that challenge the common-sense understanding of mental illness in Japan.[6]

In modern Japan, mental health patients have been institutionalized and isolated from society (Oda 2012). Indeed, there are still some 300,000 in-patients (27.3 per population of 1,000 in 2010), and more than 36,000 in-patients who have stayed over 20 years (JNGMDP 2013: 3). Bethel House's activities are very different from the Japanese mental health professionals' orthodox attitude. The characteristics of the activities there can be grasped by referring to the unique mottos invented by members of Bethel House: "taking back difficulty [*kuro*]," "admitting to weakness," "weakness as the power and the tool of solidarity," "more meetings than meals," "a life of dropping out," "a workspace to sleep on the job," and so on (Mukaiyachi and Urakawa, Bethel House 2006: 11). Bethel House is also famous for its *Hallucination and Delusion Awards,* which offers prizes for the best delusions and hallucinations of the year. The various activities and mottos of Bethel House coincide, in that they encourage mental health patients to appear in the public sphere as responsible agents without denying their weaknesses and the difficulties they have in everyday life.[7]

Against the background of the activities of Bethel House, *tojisha kenkyu* arose by chance.[8] It started when a member of Bethel House, Hiroshi Kawasaki, talked with Ikuyoshi Mukaiyachi after he "exploded." He broke the public phone in the hospital when his parents refused to order sushi and console games for him. Mukaiyachi felt bewildered and did not know what to do. Beset from all sides, he happened to say, "Well, how about studying?" The word "study" had an impact on Mr. Kawasaki, who replied with a gleam in his eye, "Yes, I would like to study" (Mukaiyachi 2005: 3; Mukaiyachi 2013a: 152; Kawasaki 2002).

Tojisha kenkyu, originally called self-study (*jiko kenkyu*) (Shimizu 2001; Kawasaki 2002), soon spread among members of Bethel House. It also gradually spread among individuals with mental illnesses outside Bethel House. Moreover, it spread among individuals with a range of conditions – addiction, cerebral palsy, and developmental disorders. Work by Satsuki Ayaya and Shinichiro Kumagaya (2008; 2010), and Harue Kamioka and Eiko Oshima (2010), as well as works by Bethel House, contributed to the distribution of *tojisha kenkyu* activities around Japan (Ishihara 2013b: 45–54).

A study consists of a sequence of information gathering, determining a hypothesis, and running trials to test the hypothesis. It is acceptable for researchers to fail to realize the expected result. Even unanticipated results are precious data for researchers. However, in clinical settings, such trials and failures are not allowed, except in clinical trials, where subjects are carefully protected so as not to be exposed to anything other than "minimal risk" and where their anonymity is secure. The anonymity of subjects and the avoidance of risk protect the subjects but also close them off from the public sphere and deprive them of their right to talk using their names and to take risks. Only the researchers appear in the public sphere (i.e., on the academic stage) with their names revealed; only the researchers publish the results gained from research with the participation of anonymous subjects. *Tojisha kenkyu* functions to give back individuals with mental health problems the right to appear and talk in the public sphere (Ishihara 2013b: 18–20).

There are no "manuals" about how to conduct *tojisha kenkyus*; *tojisha kenkyu* methods and procedures are diverse, depending on the kinds of mental health conditions, the backgrounds of the organizers, the location, and so on. In Bethel House, *tojisha kenkyus* are classified into three categories: the mono-*tojisha kenkyu*; plural-*tojisha kenkyu*; and group-*tojisha kenkyu* (Bethel Happiness Research Institute 2009: 38). Mono-*tojisha kenkyus* are those conducted alone;

plural-*tojisha kenkyus* are those conducted by more than two people, sometimes by a team of members who have the same issue; and group-*tojisha kenkyus* are those conducted at a regular group meeting (weekly or monthly). It is important for members to have a *"kenkyu"* attitude. Once they attain this *kenkyu* mindset, they will be able to conduct their research in everyday life, even when they are alone, and they will be more capable of effectively presenting the results of their research.

Mukaiyachi (2005: 4) and the Bethel Happiness Research Institute (2009: 42–45) summarized the procedures of *tojisha kenkyu* in five steps, as follows:

1   As a first step, it is essential to disconnect the problems from the person, a process sometimes called "externalization." This process of externalization is very important, because *tojisha kenkyu* is different from "self-reflection" or "introspection." By externalizing the problems, members' fears and anxieties can be relieved, thereby increasing their research motivation.

2   The next step in this process is to invent a "personal illness name" (*jiko byomei*). The *jiko byomei* is named so that *tojisha*s can face their own difficulty (*kuro*).

3   The third step is to elucidate the patterns and processes of the problems faced by the participants. This step illustrates the regularity and repetition structure of symptoms with images, artwork, or role-playing. This step helps *tojisha*s understand the meaning of their *kuro*.

4   The goal of the fourth step is to devise an actual way of protecting and helping the self and to practice these techniques in a virtual setting.

5   The fifth step is to examine the results of this practice and to specify the good and bad aspects of the study that resulted from the sessions. This information can be shared with peers in order to improve treatment sessions. This step naturally leads to the next study and the continuing practice of *tojisha kenkyu*.

So far, many *tojisha kenkyus* have been conducted and published in Japan. Many books on *tojisha kenkyu* have been published, and in a monthly journal (*Kokorono Kenko [Mental Health]* published by the Community Mental Health and Welfare Bonding Organization in Japan), articles about *tojisha kenkyu* in Bethel House are published regularly. Drawing on this material, I will summarize three *tojisha kenkyus* in order to illustrate the core features of *tojisha kenkyu*.

Rika Shimizu's kenkyu on gencho-san (auditory hallucination)

Rika Shimizu was one of the first Bethel House members to conduct a *tojisha kenkyu* and publish the results in journals and books. This section focuses briefly on a book chapter (Shimizu and Bethel House's Delusion of Persecution Research Group 2005). The purpose of her study was to elucidate how she came to realize that she had a delusion of persecution and why she had never noticed it before. First, she was interviewed by the members, and the results of this interview were written down. Then she read the interview notes and exchanged opinions with the other group members. Through her study, she found that her delusions of persecution helped her escape the emptiness of life, and she grew to depend on these delusions. She claimed it became easier for her to admit she had serious problems with delusions after she encountered the "human relationships" in Urakawa. In her concluding remarks, she says:

> Therefore, this issue is not as simple as "being cured of delusions of persecution" by a psychiatrist. Rather, it is a problem of the "way of choice," whether we choose to live in "the world of auditory hallucinations" with delusions of persecution or live in the vivid "real world" with troublesome interpersonal relationships. Auditory hallucinations bring us often various uncomfortable and challenging experiences, but, at the same time, we "depend" on them.
>
> In this sense, we are not simply "victims of delusions of persecution." We are often asked about the "choice of problems," meaning, "which problems to live with." In my experience, individuals with the most severe schizophrenia are, in principle, capable of this choice.
>
> (Shimizu and Bethel House's Delusion of
> Persecution Research Group 2005: 106–7)[9]

Masako Yoshino's kenkyu *on* satorare[10] *(Bethel Happiness Research Institute 2006)*

Masako Yoshino studied *satorare*, which is called "thought broadcasting" in psychiatry. Her personal illness name is "schizophrenia *satorare* type." She conducted her study in collaboration with Bethel House members. In order to explain her symptoms of *satorare* to others, she begged members to help reproduce the *satorare* via role-playing. She felt as if another version of her, in the body of another, is conveying her feelings. The negative feelings that arose in her were also transmitted to others, but they were not consistent with her facial expression and voice, which made it impossible for her to talk to others or even look them in the eye. Through this study, they discovered that *satorare* could be expressed as a desperate desire to share one's distress and burdens with others. In order to deal with her *satorare* problem, the group performed an experiment wherein they devised a "*satorare* sign." If the *satorare* problem began when she was in a crowd, she would raise her thumb to alert the other members, who would then give her a thumbs-up signal to let her know that everything was "All right" or "OK." This was very successful, allowing her to enter the crowd without incident: "My feelings were connected to my peers, and I received the message from them that 'I understand your feelings. Don't be afraid. I have the same feelings as you.' I felt protected, even though I was experiencing *satorare*" (Bethel Happiness Research Institute 2006: 169).

Jinen Nishizaka's kenkyu *on personality disorder (Bethel Happiness Research Institute, Personality Disorders Team 2006)*

Jinen Nishizaka, who has the personal illness name "Allergy to Humans and Addiction to Evaluation by Others," studied her personality disorder with Bethel House members. Through their study, they developed the "snowman theory of burdens" and the "principle of stones." The snowman theory explains how behaviors of people with personality disorder build on each other and grow, like snowballs. According to their study, the origins of these behaviors are simply "loneliness" or "emptiness" and their responses to everyday occurrences worsen until these responses appear as symptoms of illness that cause disturbances for the people around them. The principle of stones refers to Nishizaka's recovery process, which occurred in large part due to the self-affirming responses of her friends. When she developed her self-affirmations, she felt that "the burden is mine" and that she could escape from the cycle of destroying human relationships through her troubling, self-denial-driven behaviors. In this way, her recovery process mimics the process by which rough stones become smooth pebbles by brushing against each other as they make their way downstream to the sea. In the closing remarks, she wrote, "I hope this study will be a 'human declaration' of people who have problems that are assumed to be 'personality disorders' and it promotes new *tojisha kenkyus*" (Happiness Research Institute, Personality Disorders Team 2006: 118).

Tojisha kenkyu and the consumer/survivor movement

As mentioned above, CILs have been actively providing services to disabled persons since they were established in Japan in the 1980s. However, the consumer/survivor movement in psychiatry is not as well developed in Japan as in the United States.[11] Activities in Bethel House and *tojisha kenkyu* have been unique in Japan in that mental health patients themselves have publicly spoken. In order to clarify the uniqueness of *tojisha kenkyu*, I will compare its philosophy with that of the consumer/survivor movement in psychiatry.

It seems that the first movement for self-help/peer support and advocates in mental health care dates back to the nineteenth century. The first organization of ex-patients, the Alleged Lunatics' Friend Society, was established in 1845 in England, whose aims included campaigning for changes in the lunacy laws to reduce illegal incarceration, improving the condition of the asylum, and helping discharged patients (Hervey 1986: 253). Interestingly, the society believed that "much mental illness stemmed from the disappointments and rejections of life, and questioned the medical wisdom that the patients had to be isolated from their home associations, desiring practitioners to pay more attention to what the insane were saying" (ibid.: 254).

In the United States, the writings of E. P. W. Packard (1868) and Clifford W. Beers (1908) are often mentioned as pioneers of the ex-patients' peer-support movement (Morrison 2005: Chapter 3). Later, peer-support movements by (ex) patients of mental health, such as Recovery Inc. in Chicago in the 1930s and the Clubhouse movement in the 1950s, occurred through the first half of the twentieth century (SAMHSA 2011: 3–4). However, it was not until the 1970s that the modern mental service users/survivors movement developed (Beresford 2012: 12). In the United States, the Center for Mental Health Services (CMHS) conducted the Consumer-Operated Services Programs Multisite Research Initiative (1998–2006) (SAMHSA 2011: 29) and in the United Kingdom, national and local health care authorities have implemented a system of public and patient involvement in policy decisions for health care provision and research since the 1990s (Barnes and Cotterell 2011: xvii).

Although peer-support programs and consumer-operated service programs are very diverse, we can specify their common features or functions. SAMHSA (2011) specifies four possible functions of consumer-operated service programs: (1) providing mutual support, (2) building the community, (3) offering services, and (4) conducting advocacy activities. Campbell (2005) distinguished two functions of peer-support programs: (1) emancipatory functions and (2) caring functions.

Likewise, we can specify the functions of *tojisha kenkyu*: (1) making it possible for patients to "rest on the shelf" as well as face their problems; (2) recovering the patients' right to talk about their problems in the public sphere as responsible agents by addressing them in the form of a study; (3) recovering patients' personal histories and re-identifying them; and (4) making it possible for patients to enter into a study community and enhance connections with their peers (see Ishihara 2013b: 64–6).

Given that Bethel House's activities started as self-help/peer-support activities, the philosophy of patient and public involvement in service provision is clearly shared by the Bethel House people. However, the *tojisha kenkyu* of Bethel House still has something unique about it when compared to the consumer/survivor movement. Although the consumer/survivor movement is based on the service-user rights model, *tojisha kenkyu*'s most important principle is to study "by oneself, together with peers" (Mukaiyachi 2005: 5). *Tojisha kenkyu* includes, but is not limited to, first-person accounts. The important element of *tojisha kenkyu* is the modification of the patients' attitudes toward their problems.

Although anti-psychiatry tried to reject the orthodoxy of psychiatry and the concept of mental illness itself, *tojisha kenkyu* is not necessarily hostile to psychiatry. This is well demonstrated by Bethel House's characteristic activity of patients making personal illness names (*jiko byomei*) by themselves. They have created numerous personal illness names, which often include parodies of mental disorders in the DSM *(Diagnostic and Statistical Manual of Mental Disorders)*. In the *DSM-IV-TR* (APA 2000), schizophrenia is divided into subtypes: the paranoid type, the disorganized type, the catatonic type, and so on (although *DSM-5* [APA 2013] abandoned such subtypes). Bethel members have named their illness "schizophrenia, *satorare* type," "schizophrenia, running out type," (Ito 2009) and so on. They make use of established medical names of illness ("mental disorders") and attach subtypes to them that specify their own difficulty. Other members have named their illness without drawing on medical names. In both cases, they do not concern themselves with the hegemony of naming politics. It is true that "naming personal illness by themselves" is necessary because medical names are not sufficient for specifying their difficulty and their troubles. Professionals are authorities on medical diagnosis and medical treatment, but not on difficulty and the troubles accompanying medical diseases. However, it is not necessary for *tojishas* to take the place of professionals or to control their research. They are the authority on their own problems. At the same time, medical diagnosis is sometimes useful in naming their conditions. If they think medical names for a disorder are helpful, they can adapt them to express their conditions with necessary modifications.

Nothing about us without us?

Before concluding, I would like to discuss the issue of representation in *tojisha kenkyu*. Sometimes, it can be crucial to determine who is qualified to be involved as *tojisha*. Who should be taken into account as *tojisha*? Only severely impaired persons? How about parents, siblings, or the children of impaired persons? In this context, Nakanishi and Ueno (2003: 2) defined *tojisha* as follows: "When someone has needs, s/he is already a *tojisha*" and "*Tohjisha* refers to the end-user of the service."[12] We can easily see that their definition is based on the idea of service-user rights. This model leads to them saying "*tohjisha* know about themselves best" (Nakanishi and Ueno 2003: 12) and "*tohjisha-shuken* (sovereignty of *tohjisha*) means that I'm sovereign of myself, nobody except me – state, family, professionals – is allowed to decide who I am, what I need, on my behalf" (Nakanishi and Ueno 2003: 4). Kumagaya (2013) expresses the concept of *tojisha-undo* as follows: "It is we who know about ourselves best. We decide who we are, what we will do" (2013: 218). This echoes the international disability rights slogan: "Nothing about us without us" (Charlton 1998, 2000).

However, is it true that we know about ourselves best, especially when regarding persons with mental disorders? Are they sure of who they are? Indeed, Mukaiyachi defines *tojisha* in a different way from Nakanishi and Ueno: "In Urakawa, a contrary understanding [of *tojisha*] has been maintained. That is, 'I should not make decisions about myself alone'" (2006: 68); he also states, "It is about ourselves that it is most difficult to know" (2009: 44). This idea of *tojisha kenkyu* was expressed later by Kumagaya in a poignant way: "We don't know ourselves well. We ask ourselves who we are, what we will do, together with peers (Kumagaya 2013: 219).

In the field of disability studies in Japan as well as in the United Kingdom, the legitimacy, representativeness, and qualification of study have been discussed (Sugino 2007: 15–45). Researchers have been challenged about whether they genuinely represent the voices of disabled persons and whether they are on their side. From the perspective of the disability movement, the concerns have been about whether they should admit researchers into their community and how to control the products of research (Mercer 2002). The fact that some researchers are disabled persons themselves does not solve this tense relationship between professional researchers and disabled persons who are vulnerable to exploitation. As Barnes puts it,

> Having an impairment does not automatically give someone an affinity for disabled people, nor an inclination to do disability research. The cultural gulf between researchers and researched has as much to do with social indicators like class, education, employment, and general life experiences as with impairments.
>
> (Barnes 1992: 121–122)

In *tojisha kenkyu,* there also seems to be problems with representativeness in the form of both tense relations between disabled persons who conduct *tojisha kenkyu* and those who do not, as well as between those *tojisha kenkyu* participants who appear in the public sphere and those who rarely talk. However, in my view, the problem of representativeness is not a serious one.

The problem of representativeness stems from that of the putative privileged access of disabled persons to the experience of disability and disabled persons' endeavor to develop hegemony over disability studies by reversing the traditional hierarchy. However, such a disability movement faces an intrinsic dilemma. Given that the experience of disability is a very individual one, it would be difficult to decide who is qualified to express the experience of disability. Let us take as an example cerebral palsy. It is not difficult to discern if someone has cerebral palsy, but the experience differs from one person to another. Whose experience, whose knowledge, should be privileged? Herein lies the problem that Toyota (1998) called "*tojisha genso*" (*tojisha* myth).

In *tojisha kenkyu,* however, the establishment of hegemony over disability studies is not an important issue. The priority is the alteration of the patients' attitudes toward their suffering, facilitated by their taking part in a study community. In this sense, anyone who has problems and is ready to study her/his problems with peers can qualify as a *tojisha*.

Although *tojishas'* participation in and control over research are important issues, it is more important for *tojisha kenkyu* that patients themselves study and create or enter into communities through that study. Discussion in disability studies and *tojisha undo* has often regarded research as a "tool" to oppress or emancipate disabled persons. Such discussion fails to recognize the significance and functions of study for human beings, which are to grasp and express their conditions, to access the public sphere, and to make a community.

In Japan, some academic research fields have already begun to recognize the significance of *tojisha kenkyu*. For example, the Japanese Society of Schizophrenia, the authority on academic schizophrenia research in Japan, held its annual conference in April 2013 in Urakawa, the home town of Bethel House. Moreover, a Japanese textbook on schizophrenia (Fukuda *et al.* 2013), which was supervised by the Japanese Society of Schizophrenia Research, included a chapter, "*Tojisha kenkyu*," written by Ikuyoshi Mukaiyachi. However, although academic interest in *tojisha kenkyu* is welcome, we should be careful that academics do not interpret and modify *tojisha kenkyu* from only their own perspectives.

Conclusions

Only 13 years have passed since *tojisha kenkyu* began in the small town of Urakawa. *Tojisha kenkyu* has rapidly spread in Japan and shaken up the philosophy of mental health care systems and the social welfare system. *Tojisha kenkyu* is also gradually gathering attention abroad, for example in Korea (Kim 2013).

As discussed above, *tojisha kenkyu* provides advantages to *tojishas* by allowing them to face their own problems together with peers. The disability and consumer/survivor movements have tried to provide peer-support programs and autonomy for disabled people, and some researchers in disability studies insisted that research in disability should be conducted by disabled people. The advocates of *tojisha kenkyu* do not claim that service and research should be provided or controlled only by *tojishas*. The paramount claim of *tojisha kenkyu* is that *tojishas* should be allowed to face their own problems together with peers in a *kenkyu*-attitude and style. Academic knowledge and professional support are not to be excluded from *tojisha kenkyu* but to be used as resources. Such a flexible but consistent principle may produce a new understanding of disability and the relationships between patients and peers, caregivers, professionals, and the public.

Acknowledgments

This work was supported by MEXT KAKENHI (24119006) and JSPS KAKENHI (24300293). I would like to express my gratitude to Mukaiyachi Ikuyoshi, Kumagaya Shinichiro, Ayaya Satsuki, Mukaiyachi Noriaki, Bethel House members and staff, *Necco tojisha kenkyu kai* members, *Komaba tojisha kenkyu kai* members, and many *tojishas* for their discussion about *tojisha kenkyu*. An early version of this chapter was read at the UTCP/PhDC 1st International Conference on Philosophy of Disability, *Disability Studies and Tohjisha-Kenkyu*, March 30–31, 2013, The University of Tokyo, Komaba I Campus. I would also like to express my appreciation for the support of the Uehiro Ethics Foundation in holding this conference and other meetings to discuss *tojisha kenkyu*.

Notes

1 "Tojisha kenkyu" is pronounced as "tōjisha kenkyū". The title of this chapter might be misleading because it implies that *tojisha kenkyu* is conducted by only mental health "patients" (service users). As is suggested below, *tojisha kenkyu* is and can be

conducted not only by mental health "patients" but also by disabled persons and even "healthy persons." However, I deliberately chose this title for its conciseness as well as to indicate that *tojisha kenkyu* originated among persons with, and is mostly related to, mental health problems.

2 "Tojisha," Japan Knowledge (online), http://www.jkn21.com (accessed May 24, 2013).

3 However, as early as 1972, Nitta Kinuko used the term *tojisha* in an article on the struggle at the *fuchu ryoiku* center. "We could not do anything but stage a sit-in protest in front of the first municipal governmental building. National and municipal welfare policies and the treatment of disabled people are deceptive; they are decided upon without listening to the voices of people with disabilities themselves (*tojisha*)" (Nitta 1972).

4 Later, Ueno (2011: 66) adapted the English words "individual autonomy" for "*tojisha shuken*," as it reflects the meaning of "the right of self-governance of socially vulnerable people."

5 Please note that the Bethel Foundation in Germany (http://www.bethel.de/ueber-uns/gemeinschaft-verwirklichen.html. Accessed May 7, 2014) is Christian based while Bethel House in Urakawa is not directly connected to Christianity. However, some members of Bethel House, including Ikuyoshi Mukaiyachi, are Christian.

6 For a wonderful description of the history and persons of Bethel House in English, see Nakamura 2013. Nakamura (2013: 172–186) also describes *tojisha kenkyu* activities of Bethel House vividly. (She translates "tojisha kenkyu" by the English words "self-directed research".)

7 Although Bethel House's philosophy has been unique in Japanese mental health care settings, we could find comparable activities abroad. One example is the movement of mental health care in Italy since the end of the 1960s, led by Franco Basaglia. Basaglia's thinking is similar to Bethel House's philosophy in that he made much of working and living in the town (see Okuma 2009). Another approach worth mentioning is the "Open Dialogue Approach" (ODA) in West Lapland, Finland. ODA and Bethel House activities are similar in that they rely on the power of the dialogues of *tojishas* (clients). Interestingly, ODA began in 1984, when Bethel House was established. However, there are some differences between them. In ODA, early intervention in psychosis and family therapy are important, while in Bethel House activities, family therapy does not play much of a role and most members are chronic (ex) patients. The most important difference is that, in ODA, there is no activity similar to *tojisha kenkyu* (as distinct from group therapy) (see Ishihara 2014).

8 *Tojisha kenkyu* and the activities of Bethel House were influenced by various approaches and movements: self-help and peer-support movement, disability movement, cognitive behavior therapy, Social Skills Training (SST), and Victor Frankle's existential analysis (see Ishihara 2013b: 23–36). However, *tojisha kenkyu* is unique and different from all of these movements and approaches.

9 Here, she pointed out that the main problem was the way she, herself, chose to act. However, at the same time, she mentions the importance of the fact that she was "chosen" more than that she chose. She said what opened her up to herself more than anything else did "was the mysterious experience of being 'chosen' beyond my own choice" (Shimizu and Bethel House's Delusion of Persecution Research Group 2005: 107).

10 The word *satorare* seems to stem from the title of a Japanese comic book series (Sato 2001), in which the thoughts of characters with a fictional brain disease are broadcast without their knowledge. The comic was filmed and broadcast as a dramatic series.

11 In Japan, the Japan National Group of Mentally Disabled People was organized in 1974 (Nagano 2001) and has been active in "fighting against the Japanese Ministry of Health and Welfare, evil mental hospitals and psychiatrists, and those who discriminate against mental disease patients" (see the website of JNGMDP: http://www.jngmdp.org/). In 1993, Zenseiren (Japan Federation of Mentally Disabled

People's Associations) was established (Kato 2001). Moreover, in the early 1990s, the "Clubhouse" movement was introduced in Japan (see the website of the Japan Clubhouse Coalition: http://www.clubhouse.or.jp/).

12 Note that Nakanishi and Ueno (2003: 2–33) think *tojisha* is not a synonym for "the person who has problems." If s/he adapts to the society that creates the problems, s/he is not *tojisha*. It is not until s/he makes and needs the concept of an alternative society that s/he becomes *tojisha*. Later, Ueno (2011) defined *tojisha* as "a subject who [consciously] regards oneself as the bearer of one's needs" (Ueno 2011: 79).

References

Citations in the text from Japanese literature were translated into English by Ishihara. The titles of Japanese literature were translated into English by the author and parenthesized by the author unless they have original English titles (the original English titles are marked with an asterisk★).

APA (2000) *Diagnostic and Statistical Manual of Mental Disorders (DSM-IV-TR)* (4th, Text Revision ed.), Washington, D.C., American Psychiatric Association.

APA (2013) *Diagnostic and Statistical Manual of Mental Disorders* (5th ed.), Washington, D.C., American Psychiatric Association.

Asahi Shimbun (1968) Kakkitekina Shogaisha-shisetsu Raigetsu Misebiraki (A Groundbreaking Institute for Disabled People will Open Next Month). March 6, 1968, evening 3rd ed., p. 10. Retrieved from *Kikuzo II Visual*. (Japanese)

Ayaya, S. and Kumagaya, S. (2008) *Hattatsushogai Tojisha Kenkyu. Yukkuri Teineini Tsunagaritai (A* Tojisha Kenkyu of *Developmental Disorders. How to Connect Slowly and Carefully)*, Tokyo, Igakushoin. (Japanese)

Ayaya, S. and Kumagaya, S. (2010) *Tsunagari no Saho. Onaji demonaku Chigau demonaku (The Manners of Connecting. Not the Same, Not Different)*, Tokyo, NHK Shuppan. (Japanese)

Azumi, J., Okahara, M., Onaka F., and Tateiwa, S. (2012) *Seino Giho (Ars Vivendi)*, 1990, 3rd. ed., Seikatsushoin, 2012. (Japanese)

Barnes, C. (1992) Qualitative Research: Valuable or Irrelevant? *Disability, Handicap, and Society* 7(2): 115–124.

Barnes, M. and Cotterell, P. (eds) (2011) *Critical Perspectives on User Involvement*. Bristol, UK, The Policy Press.

Beers, C. W. (1908) *A Mind That Found Itself: An Autobiography*. Retrieved from https://archive.org/details/39002010727783.med.yale.edu (Accessed May 5, 2014).

Beresford, P. (2012) Psychiatric System Survivors. An Emerging Movement. In N. Watson, A. Roulstone and C. Thomas (eds), *Routledge Handbook of Disability Studies*, London: Routledge, pp. 151–164.

Bethel Happiness Research Institute (Bethel Shiawase Kenkyujo), Personality Disorders Team (Jinkaku Shogaikei Kenkyu Team). (2006) Jinkaku Shogai no Kenkyu Sono Ichi (Studies of Personality Disorders, Part 1). Presented by Nishizaka Jinen in collaboration with Yamamoto Kayo, Akiyama Satoko, Katogi Shoko, Yoshida Megumi, Mukaiyachi Ikuyoshi, Shimono Tsutomu, Monju Shiro and Monju Yayoi. In I. Mukaiyachi and Urakawa Bethel House 2006, pp. 103–119. (Japanese)

Bethel Happiness Research Institute (2006) Satorare no Kenkyu. Satorare kara Satorase e (A Study of *Satorare*. From *Satorare* to *Satorase*). Presenter: Yoshino Masako. Collaborator: Yoshino Masako, Akiyama Saoko, Katogi Shoko, Tachibana Hideki,

Sakai Akira, Hirose Hideyuki, and Shimizu Rika. In I. Mukaiyachi and Urakawa Bethel House 2006, pp. 160–170. (Japanese)

Bethel Happiness Research Institute (2009) *Let's Tōjisha kenkyu*, Vol. 1. Ichikawa: COHMBO (Community Mental Health and Welfare Bonding Organization). (Japanese)

Campbell, J. (2005) The Historical and Philosophical Development of Peer-run Support Programs. In S. Clay (ed.), *On Our Own Together. Peer Programs for People with Mental Illness,* Nashville, Vanderbilt University Press, pp. 17–64.

Charlton, J. I. (1998, 2000) *Nothing About Us Without Us: Disability of Oppressions and Empowerment,* Berkeley, Los Angeles/London, University of California Press.

Fukuda, M., Murai, T., Itokawa, M., and Kasai, K. (eds) (2013) The Japanese Society of Schizophrenia Research (supervised), *Tōgo-shiccho-sho (Schizophrenia)*, Tokyo, Egakushoin. (Japanese)

Hervey, N. (1986) Advocacy or Folly. The Alleged Lunatics' Friend Society, 1845–1863. *Medical History,* 30(3): 245–275.

Ishihara, K. (ed.) (2013a) *Tōjisha kenkyu no Kenkyu. (The Study of* Tohjisha Kenkyu), Tokyo, Igakushoin. (Japanese)

Ishihara, K. (2013b) Tojisha Kenkyu towa Nanika. Sono Rinen to Tenkai (What is *Tōhjisha Kenkyu?* Its Philosophy and Development.) In K. Ishihara (ed.) 2013, pp. 12–72. (Japanese)

Ishihara, K. (2014) Open Dialogue to Bethel. Open Dialogue UK Seminar Sanka Hokoku. (Open Dialogue and Bethel. A Report on Participation in an Open Dialogue UK Seminar.) *Seishinkango* 17(4): 19–23. (Japanese)

Ito, N. (2009) Zenryoku-shisso no Kenkyu (A Study of Running Out), in Bethel Happiness Research Institute and Mukaiyachi 2009, pp. 130–139. (Japanese)

Japan Council on Independent Centers (eds) (2001) *Jiritsu-seikatu-undo to Shogai-bunka. Tojisha karano Fukushiron (Independent Living Movement and Disability Culture. Studies of Social Welfare from the Perspective of* Tojisha*)*, Tokyo, Gendaishokan. (Japanese)

JNGMDP (2013) The Parallel Report to CAT committee by Japan National Group of Mentally Disabled People in 2013. http://www.jngmdp.org/e/index.php?CAT%20 Report%202013 (Accessed July 6, 2014).

Kamioka, H. and Oshima, E. (2010) *Sonogo no Fujiyu. Arashi no Ato wo Ikiru Hitotachi (Subsequent Inconvenience. Survivors after the Storm)*, Tokyo, Igakushoin. (Japanese)

Kato, M. (2001) Yes. Self-help wo Ikiru. Zenseiren no Ayumi wo Furikaette. (Yes. Living with Self-Help. Looking back on the History of Zenseiren). In Japan Council on Independent Centers (2001), pp. 123–132. (Japanese)

Kawasaki, H. (2002) Bakuhatsu no Kenkyu. Boku no Bakuhatsu no Kiseki kara (A Study of the Explosion. Learning from the trajectory of my explosion). *Seishinkango* 5(1): 45–48.

Kim, D. (2013) Kankoku niokeru Seishin-shogaisha niyoru Tojisha Kenkyu no Genjo (The Current Situation of *Tojisha Kenkyu* by Persons with Mental Illness in Korea). Translated into Japanese from Korean by Moon, Kyungnam. In K. Ishihara and M. Inahara (eds), *UTCP Uehiro Booklet,* No. 2, *Philosophy of Disability & Coexistence: Body, Narrative, and Community,* pp. 175–182.

Kumagaya, S. (2013) Itami kara Hajimeru Tojisha Kenkyu. (*Tōhjisha kenkyu*: Starting from Pain.) In K. Ishihara (ed.) 2013a, pp. 217–280. (Japanese)

Makiguchi, I. (1986) Tojisha Undo to Volunteers (*Tōjisha Undo* and Volunteers). In K. Uda and E. Okamoto (eds), *Volunteer Katsudo no Jissen (The Practice of Volunteer Activity)*, Tokyo: Chuohoki Publishing, pp. 292–306. (Japanese)

Mercer, G. (2002) Emancipatory Disability Research. In C. Burnes, M. Oliver, and L. Barton (eds), *Disability Studies Today*, Cambridge, Polity, pp. 228–249.

Mobilizing the Human Spirit (2012) *Clifford W. Beers. The Founding of Mental Health America 1908–1935. Telling the Story and Showing the Way*. Washington, DC, National Human Services Assembly.

Morrison, L. J. (2005) *Talking Back to Psychiatry. The Psychiatric Consumer/Survivor/ Ex-Patient Movement*, New York & London, Routledge.

Mukaiyachi, I. (2005) Tojisha Kenkyu towa Nanika (What is Tojisha Kenkyu?). In Urakawa Bethel House 2005, pp. 3–5. (Japanese)

Mukaiyachi, I. (2009) *Giho Izen (Before Technique)*, Tokyo, Igakushoin. (Japanese)

Mukaiyachi, I. (2013a) Tojisha Kenkyu ga Dekirumade (The Birth of *Tojisha Kenkyu*). (Interview). In K. Ishihara (ed.) 2013a, pp. 150–175. (Japanese)

Mukaiyachi, I. (2013b). Bethel no Roots wo Tazuneru Tabi (A Journey to the Roots of Bethel House). *Bethelmonde* 6: 4–6. (Japanese)

Mukaiyachi, I. and Urakawa Bethel House. (2006) *Anshin Shite Zetsubo Dekiru Jinsei (Desperate Lives with Ease)*, Tokyo, NHK publishing. (Japanese)

Nagano, E. (2001) Zenkoku 'Seishinbyo'-sha Shudan no Tatakai. (The Struggle of the Japan National Group of Mentally Disabled People). Japan Council on Independent Living Centers (2001), pp. 114–122. (Japanese)

Nakamura, K. (2013) *A Disability of the Soul: An Ethnography of Schizophrenia and Mental Illness in Contemporary Japan*, Ithaca, NY, Cornell University Press. (Japanese Translation: *Crazy in Japan. Bethel no Ie no Ethnography*. K. Ishihara and T. Kono [Translation Supervisors], K. Ishihara, M. Mizutani, R. Iizuka, T. Ikeda, K. Takae, T. Kono, M. Takahashi, M. Kataoka, and M. Inahara [Translators], Tokyo, Egakushoin, 2014.)

Nakanishi, M. (1993) Tojisha Shutai no Fukushi Service no Kochiku. Shogaisha ga Chiiki de Kurasu Kenri to Hosaku. Jiritsu Seikatu Center no Katudo wo Toushite (Building a *Tojisha* Oriented Welfare Service. Rights and Methods of Disabled Persons Living in the Community. Learning From the Activities of the Independent Living Center), *Shakai Fukushi Kenkyu (Social Welfare Studies)* 57: 48–53. (Japanese)

Nakanishi, M. and Ueno, C. (2003). *Tohjisha Shuken* (Tohjisha *Sovereignty*), Tokyo: Iwanamishoten. (Japanese)

Nakanishi, S. (2014) *Jiritsu Seikatsu Unodo-shi. Shakaihenkaku no Senryaku to Senjutsu (The History of the Independent Living Movement. Strategies and Tactics of Social Change)*, Tokyo, Gendaishokan. (Japanese)

Nitta, K. (1972) Watashitachi wa Ningyo ja nai (We Are not Doles), *Asahi Journal*, Nov. 17, 1972: 52–3. Available at http://www.arsvi.com/1900/7211nk.htm (Accessed May 5, 2014). (Japanese)

Oda, J. (2012) *Naze Nihon wa Seishinkabyoin no Kazu ga Sekaiichi Nanoka (The Reason Why Japan is the World's Leading Country in Mental Institutions)*, Tokyo, Takarajima. (Japanese)

Okuma, K. (2009) *Seishinbyoin wo Suteta Italia, Sutenai Nihon (Italy Abolished Mental Hospitals; Japan Maintains)*, Tokyo, Iwanamishoten. (Japanese)

Packard, E. P. W. (1868) *The Prisoners' Hidden Life, or Insane Asylums Unveiled. As Demonstrated by the Report of the Investigating Committee of the Legislature of Illinois together with Mrs. Packard's Coadjutors' Testimony*. Retrieved from https://archive.org/details/prisonershiddenl00inpack (Accessed June 21, 2014).

SAMHSA (Center for Mental Health Services, Substance Abuse and Mental Health Services Administration, U.S. Department of Health and Human Services) (2011). *Consumer-Operated Services: Evidence*. Retrieved from http://store.samhsa.gov/product/

Consumer-Operated-Services-Evidence-Based-Practices-EBP-KIT/SMA11-4633CD-DVD (Accessed Dec. 27, 2011).

Sato, M. (2001) *Satorare* (1). Kindle edition, 2012. Tokyo, Kodansha. (Japanese)

Shimizu, R. (2001) Higaimoso tono Deai to Jiritsu (Encounter with and Independence from Delusion of Persecution), *Seishinkango* 4(6): 31–34.

Shimizu, R. and Bethel House Delusion of Persecution Research Group (2005) Higaimoso no Kenkyu. Genchosan datte Jiritsururu (A Study of Delusion of Persecution: Even Auditory Hallucination Becomes Independent), In Urakawa Bethel House 2005, pp. 93–107. (Japanese)

Sugino, A. (2007) *Shogaigaku. Rironkeisei to Shatei (Disability Studies. Theoretical Issues, Background, and Scope*)*. Tokyo, University of Tokyo Press.

Tateiwa, S. (1990) Hayaku, Yukkuri. Jiritsu-seikatu-undo no Seiritsu to Tenkai. (Early, Slowly. The Birth and the Development of the Independent Living Movement.) In J. Azumi *et al.* 2012, pp. 258–353. (Japanese)

Tateiwa, S. (1995) Jiritsu Seikatsu Unodo no Chosen. (The Challenge of the Independent Living Movement.) In J. Azumi *et al.* 2012, pp. 414–498. (Japanese)

Toyota, M. (1998) Tohjisha-genso-ron. Aruiwa Minority no Undo niokeru Kyodogenso no Ronri (A Study of the *Tojisha*-phantasm. The Logic of the Shared Phantasm in the Minority Movement), *Gendai Shiso*, 26 (2): 100–113. (Japanese)

Ueno, C. (2011) *Care no Shakaigaku. Tojisha Shuken no Fukushi Shakai e (Sociology of Care. Towards the Welfare Sociology of Individual Autonomy)*, Tokyo, Ota Shuppan. (Japanese)

Ueno, C. (2013) 'Tojisha' Kenkyu kara 'Tojisha Kenku' e. (From the Study of *'Tojisha'* to *'Tojisha Kenkyu'*). In Y. Soeda (ed.), *Tousousei no Fukushi-shakaigaku. Dramaturgy toshite (Welfare Sociology of Conflict: Society as Dramaturgy*)*, Tokyo, University of Tokyo Press, pp. 25–46. (Japanese)

Urakawa Bethel House (*Bethel no Ie*) (2002) *Bethel no Ie no Hi-enjoron. (The Theory of Non-Help at Bethel House)*. Tokyo, Igakushoin. (Japanese)

Urakawa Bethel House (2005) *Bethel no Ie no Tojisha Kenkyu* (Tojisha Kenkyu *at Bethel House*), Tokyo: Igakushoin. (Japanese)

Watanabe, M. (1985) Shogaisha/Tojisha no Seikatsu to Ishiki no Kouzouteki-haaku. "Seikatsu-kozo to Shakai-fukushi Needs nikansuru Jisshotekikenkyu": Chukan-hokoku (A Dynamic Structural Approach to the Life and Consciousness of Physically Disabled People as the Concerned Subjects: An Empirical Study on their Life-Structure and Social Welfare needs – an interim report*), *Tokyogakugeidaigaku Kiyo Daisanbumon: Shakaigaku (Bulletin of Tokyo Gakugei University. Section III, Social sciences*)*, 37: 83–164. (Japanese)

Yokotsuka, K. (2007) *Haha yo Korosuna (Mother! Do not Kill me!)*, 1975, 198, Seikatsushoin, 2007. (Japanese)

Yomiuri Shimbun. (1967) Kono Chichi wo Oitsumetamono. Ishi no 'Anrakusatujin'. Sukuenai Jusho-shinshosha. (What Drove Father into the Corner? 'Mercy Killing' by a Doctor: No Help for Severely Disabled People.) August 7, 1967, morning 14th edition, 15. Retrieved from Yomidas Rekishikan. (Japanese)

Yomiuri Shimbun. (1968) Shinshin-shogaisha Shisetsu 'Fuchu Ryoiku Center' Asu Kaisho (*Fuchu Ryoiku* Center: Institute for Mentally and Physically Handicapped People is Opening Tomorrow). May 31, 1968, evening 4th ed., 10. Retrieved from Yomidas Rekishikan. (Japanese)

3

THE PSYCHO-SOCIAL IMPACT OF IMPAIRMENTS

The case of motor neurone disease

Jo Ferrie and Nick Watson

Introduction

There is currently a great deal of debate within both disability studies and medical sociology with regard to what Carol Thomas (2012) has termed *The Disability Question*. At the heart of this question is whether the emphasis of research on disability should be placed on the impact that a particular impairment has on an individual, which Thomas has termed 'impairment effects', or on how societal organisation and cultural values act to exclude people with an impairment, which Thomas and others have termed 'disablism'. Medical sociology has traditionally been dominated by the former, whilst in disability studies attention has been placed on the latter. More recently in disability studies, the emerging Critical Disability Studies approach has added a third element to this debate with a focus on the discourses that surround impairment and the cultural values that reproduce these discourses. Here the emphasis is placed on critiquing how these affect people with impairment, a concept that is also known as 'ableism' (Goodley 2011; Chouinard 1997).

In this chapter, we use data drawn from a project on living with motor neurone disease (MND) funded by Motor Neurone Disease Scotland to explore the relative merits of these approaches and examine their applicability to an impairment group that straddles the boundaries of chronic illness, terminal illness and impairment. The aim of our study was to document the experiences and perceptions of people with MND and their partners about what it was like living with the condition. We sought to explore what they thought was important in their day-to-day life, including the management of the symptoms associated with MND and their temporal nature, the services they received and the service providers. We also wanted to investigate how people felt that having the condition changed their social relationships with family, peers and professionals, and their ability to participate in the mainstream.

To date there has been little research from within disability studies on people with MND or on the experiences of those with degenerative disabilities and terminal conditions in general (Scambler 2005). From medical sociology, Simon Williams has argued that disability studies has simplified the disability problem to such an extent that it only applies to those without a chronic illness and that it has ignored the needs of those with chronic and or progressive conditions (Williams, 1999: 812). With chronic or progressive conditions, people's needs, their experiences and their perceptions may be different from those with a so-called static condition, and if disability studies is to attempt to include all disabled people then this knowledge gap needs to be filled.

Thomas has attempted to answer her own query, and to meet these critiques from medical sociology, by developing a two-pronged solution to the disability question through modifying the social model of disability into what she terms the social relational model of disability (1999, 2007). Disability is, she argues:

> a form of social oppression involving the social imposition of restrictions of activity on people with impairments and the socially engendered undermining of their psycho-emotional well-being
>
> (Thomas, 1999: 3)

Further she suggests that some disability theorists have misread the original UPIAS definition which stated that disability was something imposed 'on top of impairments' and makes the case that some of the restrictions experienced by people with an impairment are not social in origin. These restrictions are not disabilities but are the result of what she calls 'impairment effects', which she defines as non-socially imposed restrictions. Thomas accepts that impairments are not irrelevant and that their effects combine with disablement. She concludes that disability research must engage with both (1999: 137).

Alongside this, Thomas has called for an exploration of what she terms the psycho-emotional dimensions of disability, by which she means the consequence of living with an impairment in a society that does not easily accommodate people who are different, or who have different needs. If the social model is about the oppression people face on the outside (attitudes and physical barriers), the psycho-emotional dimension refers to oppression on the inside. As Thomas says:

> it is about being made to feel of lesser value, worthless, unattractive, or disgusting as well as about 'outside' matters such as being turned down for a job because one is 'disabled'.
>
> (Thomas, 2004: 38)

Thomas theorises that this form of oppression, because it becomes internalised, affects what people can be, who they believe they are, and so affects what they can do. Donna Reeve (2012) has further developed this concept, which she sees as being triggered by stigma and latent oppression in society. Psycho-emotional disablism is both absorbed from outside and is learnt through a loss of opportunities, experiences (such as being stared at) or the absence of experience, for example not getting a job or being prevented from forming a relationship.

Thomas argues that to answer the disability question we need an approach that allows for the incorporation of both a sociology of impairment and impairment effects, and a sociology of disablement, to use her distinction. She argues that this will enable the development of an understanding of both the social oppression experienced by people with an impairment, and the embodied experience of living with an impairment. Both ideas developed from within medical sociology as well as those from disability studies are needed.

In this chapter, we critically reflect on the ideas of Thomas, Reeves and others concerning the concept of impairment effects and psycho-emotional disablism, and argue that whilst these writers have explored how disablism has produced psycho-emotional impacts, they have failed to explore how impairment itself can have a similar effect, disabling people in private spaces and in their private lives. MND is a very brutal and severe condition, and the lived reality of its impact on those with the disease and their families cannot be explained without a full engagement with the condition. We begin with a brief description of the condition and then move on to discuss how medical sociology has examined MND.

Motor neurone disease

Describing the symptoms associated with a condition and discussing how these symptoms affect individuals is something that is not usually 'done' in disability studies, particularly in the UK where the body has disappeared from much theoretical work. With some exceptions (for example Shakespeare *et al.* 2009), the visceral experience of impairments, of what it is actually like to live with an impaired body, is generally bracketed in favour of structural factors. Even in approaches from within Critical Disability Studies which claim to focus on embodiment lived experience is absent, with emphasis instead on the cultural production of the disabled body (Vehmas and Watson 2014). However, such approaches only give partial accounts of what it is like to be a disabled person or to live with a chronic condition (Shakespeare and Watson 2010).

MND, sometimes called Amyotrophic Lateral Sclerosis (ALS) is a term applied to cover a range of different neurodegenerative syndromes all of which share a common neuropathology, in particular the progressive degeneration of motor neurones. It is a progressive, terminal condition that in the UK affects approximately one in 50,000 people: at any one time there are roughly 3,000 people with the condition (Forbes *et al.* 2007). Incidence increases sharply as people age, reaching a peak in the seventh decade, although the incidence in the very elderly is uncertain and it is less common in people under 50 (Ibid.). Although the condition is very rare, the impact it has on the population is much larger with one report suggesting that for every person affected by MND another 14 close family or friends are affected (MND Association of Victoria, 2008).

MND affects motor neurones which undergo progressive degeneration and die. There are four common forms of onset:

- primary lateral sclerosis (PLS)
- progressive muscular atrophy (PMA)
- amyotrophic lateral sclerosis (ALS)
- bulbar palsy.

The symptoms people experience vary according to the mode of onset. Bulbar onset affects breathing and eating whilst PLS, PMA and ALS predominantly affect the upper and lower limbs and walking and movement, termed spinal onset. Most people experience a combination of both spinal and bulbar symptoms.

MND initially causes motor weakness, often beginning with fairly minor symptoms like a drop foot (increasing the risk of tripping) or slurred speech. New symptoms emerge every few weeks or months, and the physical decline in some cases can be very rapid. Normally, within a matter of months of diagnosis, adults with MND experience extensive motor weakness across their whole body to the extent that they can no longer turn in bed, cough, breathe, eat, talk, walk or hold themselves upright in a chair. In addition to the soreness associated with not being able to move position, muscle spasms can cause sharp pain. It is consequently a very distressing condition, although there is a great deal of variety, both in the symptoms people experience and in the speed of progression. The historian Tony Judt (2011: 15) described his own experience of the condition as 'progressive imprisonment without parole'. MND can also affect cognitive skills and mental health, although there is some debate as to whether this is a consequence of the use of oxygen to ease breathing difficulties and the drugs to fight spasms and pain, which can leave individuals in an 'altered state', or the condition itself.

Death usually results from respiratory failure, and generally occurs within 18 months of diagnosis. Although the disease has a quick progression, many people with MND are not given a prognosis at diagnosis. Some people do not survive six months after diagnosis, whilst others can survive for up to five years.

The sociology of MND

Whilst disability studies has to a large extent ignored conditions such as MND, the same is also to an extent true of medical sociology. Much of the previous research on MND has focused on the medical aspects associated with the condition, such as how the disease progresses and how the disease can best be managed. In their recently published systematic review of qualitative research with people with MND, Sakellariou *et al.* (2013) emphasised that we only have limited knowledge of how people live their lives with MND. However, there have been a few studies which have sought to explore how MND is experienced from the perspective of those with the condition and their family and carers. A series of relatively small-scale studies in England by Brown (2003), Hugel *et al.* (2006), Hughes *et al.* (2005) and Brown and Addington-Hall (2008) have documented the lived experience of those with MND and the care and support that those with the condition and their carers receive.

All of these studies describe the emotional trauma associated with MND and how living with the condition produces uncertainty. As a consequence, people prefer to live in the 'here and now' rather than think about the future (Sakellariou *et al.* 2013). Brown (2003) documents what she calls the 'existential shock' of the diagnosis and the impact that it has on both those with MND and on their families and their friends. Hughes *et al.* (2005) comment on how the rapid physical deterioration associated with the condition affects the emotional and physical well-being of both the individual with the condition and their family and how these two combine and make coping with the condition very difficult. As the condition progresses, people start to lose touch with their friends and stop their usual social activities (Brott *et al.* 2007). However there is evidence to suggest that people with MND continue to want to be in control of their lives and to be involved in decisions about their care and support and about their opportunities (King *et al.* 2009). People want to be enabled to be in charge and to maintain their sense of self and self-identity.

Problems in the delivery of care and support are also often highlighted. In the UK, the shift to primary care as the main deliverer of support, whilst welcome in some areas, can create difficulty for people with MND. For example, although General Practitioners (GPs) will invariably be involved in the care of MND patients, often they have little or no prior experience of working with people with MND and may lack adequate knowledge of this rare condition (Oppenheimer 1993; Robinson and Hunter 1998; Van Teijlingen *et al.* 2001; Brown *et al.* 2005). A general practice with 10,000 patients is likely only to encounter a case of MND every two to three years (Shaw 1999) and an individual GP can expect to see one patient in their career (Levvy 2000). The provision of good care and support is critical during the early and late stages of the condition (Sakellariou *et al.* 2013).

Methods

The data presented here are drawn from a three-year project that aimed to assess what it was like to live with MND in Scotland. We adopted a two-pronged approach, running a series of focus groups with those who had recently cared for a partner, parent or other who had died. We spoke to 22 people in this stage of the study, the purpose of which was to sensitise us to the key issues faced by those with MND and their families. In the second stage of the study, we interviewed people from across Scotland with the condition. In all we recruited 43 people to act as our key informants (around 400 people live with MND in Scotland currently so this is a sizeable proportion). We interviewed each key informant and their family members up to four times over the course of the study. By adopting this longitudinal approach to the research, we were able to document how their views and experiences changed over time. According to our extensive review of the literature, this longitudinal strategy has not previously been used to explore the impact of MND on people and their families. Ours was also the largest study in terms of the number of voices heard that we can find globally.

All those we spoke to were interviewed in their own homes, and we documented their experiences as the disease progressed. Most of the interviews were joint interviews with their husband, wife or (adult) child, and in a number of cases where the participant had little or no spoken communication the partner answered most of the questions. However, we were careful to ensure that the person with MND was included in the interview and all questions were directed to him or her. Some participants communicated through pen and paper or used equipment such as a light reader. No one was excluded because they faced barriers to communication: interviews just took longer to accommodate their needs. All interviews were taped and transcribed. The informants and their family members were active participants in the research process shaping both the content and the direction of the research as they identified practices, events and processes that were important to them.

The interviews were analysed using standard qualitative methods and an inductive comparative analysis of the data was carried out (Silverman, 2010). The transcripts were read and coded and themes and topics of particular importance to individual participants were identified. The categories evolved as more and more transcripts were analysed. By using this coding system we were able to identify patterns, breaking the data down into manageable units and regrouping this data as emergent themes (Atkinson 1992). We now turn to a discussion of these themes.

Living with motor neurone disease

Impairment effects

The effect of MND, and how its intersection with and affect on day-to-day life, was the most common theme running through all of the interviews and was the single most important issue for all those we spoke to. One of the most difficult aspects, and the most commonly discussed topic for people with MND and their families, was the fast progression and rapid decline that was often associated with the condition. This, coupled with a lack of prognosis, unsettled individuals and generated a sense of the future being uncertain. This often meant that many people were unable to move beyond their impairment. It overwhelmed everything, all they did and all that they were.

Several participants described how unpredictable their life had become, and how in the absence of a timeline or a prognosis they could not anticipate what would happen to them, or plan for the future. Despite not being given a prediction of how their condition would progress by medical practitioners, and also being advised by them and by other health and social care workers not to seek out alternative information, many had gone to websites, used web-based discussion groups or had accessed other sources of information: all were aware of the approximate 18 month average life expectancy post diagnosis that is commonly quoted. Imminent and inevitable death was for many the only certainty: uncertainty was confined to the speed of progression and the pattern of decline. The uncertainty associated with the condition, coupled with its rapid progression and the fact that it is terminal, left many people feeling abandoned. There was no time for people to 'get used' to this information and to undergo what Williams (1984) terms 'narrative reconstruction'. So one family member told us,

> and she helped me fill in the form [for Disability Living Allowance] and [the Finance Advisor] said … "I'm not asking you to lie, but I'm asking you to fill in the form for the worst case scenario", and like three months later it *was* the worst case scenario.
>
> (Jenny, talking about her mother Kate)

The fast progression prevented people being able to assimilate and normalise their impairment and to create a new identity: people had no time to get 'used' to living with an impairment and its consequences. In this way, the body was more significant than social barriers.

The limitations resulting from MND often made it impossible for people to carry out what previously had been key activities or identifiers in their lives:

> He had been a wood carver and had painted and he was just giving it all up. And I would ask "Why are you not doing it?" and he would say "Because I can't hold things".
>
> (Grace, talking about her husband Ron)

It was not just Ron's inability to carry out a practised task, but the inability to perform at his normal level and to produce quality craftsmanship that caused him to stop working with wood. Similarly Patsy, a knitter and wool spinner, had stopped knitting as she became more aware of her failing skill and speed, and was no longer able to operate at the level she had previously.

This reaction was not just confined to tasks, it affected whole swathes of people's lives, with many giving up activities that had once defined them. For example, Rachel talked about the loss of anticipation:

> You know there are things that you are never going to do again that you miss … I mean sometimes you are watching the television and a nice

programme is on and somebody is there and they are down the beach? And they're walking in the water, and I think "I'll never do that again ..." "I'll never swim in the sea again ..." There's all that ... You know? People going out for a walk? We used to love going for walk when we were on holiday we just used to walk – never do that again, it'll never happen. That's what I'm saying, there's all that ... Everything is tainted by it, every single aspect of your life is tainted by this disease – no, just the mobility, everything of it, everything about it. God forgive me, I say to Rick "See if I had cancer? At least I'd be able to get about ..."

(Rachel)

The terminal nature of MND was also central to this. For example, a number of people commented on the futility of hope, or of maintaining a positive attitude, or of fighting the progression of the condition. This hopelessness was also highlighted by Rachel, who said:

There's always an element of hope with cancer you know, for us, it's nothing.

(Rachel)

Challenging impairment effects

A minority of our respondents took a different perspective and were more able to live a life beyond their impairment effects. For people in this group, their very extensive levels of impairment did not appear to overwhelm them in the same way as others. This was achieved in a number of ways. For some, the only way to face the challenges presented by living with MND was to avoid any discussion of the condition at all and to bracket the impairment and its effects:

her approach was, right from the very first day after she was diagnosed, was to just get on with life and not go over it or to even talk about it to me. She just simply blanked it out. That was her way of dealing with it.

(Brian, talking about his wife Eilidh)

Some people railed against their impairment effects and tried to continue as they had done previously:

you know when your fingers go ... he couldn't fasten buttons and he would say "No! I'll do it myself." He would get on with it and even if it took him 10–15 minutes, he would be determined.

(Vicky, talking about her husband Cameron)

The refusal to talk about the condition featured in many narratives. Whilst it was a way of managing life with MND, it was also a way of people ensuring that who they were did not become lost, so that they could maintain their identity and their social role:

> I'd like to talk to someone to bawl my eyes out or whatever, but I can't ask for it. So I never talk about it. I'd never say, that's my arms going or you know my hands are getting weaker ... because you're always on the verge of tears, it sits there all the time. Who wants to know it's getting worse? ... I can't let [family] see me upset, they can't see it get to me. Because I'm the Mammy, they feed off me.
>
> (Emma)

From these quotes, it may be argued that the participants were under some social pressure to minimise the impairment effects, even if it was self-imposed. This avoidance of support sometimes extended to a rejection of some assistive technologies. Many described the presence of equipment like hoists, hospital beds, reclining chairs, commodes and so on as an intrusion into their lives, and actively resisted the use of equipment or adaptations that they felt interfered with their independence. Some rejected equipment designed to extend life because it took away an element of control:

> He was trying to get used to his breathing machine, Craig was thinking I have to breathe when I want to breathe. Not when it tells me to breathe.
> (Julie, talking about her husband Craig)

Many people used comedy, and a very dark humour to deny the inevitability of MND:

> and I suppose one final laugh, well we probably shouldn't laugh at it but last year at Christmas time we knew it was a matter of days, Kate's ... um ... brother bought her a calendar for 2010 as a Christmas present which was extremely ill advised but we could see the funny side of it ... [Kate said] "what the hell do you think we are going to do with that?"
> (Calum, talking about his mother-in-law Kate)

In other cases, humour was used to show how relationships were still central. For example, two people we interviewed used an electronic speech board to communicate, and in both cases their teenage children had switched off their parent's machine when they were getting told off or were being asked about homework. In telling these stories, the parents found great humour and pointed to the normality of their relationship with their respective 13-year-old children. But we argue that maintaining this normalcy was at the cost of acknowledging the corporeal experience.

Disablement and disablism

As discussed, social model theory has helped the concept of disablism to emerge as social barriers are highlighted. Within our research, examples of direct disablism were rare. This may be both because many of the informants were older and that very rapidly their level of impairment meant they were unable to access the mainstream, and thus simply did not experience barriers. Where people did access the mainstream, it appears that they tended to modify their lives and only to go to accessible environments: disablism may have shaped their choices, but they did not talk about this. For example people went to different restaurants from those they might have visited previously, or they changed their normal shopping habits, which may explain why we did not hear very many stories about access issues. Also, many had already retired or were in their final years at work, and only a few participants talked either about a desire to be in work, or complained about being forced to retire. Some even commented about how understanding their employer had been, and how they or their partner had received more than the minimum entitlement to sick pay. This is not to say that disablism was absent, or that it did not affect people's well-being, as we discuss below.

However, disablism was encountered in other areas, coming to the fore particularly around access to support services, for example around the entitlement to live as part of a couple. In one case, we were told how a couple had to fight for their right to an accessible route into their first-floor flat, and how for a period the husband had to give his wife fireman's lifts in order to get home:

Martin: When [Joanne] was first diagnosed ... em ... it wasn't good at all. We had a terrible run in with ... we had wanted a stair lift fitted and they wouldn't do it. Despite being approached by the MSP and everything, they wouldn't do it ... eh ...

Jo: And what reason did they give?

Martin: They didn't think basically ... and again this 5 year thing came into the equation ... to cut a long story short they basically didn't think they would get their money's worth out of it.

Many couples were required to move from their first-floor bedrooms to smaller, often single occupancy downstairs rooms because local authorities preferred to build wet rooms than to provide stair lifts. Others talked about the issue of shared beds, and the difficulties they had in getting funding from the local authority to buy a double bed that would meet their needs. Some Scottish local authorities apply a five-year rule to the provision of adaptations, only funding work if they believe that the benefits will last for more than five years. This ruling discriminates against anyone diagnosed with MND, and several people reported being turned down because they were considered an 'invalid use of budgets'.

We had to fight, fight for a wet floor shower room to the extent of "Well, you're not entitled." Based on what? I had people say to my face about that. I've also had people say to my face "Well, he's not got cancer so we've not got all of these things in place." I actually said to them, "So you're actually grading life limiting illness now are you?" I said that to them and there was silence.

(Nadine, talking about her brother Laurence)

The provision of appropriate and accessible toilets was also a major concern. Whilst these policies are clearly unjust, they could, as Bury (2010: 175) has argued, be driven by a desire to control the financial implications of managing health problems in the community, rather than those arising from disablism. Nevertheless and whatever its origin, this denial of service clearly had effects on their psycho-emotional well-being but these were perhaps more indirect than direct (Reeve 2012). It is to a discussion of psycho-emotional disablism that this chapter now turns.

MND and psycho-emotional dimensions

People with MND and their families faced a wide range of psycho-emotional disablism and its effect and potential to harm was considerably more detrimental and disruptive to the lives of those with MND than direct disablism. In the rare occasions where people described such disablism, it was the potential 'embarrassment' that people commented on rather than the denial of the actual opportunity:

I did go to another restaurant between Christmas and New Year with a group of friends but I forgot that there was three steps going up to it. And whilst there is a hand rail, the hand rail stops short ... So, I got up the first two steps ok and then I had to get the other boys to give me a hand up the third step which was ... it was quite embarrassing you know. I am still at the stage ... I mean, I know that it is daft a lot of the times but I do still ... I don't know how to say this – I am still quite self-conscious about ... eh ... being able to do things and being self-sufficient basically.

(Andrew)

Whilst the cause of this discrimination is structural in origin it is not the actual discriminatory act (the absence of a full handrail) that is the problem; it is the felt effect this has on his identity. As Thomas would put it (2007) it is more a barrier to being than a barrier to doing.

The impact of MND on interactions with others either on a formal or informal basis, particularly with non-family members, was a major concern for many of our informants. For some, the fear of meeting people and of their reaction to them was so overwhelming that they withdrew from almost all social contact. Rachel for example described how 'embarrassed' she felt when going out in public:

Rachel: I felt embarrassed at neighbours seeing me. Embarrassed at friends seeing me. Crazy! Why should I? But I do.

Jo: Because of their reaction to you?

Rachel: No! they've been great, it's me. I'm embarrassed.

Jo: But if it was them …

Rachel: I'd be there, with them! But the shoe is on my foot and I'm embarrassed to have this illness. I'd rather die tomorrow that have to deal with this. You have to mentally adjust all the time, it's too much.

Rachel had stopped leaving the house because she did not want people to see her. Here, and in many other cases, the stigma that caused this disablism was, to use Scambler's terms, 'felt' rather than 'enacted' (1986). Although many people used the term 'stigma' to describe their position, few attributed this to any specific episode or to any particular action.

For many of our respondents, it was not the physical or the built environment that excluded people and nor was it the attitudes of others. It was more a fear of exposure or of being the centre of attention:

> if some friends maybe come in and they're just sitting in the chair and maybe I have been in the living room and I make my way through … When I come in and I see them all looking like this … Do you know? And I want to say "Don't … Don't do that … You're making me feel … Don't look at the way I'm walking … I know I'm walking and I'm always getting worse but you're sitting and going like … this is drawing attention to me …" I would never say to them, I would never say to them … But I do feel … and then I start to feel embarrassed … But all they're doing is … "Oh God, look at him walking …" That's what they are obviously thinking but to me I don't like them staring … they're no' staring … But the looking and I get embarrassed about that …
>
> (Tim)

People felt that they stood out because of their impairment and became the centre of attention out of a fear that was driven in part by the different ways that they now needed to do activities. For example, people told us how they no longer ate out in restaurants because of the way that they had adapted their eating practices.

In the above examples, we have documented three elements of the disability experience as postulated by Thomas. There was for our informants a fourth element, which we have called psycho-emotional impairment effects: we have coined this term to explain aspects of living with MND which are distinct from either the effects of the impairment or the different experiences of disablement.

Psycho-emotional impairment effects

One of the most profound themes to emerge from our analysis of the data was about fear. Living with MND generated a level of fear that prevented many people from actually doing or being. This fear was represented in a range of ways. People were scared of the future; of how impaired the condition would actually make them; of how much they would suffer; and in particular, of how they would die. People were very aware that MND was a terminal condition with a poor prognosis, as Marie said:

> And God forgive me I used to say to Stephen [husband] "Do you know Stephen it would be better if I had cancer ..." and I know I don't mean ... but there is always a certain element of, for people with cancer ... because there is treatments and there is this and there is that. It's everywhere ...

There was an almost universal fear of not being able to breathe and suffocating. However this fear was not just confined to the end of life. Many participants talked about how MND affected their breathing and swallowing, expressing an acute fear about being unable to get a breath, being unable to cough, and being unable to stop choking. Such coughing or choking fits were common, and each time they occurred they reminded people of the terminal nature of their condition and the precarious nature of their existence. For example, for Betty the fear of choking became so real that it prevented her from doing anything, as her husband Robert told us:

> and one of the strange feature of this was that we had to avoid any sort of emotional situations because physically, if Betty was to cry it would probably have choked her ... if she was to burst into tears it could've possibly have killed her ...

Here there is an interplay between fear, impairment effects, psycho-emotional disablism and disability. All these combine to reinforce each other. Betty had to avoid emotionally exposing herself to the reality of her situation, to the experience of having MND, because to be upset could trigger a choking fit severe enough to cause death.

Conclusion

In this conclusion we reflect on how these data and the analyses presented here can help in answering the disability question posited at the start of this chapter. For Thomas, disability is a socially constructed barrier to being which has a psycho-emotional element (2004: 43). The evidence from this study suggests that disability can be an impairment-related barrier too, as the psycho-emotional dimensions of living with such limiting impairments create, in and of themselves, a barrier to being. Because of the severity of impairment, many participants lived in fear of the final stages of the condition: they feared being trapped, in pain, unable to move, unable to speak, choking for breath. This was worse than the idea of dying. For many of those we spoke to, living with MND became all-embracing. As Brown and Addington-Hall describe, they were forced 'to turn inward, to face death in an increasingly difficult day-to-day life' (2008: 211). In the case of MND, it would appear separating out this fear, the cause of this fear, and the experience of this fear, and disaggregating it into one of Thomas's three categories is impossible, as Shakespeare has argued in relation to MS (2013: 24). Scambler and Newton (2010: 103) have argued that with some impairments the social oppression can become secondary to the biological effects of the condition.

Our participants understood their impairments stopped them 'doing'. They also understood their impairments as a barrier to 'being', as they hid from society and stopped activities. Here they were not responding to ablism: they did not consider themselves inferior to other people and did not recount stories to suggest that others thought of them in this way, nor did they think that disabled people were inferior. But they did think they were inferior to themselves as they had been, to the preserved echo of an identity of someone pre-MND.

Thomas connects her ideas to a Social Relational Theory of disability which allows a bridge to be built between those 'socially identified as impaired and those deemed non-impaired or 'normal' (Thomas 2004: 41). Here Thomas draws a hypothetical line between all people. In the case of MND, though, this line has to be drawn between the person's history of life without impairment, their present life with impairment and their future lives of more severe impairment.

The progressive nature of MND and the severity of symptoms impacted on our respondents' stories, meaning that the body could not be ignored or even conceptually sidelined. As a prognosis was lacking, so the body became the evidence base, the primary indicator of how much time was left. To paraphrase Charmaz (2010: 19) 'The vicissitudes of MND can make meanings fragile, not only of illness but of self, situations and relationships'.

Our research shows that 'barriers to being' are impacted directly by impairment effects, though the fear of social situations exacerbated this and further limited our participants' desire to be in social spaces or situations. Impairments have a psycho-emotional impact. In addition to the challenge of progressing symptoms and facing end of life, many participants also spoke of there being an emotional element directly connected to the biomedical state of the body. The fear of choking for example caused distress which would not be captured by the notion of psycho-emotional disablism. It is difficult to entirely distinguish between the psycho-emotional impairment effects (triggered by the body) and psycho-emotional dimensions (triggered by disablism) (Watson 2012; Shakespeare 2013). Avoiding a scrutiny of the psycho-emotional impact of the physical, biological and psychological elements of their impairment brackets these experiences entirely from the gaze of disability studies.

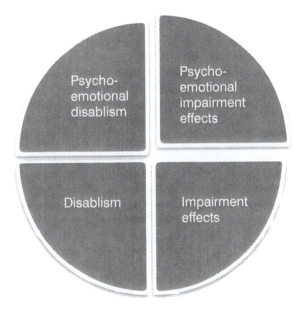

FIGURE 3.1 Re-engaging with the body: the full scope of the Social Relational Model

What we are proposing is an additional element to Thomas's original conceptualisation, one that incorporates the psycho-emotional effect of the impairment and a focus on limitations in private spaces (see Figure 3.1). This will allow us to analyse the data more fully and to ensure that we produce a picture that will incorporate or include all of their lives. Potentially, it also supports the development of interventions that can help at all of these levels, including counselling. Sian Vasey (1992) in her defence of the social model argues that there is nothing that the disabled people's movement can do for people in distress or in pain and that it is therefore not worth including these private areas of life. This enormously reduces the issues which the disability movement can mobilise around and disability studies explore.

Following Watson and Shakespeare (2002) and Shakespeare (2006), we argue that disability studies must re-visit the experience of impairment in order to fully represent the complexity and heterogeneity of the experience of disability. If we take this more extensive approach, pressure can then be placed on services to help people at this level. Without such help, many of those with long-term chronic conditions will not be able to take part in society, no matter how accessible or welcoming that society is. Our approach is novel because we are articulating the importance of the psycho-emotional impacts of impairment, as a concept distinct from psycho-emotional disablism.

References

Atkinson, J. (1992) The ethnography of a medical setting: reading, writing and rhetoric, *Qualitative Health Research* 2(4):451–474.

Brott, T., Hocking, C. and Paddy, A. (2007) Occupational disruption: living with motor neurone disease, *British Journal of Occupational Therapy*, 70: 24–31.

Brown, J. (2003) User, carer and professional experiences of care in motor neurone disease, *Primary Health Care Research Development*, 4: 207–17.

Brown, J. and Addington-Hall, J. (2008) How people with motor neurone disease talk about living with their illness: a narrative study, *Journal of Advanced Nursing*, 62, 2: 200–8.

Brown, J. B., Lattimer, V. and Tudball, T. (2005) An investigation of patients and providers' views of services for motor neurone disease, *British Journal of Neuroscience Nursing*, 1, 5: 249–52.

Bury, M. (2010) Chronic illness, self-management and the rhetoric of empowerment, In G. Scambler and S. Scambler (eds), *New Directions in the Sociology of Chronic and Disabling Conditions: Assaults on the Lifeworld*. London: Palgrave Macmillan.

Charmaz, K. (2010) Studying the Experience of Chronic Illness Through Grounded Theory. In G. Scambler and S. Scambler (eds), *New Directions in the Sociology of Chronic and Disabling Conditions: Assaults on the Lifeworld*. London: Palgrave MacMillan.

Chouinard, V. (1997) Making space for disabling difference: challenging ableist geographies, *Environment and Planning D: Society and Space*, 15: 379–87.

Forbes, R. B., Coville, S., Parratt, J. and Swingler, R. J. (2007) The incidence of motor neurone disease in Scotland, *Journal of Neurology*, 254, 7: 866–69.

Goodley, D. (2011) *Disability studies: An inter-disciplinary introduction*. London: Sage.

Hugel, H., Grundy, N., Rigby, S. and Young, C. A. (2006) How do current care practices influence the experience of a new diagnosis of MND? A qualitative study of current guidelines based practice, *Amyotrophic Lateral Sclerosis*,7, 3: 161–166.

Hughes, R. A., Sinha, A., Higginson, I., Down, K. and Leigh, P.N. (2005) Living with motor neurone disease: lives, experiences of services and suggestions for change, *Health Social Care Community*, 13, 1: 64–74.

Judt, T. (2011) *The Memory Chalet*. London: Vintage.

King, S. J., Duke, M. M. and O'Connor, B. A. (2009) Living with amyotrophic lateral sclerosis/motor neurone disease (ALS/MND): decision-making about 'ongoing change and adaptation', *Journal of Clinical Nursing*, 18: 745–54.

Levvy G. (2000) The role of the lay associations. In R. H. Brown, V. Meininger and M. Swash (eds), *Amyotrophic Lateral Sclerosis*. London: Martin Dunitz.

MND Association of Victoria (2008) *Motor Neurone Disease and Palliative Care: Interim Report on the MND Pathway Project*, Online Publication, http://docs.health.vic.gov.au/docs/doc/Motor-Neurone-Disease-and-palliative-care:-Interim-report-on-the-MND-Pathway-Project (accessed April 2013).

Oppenheimer, E. A. (1993) Decision-making in the respiratory care of amyotrophic lateral sclerosis: should home mechanical ventilation be used? *Palliative Medicine* 7: 49–64.

Reeve, D. (2012) Psycho-emotional disablism: the missing link? In N. Watson, A. Roulstone and C. Thomas, *Routledge Handbook of Disability Studies*. Oxford: Routledge.

Robinson, I. and Hunter, M. (1998) *Motor Neurone Disease, the Experience of Illness Series*. London: Routledge.

Sakellariou, D., Boniface, G. and Brown, P. (2013) Experiences of living with motor neurone disease: a review of qualitative research, *Disability and Rehabilitation*, 35, 21: 1765–73.

Scambler, S. (2005) Exposing the limitations of disability theory: the case of Juvenile Batten Disease, *Social Theory and Health*, 3: 144–64.

Scambler, S. and Newton, P. (2010) Where the biological predominates: habitus, reflexivity and capital accrual in the field of Battens disease. In G. Scambler and S. Scambler (eds), *Assaults on the Lifeworld: New Directions in the Sociology of Chronic and Disabling Conditions*. London: Palgrave Macmillan.

Shakespeare, T. (2006) *Disability Rights and Wrongs*. London: Routledge.

Shakespeare, T. (2013) *Disability Rights and Wrongs Revisited*. London: Routledge.

Shakespeare, T. and Watson, N. (2001) The social model of disability: an outdated ideology? exploring theories and expanding methodologies, *Research in Social Science and Disability* 2, 9–28.

Shakespeare, T. and Watson, N. (2010) Beyond Models: understanding the complexity of disabled people's lives. In Scambler, G. and Scambler, S. (eds), *New Directions in the Sociology of Chronic and Disabling Conditions*. London: Palgrave Macmillan.

Shakespeare, T., Thompson, S. and Wright, M. J. (2009) No laughing matter: medical and social factors in restricted growth, *Scandinavian Journal of Disability Research*, 12, 1: 19–31.

Shaw, P. J. (1999) Motor neurone disease. *British Medical Journal*, 318: 1118–1121.

Silverman, D. (2010) *Qualitative Research*. London: Sage.

Thomas, C. (1999) *Female Forms: Experiencing and Understanding Disability*. Buckingham: Open University Press.

Thomas, C. (2004) How is disability understood? An examination of sociological approaches. *Disability & Society*, 19, 6: 569–83.

Thomas, C. (2007) *Sociologies of Disability and Illness: Contested Ideas in Disability Studies and Medical Sociology*. Basingstoke: Palgrave Macmillan.

Thomas, C. (2010) Medical sociology and disability theory. In G. Scambler and S. Scambler (eds), *New Directions in the Sociology of Chronic and Disabling Conditions. Assaults on the Lifeworld*. Basingstoke: PalgraveMacmillan.

Thomas, C. (2012) Theorising disability and chronic illness: where next for perspectives in medical sociology? *Social Theory & Health*, 10, 3: 209–28.

Van Teijlingen, E. R., Friend, E. and Kamal, A. D. (2001) Service use and needs of people with motor neurone disease and their carers in Scotland, *Health and Social Care in the Community*, 6: 397–403.

Vasey, S. (1992) A response to Liz Crow, *Coalition* September, 42–44.

Vehmas, S. and Watson, N. (2014) Moral wrongs, disadvantages and disability: a critique of critical disability studies. *Disability and Society*. 29, 4: 638–650.

Watson, N. (2012) Researching disablement. In Watson, N., Roulstone, A. and Thomas, C. (eds), *Routledge Handbook of Disability Studies*. London: Routledge.

Williams, G. (1984) The genesis of chronic illness: narrative re-construction, *Sociology of Health & Illness*, 6: 175–200.

Williams, S. (1999) Is there anybody there? Critical realism, chronic illness and the disability debate, *Sociology of Health and Illness*, 21, 6: 797–819.

PART II
Disabling processes

4

ITALIAN STRATEGIES FOR JOB PLACEMENT OF PERSONS WITH DISABILITIES

A network case

Fabio Corbisiero

Introduction

The recent public debate about the inclusion of disabled persons in the labour market has involved much theoretical reflection as well as some important empirical studies on the relationship between disability and work (Heymann *et al.*, 2014; Barnes, 2012). Several different paradigms have been formulated, but research and policy have converged on the so-called process of 'disablement', that is to say the role of the environment (physical, social and relational) as one of the causes of disability and the resulting restriction or elimination of a person's opportunities for employment. While traditional models of disability proposed an indissoluble bond between a bodily pathology and the absence or reduction of opportunities for work (Oliver, 1990), the more recent models analyse the complex dynamics that are created between these dimensions (WHO, 2001). As a result, the role of environmental factors in increasing and enhancing the possibilities for employment has been progressively incorporated into the analysis.

The approval in 2006 of the UN Convention on the Rights of Persons with Disabilities (CRPD) was a watershed in this debate, because it favoured an approach centred on the protection of the human rights and the fundamental liberties of every disabled person. Already in the Preamble, disability is no longer conceived of as a mere 'deficiency' with respect to 'normality', but rather as something that 'results from the interaction between persons with impairments and attitudinal and environmental barriers that hinders their full and effective participation in society on an equal basis with others' (UN, 2006, Preamble, Paragraph *e*). The Convention as a whole sees the breaking down of these barriers as the main goal. Starting out from the recognition of specific rights, already embodied in other international conventions, which apply also to people with disabilities, it proceeds to a reformulation of concepts that responds to a new model of disability and the related process of social inclusion (Griffo, 2007). A person's disability is interpreted as a 'dual social disadvantage', characterised both by a functional/structural impairment (relative to the person) and by environmental factors (relative to society), which limit that person's activities and restrict their participation in social relationships, even if only temporarily. For instance, people with disabilities face dual disadvantages as individuals with disabilities are more likely to live in poverty, including in developed countries such as the United States (U.S. Census Bureau, 2008). Additionally, households with members with disabilities generally have lower incomes than other households and are at a significantly higher risk of living below the poverty line (Loeb and Eide, 2004; Hoogeveen, 2005). As parents and family members take on care-giving roles, at least one parent or family member (mostly women) in many households may have to give up employment or sustainable livelihood activities due to limited government support, inaccessible community infrastructure, and financial limitations to pay for personal assistants. This paradigm shift should not omit the importance of impairments themselves, even after the hypothetical and desirable dismantling of disabling barriers (Crow, 1996; Brandt and Pope, 1997). Rather, the shift invokes the collective responsibility of society as a whole, which is called upon to implement the environmental changes necessary for the full participation of disabled persons in all arenas of social life. In this way, one gets beyond a merely medical discourse on disability and one sees it as a multifaceted social process, in which the environment plays a fundamental part.

This approach underlies the WHO's revision of the International Classification of Impairments, Disabilities and Handicap (ICIDH) and the later development of the International Classification of Functioning (ICF). On a theoretical level, the ICF is a synthesis of the medical and social models, providing a survey of various perspectives on health through a broader conception of disability. The ICF, unlike the ICIDH, is not a classification of the 'consequences of illness' but rather a classification of the 'components of health'. These are understood as being the constitutive factors of health and well-being. This new framework for classifying disability has been developed on the basis of a set of precise and 'politically correct' requirements, namely: disability viewed as a universal aspect of humanity; environmental factors incorporated into the scheme of classification; all potentially stigmatising terminology removed and positive classifications of levels of human functioning adopted; any distinction between physical and mental dimensions abolished and all levels of disability defined as equal, regardless of their root cause; greater attention to the analysis of personal, social and physical contexts.

Although several authors have argued that the ICF holds considerable promise both as a nosological tool and as a heuristic in guiding rehabilitation research, others have expressed reservations and concerns. For example, Nordenfelt (2003) critically analysed the conceptual platform of the ICF, focusing on the definitions of Activity and Participation. He concluded that these ICF framework areas rest partly on confusion between capacity for action and the actual performance of that action and therefore need to be revised from a conceptual perspective. Yet, Imrie (2004) evaluated the theoretical underpinnings of the ICF, arguing that the ICF fails to specify in detail the content of some of its main claims about the nature of impairment and disability, which may limit its educational capacity and influence. Imrie opined that the ICF needs further conceptual clarification and development in several key areas. Despite widespread diffusion of the ICF, the WHO itself recognises that even the most cautious definitions and terms used to classify and describe disabled persons can become stigmatising. The risk of passing off ideologically or ethically motivated definitions as scientific descriptions is what the OECD has termed a packaging of disability (Prinz, 2002). Acknowledging the variety of individual experiences of disability, the ICF eschews a rigid approach, reinforcing the WHO's principle that individuals have a right to be called according to how they choose to self-identify.

The use of ICF in job placement policy for disabled persons

The theoretical framework of the ICF and its bio-psycho-social model, strengthened by the signing and ratification of the UN Convention on the Rights of Persons with Disabilities (CRPD), are gradually fostering job placement policies for disabled persons. Full social and economic participation of disabled subjects is essential if the European Union is to ensure the success of the 2020 Europe strategy (European Commission, 2010) for sustainable and inclusive growth. Indeed, labour market integration of disabled persons has become a paradigmatic case for the EU's 28 member states. A recent Action Plan (2007) states: 'The European Union views disability as a social construction. The social model of disability of the EU highlights the environmental and social barriers that prevent disabled persons from engaging fully in society. These barriers must be removed.' On the one hand, workplace integration in the EU's open market – also of disabled persons – is still considered a priority. On the other, the growing emphasis on productivity – under the pressure of globalization and the current global crisis – has fostered a widespread awareness of the risks and problems of identifying labour market integration with a standard model of the labour market, one that is resistant to the integration of disabled people. To counter this, recent European positions regarding the relationship between work and disability have focused on enabling disabled persons to exercise all of their legal rights and to participate fully in society and in the European economy, by creating a market that is accessible to all.

In Italy, the second National Conference on Disability (Bari, February 2003) identified, for the first time, the ICF as its frame of reference for developing policies to promote the integration of disabled persons. Italy is particularly interested in the integrative approach of the ICF framework, which implicates all fields of public policy and intervention, particularly welfare and labour policy, because of the conviction that only collaboration across sectors can effectively reduce the disadvantages disabled persons face. Before 2003, workplace integration of disabled persons had been underpinned by two prescriptive laws: Law 104/1992 and Law 68/1999. This legislation did not adequately meet the demands expressed by the movements for the rights of disabled persons and the associations that represented them, nor did it look closely enough at the process and models of integration that were being developed by the Italian regions. Yet, despite these limitations, Law 68 remains the most recent and probably the most important systematic reform in Italy to have dealt with disabled persons' right to work, predating the adoption of the European Directive on Non-Discrimination (78/2000, implemented in Italy by a legislative decree in 2003) and the ratification of the CRPD in 2009.

Law 68 is based on the concept of 'collocamento mirato ('targeted placement'), a concept that speaks to the desire to harmonise two approaches: on the one hand, grounding the path to workplace integration in an assessment of the social, educational and professional history of the disabled person, along with a valuing of his or her skills; on the other, using technical and support tools to make an effective assessment of the employment capacities of the person with disabilities so that s/he gets placed in the 'right job'. These tools include the analysis of available jobs, personalised support programmes and the resolution of physical and/or interpersonal problems in the workplace environment. On a theoretical level, then, the structure of Law 68/99 already anticipates some of the guidelines and multidisciplinary approaches contained in the ICF. An example of this is the role of the 'specialised offices' for targeted placement. The specific role of these offices is delegated to regional legislators, who are responsible for planning, delivering and monitoring the placement in jobs of disabled people, in liaison with the social, medical, educational and other services offered in the area. On the other hand, the assessment of a disabled person's employable skills and the services necessary for workplace integration are entrusted to a 'technical committee' made up of social, medical and legal experts from provincial labour policy boards. This law therefore appears to tackle head-on the problems of an integrated approach to policies and services for disabled people, in order to overcome the notion that diminished psychological or physical abilities lead to a reduction in one's ability to work and generate income. Through targeted placement, Italian law promotes and supports, at least theoretically, the individualised integration of disabled persons into the labour market. This integration is based on an assessment of each individual's ability to work, as well as of the characteristics of the workplace, and it encourages the removal of environmental and social barriers that make integration difficult.

In practice, however, the targeted placement of people in jobs remains a long and indirect process because it comes up against a complex set of requirements to do with the particular users involved (disabled persons and businesses subject to hiring obligations), the compliance standards required by the law, and inequalities between regions (particularly between North and South of Italy) that characterise job placement services in Italy. In fact, it is precisely these territorial differences that bring us to the typically Italian difficulty of putting a law into effect without reference to concrete network strategies that involve the various national and local stakeholders in policy decisions and in workplace integration services. For example, the Third Report to Parliament of the Ministry of Labour and Social Welfare in 2006 praised the network strategies of Job Centres in the Italian provinces: 'many of these centres place themselves within structured local networks and take on the principal characteristics of each region' (Ministero del lavoro e della previdenza sociale, 2006). The aim of the Ministry of Labour government's employment policies is to ensure a higher proportion of disabled people in work; and so, in a regime lacking financial resources at the national level, the Italian government discharges the burden of the disabled into the local networks. The networks policy is, on the one hand, a kind of symbolic politics which aims at national-level responsibility away from management of the total network of stakeholders; on the other hand, it is also a way to encourage institutions and local stakeholders in the 'job networking' that the law 68/99 mandates.

An Italian new deal for disabled people: the ICF Italia Lavoro project

As we have seen, since its global circulation in 2001, the ICF has been favourably received also in Italy because it introduces a methodology of analysis and interpretation that can improve the impact of policies and services of inclusion of disabled people in the labour market. At the second National Conference on Disability in Bari in 2003 (also European Year of People with Disabilities), the ICF methodology was identified as the starting point for a 'renewal' of the targeted placement system and the basis for implementing a pilot project on labour policy: Progetto ICF Italia, promoted by the Ministry of Labour and Social Policy and entrusted for implementation to the ministry's technical agency 'Italia Lavoro spa'.

This pilot project raises awareness throughout Italy of the ICF framework as an innovative strategy for workplace integration of disabled persons. In its first phase, the project circulated an 'ICF-checklist' that lists the physical, environmental and social conditions that constitute a condition of disability. Moreover, the pilot project establishes the basis for an integrated approach that brings together targeted placement and the supply chain of actors who implement the services of entry into the labour market. The first phase of this trial, which ended in 2006, was a moderate success: 17 regions and 78 provinces were involved; 176 disabled persons were employed with temporary contracts and 202 ICF-forms were filled out both by employers and workers. Despite efficient project management and the readiness of districts to adopt the pilot project presented by the ministry, this initial trial highlighted many of the problems inherent in the targeted placement system based on the over-bureaucratised models of Law 68/99 and the fact that its recognition of the right to work was based exclusively on a medical assessment. Though the ICF pilot project is still far from being a holistic and multidimensional evaluation of the disabling condition, it advocates for an important change in the way integration into the labour market is organised. In the territories involved in the pilot, new tools (the ICF) and methods (the integrated approach) are to be adopted that seek to combine application of the legal requirements, the work environment and the needs of the disabled person.

In 2008 and 2009, on the basis of this pilot project, Italy put forward a new project called 'Messa a punto di protocolli di valutazione della disabilità basati sul modello bio-psicosociale e della struttura descrittiva della Classificazione ICF' ('Refining Disability Evaluation Protocols Based on the Bio-Psycho-Social Model and the Descriptive Framework of the ICF'). The project was promoted by the Friuli-Venezia Giulia region, co-funded by the Italian government and managed by Italia Lavoro. Its goal was to provide a definition of ICF modalities and identify tools with which to assess health and disability when carrying out integrated socio-medical healthcare programmes. These projects, taken together, have brought about significant methodological advances, including the development of the WHO checklist with its definition of an ICF 'specialised protocol'. Further analysis of the potential of the ICF, along with the honing of tools used in these pilot projects, generates two protocols for workplace integration: one aimed at the employee and another at the employer.

The first protocol permits the assessment of the employee's characteristics by outlining their 'profile of functioning'. The second analyses the resources provided by the employer in order to comply with the law (68/99) and describes the work environment. The latter is the more significant component: for the first time the 'workplace' and the resources provided in it are evaluated on the basis of the bio-psycho-social approach. This experiment promotes the notion of a 'personalised project' as a dynamic tool that does not strictly adhere to the rigid classifications of functioning defined by the ICF framework.

As well as improving the implementation of the ICF in labour market integration practices, the experimental path being carved out by these Italian projects is also evolving towards a networking approach involving the entire chain of actors involved in targeted placement. The ICF framework, its language, its practices and its tools are gradually gaining traction within the targeted placement process. The actors involved in the job placement of a disabled person now realise that they each play an essential and different role within a unified network. Indeed, the fifth report to Parliament (2008–9) on the implementation of Law 68/99 emphasises the concept of the network as a cornerstone for streamlining organisational models and bringing together the various actors in the targeted placement system.

In 2009–11 the two Directorate-Generals of the Italian Ministry of Labour (DG Social Policy and DG Labour Market) launched a third and more important pilot, the ICF4 Project 'Sviluppo dell'applicazione dell'ICF e di strumenti da esso derivati alle politiche attive di inserimento lavorativo delle persone con disabilità' ('Development of ICF Implementation and ICF-derived Tools for Active Policies of Workplace Integration for Persons with Disabilities'). This project is being carried out in 11 regions (Piedmont, Liguria, Veneto, Friuli-Venezia Giulia, Abruzzo, Marche, Basilicata, Campania, Calabria, Puglia, Sicily) through a 'pilot' province in each region (respectively Asti, Genoa, Padua, Pordenone, Teramo, Ascoli, Potenza, Avellino, Catanzaro, Foggia, Catania). This new project envisages a training programme for using the ICF framework, together with the employee and employer protocols discussed above, so that users will be able to read and interpret the profile of functioning of the disabled person and the profile of the work environment. The final aim of this new project is to improve the efficiency of targeted placement and the efficacy of its own services, providing technical and methodological support to businesses whose organisational labour model does not yet fully comply with the law.

One of the innovative methods employed by the ICF4 project is the application of Social Network Analysis (SNA), a methodology that interprets social reality on the basis of its network structure, taking the social relationship as the minimum unit of observation (see Wasserman and Faust 1994). From this methodological perspective, social structure is viewed as a set of relations between social positions persisting over time. It consists of networks, made up of nodes (members of the social system) and links connecting them. Taking up Simmel's metaphor of 'social circles' (Simmel 1890) we might say that SNA views actors as moving through social spaces created by the intersection of various relational spheres; in each of these, the subject plays a distinct social role and assumes a different position. SNA aims to elicit the concrete structures of social relationships, both formal and informal, while relativising the role of positional logic in explaining and understanding social behaviour. In other words, for structural analysis, no variable or social position is ever absolutely determined; rather, it exists in geometrical relation to the networks in which the subject plays various roles and assumes different positions, depending on a given situation.

The ICF4 project was fully aware of the heuristic potential of SNA for analysing a complex system, such as that of integrating disabled persons into the labour market. Through the analysis of social networks, SNA opens up the possibility of discovering a 'new' model of intervention based on the integration between policy actors and those who provide social, medical, labour and training services. Furthermore, this new model aims to overcome fossilising situations that limit the disabled person's placement in the 'right' job. In order to demonstrate this methodology's practicability, the present author and his team were tasked with acquiring data on the 11 territories participating in the ICF4 project in order to discover how different organisational models are employed. The main objective of the empirical research we carried out was not to assess the strength of the network model on the integration of disabled persons into the labour market, since that would have required observation over a long period. Rather, the objective was to conduct a macro-analysis of

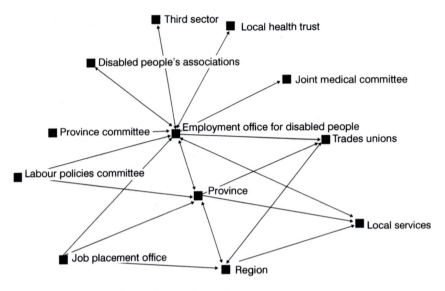

FIGURE 4.1   National Regulatory Network

the disconnection between the chain of service providers involved in targeted placement, as prescribed by national regulations, and the potential models of networking of those same actors that the local territories could create, bringing together into a system of communicative nodes a series of 'specialised offices' that would otherwise be separate. The networks presented in this chapter emerge from a research project carried out between 2010 and 2012, within the context of these pilot projects, by the methodology group of the Area for Social and Labour Inclusion of Italia Lavoro. Specifically, the networks were constructed with the norms of Law 68/99 as guiding criteria, with the aim of reconstructing the relationships among the diverse actors who participate in the process of targeted employment. Starting from the functions assigned to the actors by national norms on access to work, the construction of these networks aimed to assess the morphology of this process and to identify which actors actively participated (see Figure 4.1).

In referencing the different actors, we used the terminology of Law 68/99, which may or not differ from that adopted by the regional government when implementing the national law. The networks were obtained by drawing up a square matrix (actor by actor) that identified the symmetrical relations of all actors. The matrix identifies four kinds of ties:

1   *Normative*: those deriving from Law 68/99. They include all relations expressed by default but not necessarily acted upon (represented in the matrix by =).
2   *Formal*: relations between subjects formalised by specific actions or voluntary wilful expressions (e.g. agreements, conventions, memoranda of

understanding, etc.) not necessarily made in order to comply with legal requirements (represented in the matrix by +).

3   *Informal*: relations between actors, expressed in the form of collaboration through 'autonomous initiative' (represented in the matrix by -).

4   *Multiplex*: multiple relations between actors, containing a dichotomous dimension, which sums up the formal and informal ties between actors. This kind of tie (represented in the matrix by + -)[1] describes all ties wherein the actors initiate practices and actions that go beyond the exclusively formal agreement in order to facilitate the process of targeted placement. A different matrix was developed, for each region analysed, using UCINET 6.0 software (for an introduction see Borgatti *et al.*, 2002), which allows one to represent sociograms and calculate a large number of classical descriptive and network statistics (mean, standard deviation, density, centrality, social cohesion).

The case study: Teramo province

Among the 11 territories included in Italia Lavoro research project, we selected Teramo province, in the Abruzzo region as the case study. Both in its application of the legislative norms and in the way it organises its job placements, Teramo represents one of the most accomplished implementations of the ICF framework. In applying the norms, the regional government's approach has been to confront the various forms of disadvantage through a single institutional plan. An excellent example of this is the establishment of SILUS (Servizio lavorativo utenza svantaggiata – Labour Service for Disadvantaged Users), tasked with carrying out functions related to targeted employment. The regulatory network presented in Figure 4.2 highlights the first level of this region's accomplishments. The centrality of targeted placement (specialised offices) and the dense network of links of the Employment Centre (where SILUS is headquartered) demonstrate the effectiveness of national and regional regulations. Transferring their powers and duties to the provinces, these regulatory bodies have created the conditions for such tasks to be fulfilled via a network of complementary services, promoting the employment of disadvantaged persons by establishing ties among stakeholders. Nevertheless, the regulatory network demonstrates a markedly low density, due for the most part to the presence of various isolated nodes (INAIL, INPS, Agenzia per il lavoro and other brokers) that do not actively participate in labour implementation within the network. On a theoretical level, this low density highlights the fact that the onus of labour market integration of persons with disabilities rests with the offices that have 'historically' been called upon to perform this function.

From this critical perspective, the use of SNA reveals an organisational architecture that disregards the norm, and indeed, even destroys it in favour of a model based on a set of formal and informal ties that facilitate the process of targeted placement and specialised offices. Figure 4.3 highlights several analytical

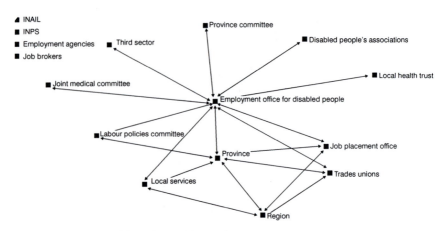

FIGURE 4.2 Regional Regulatory Network

issues; primarily the co-presence of two significant levels of stakeholders. On the one hand, there are those at the institutional level, made up of the set of local entities (regional, provincial and all offices tasked with labour market integration); on the other, there are non-institutional stakeholders made up of associative foundations and work placement agencies. On the level of relationships within the network, we can observe three kinds of connections made up of formal, informal and multiplex ties. These ties make the Province of Teramo an important case for understanding the gap between organisation based on a regulatory approach and organisation based on a layering of local practices and procedures. The Teramo network displays a relational sphere that is structurally weak in terms of formal ties. Legal possibilities – formal agreements, protocols and conventions among actors – remain partially unrealised. It is, therefore, not accidental that many of the relationships displayed in Figure 4.3 are the informal ties that exist between actors in the supply chain of targeted employment.

In this case, the gap between formal and informal ties undermines the legal framework and reinforces the thesis that the efficiency and efficacy of any project integrating disabled persons into the labour market necessarily depends on connections between the various actors. Here, it is clear that this newly visible network of abilities would be able to capitalise fully on resources, should these informal and multiplex ties be transformed into systemic actions.

From this perspective, their formalisation could guarantee the effectiveness of the principle often expressed in regional regulations: pursuing regional labour policies through coordination between all actors involved in the network. Trade unions, the non-profit sector and work placement agencies can be especially helpful in this regard. Their involvement in this process not only reinforces the relationships and meaningful exchanges between all actors in the network, it also undermines the centrality of a purely legal/institutional approach. Measurement of the index of centrality (degree)^2 supports this perspective: voluntary organisations, including associations of disabled persons, demonstrate

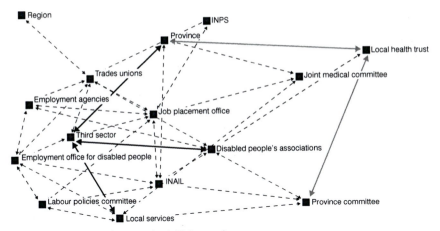

FIGURE 4.3 Multiplex Provincial Network

a higher centrality index (64.3 per cent) than any other actor in the network. The centrality index of the Employment Centre of Teramo (Giulianova, Roseto degli Abruzzi and Nereto) is lower (57.7 per cent).

The implementation of targeted employment services through the activity of local networks is therefore one of the fundamental aspects that make the case of Teramo an organisational model that can be used to analyse other cities involved in the ICF pilot project. From a strictly quantitative perspective, it is impossible to assess the efficacy of the network model in Teramo's targeted employment programme.[3] However, the data that emerges from the forms distributed to targeted employment offices in this province tell of a process that has made the national law more 'fluid', transforming a chain of fundamentally separate actors into an interconnected network whose ties potentially facilitate the job placement of disabled persons. Moreover, this network bears a far greater resemblance to actual social practices than the regulatory model does.

Concluding reflections

As this chapter has shown, the transition from the medical paradigm to the bio-psycho-social model has revolutionised the discourse on disability. The new meanings linked to the existence and well-being of a disabled person recognise that anyone can experience problems of 'functioning' at any point in their life. They highlight the fundamental importance of environmental factors – attitudes, physical or social barriers – in bringing about the disabling condition. We thus arrive at a definition of disability as a health condition in an unfavourable environment. With regard to job placement of persons with disabilities, it is beyond a doubt that the ICF approach and its accompanying methodology have breached the rigid medical-health apparatus that formerly dominated work placement. For over a decade, the practice of health assessments had caused a substantial medico-legal 'drift' in the Italian organisational models linked to Law 68/99. These models, furthermore, were influenced by the assessment of an individual's degree of 'handicap', which was tied to a recognition of 'impairment/dysfunction' rather than to a real identification of a condition of social and environmental disadvantage. However, in the legislative sphere there was an element of novelty, which came on the heels of Law 68/99, namely the Framework Law (*legge quadro*) on the integration of social and local services was passed (Law 328/2000). This law takes a holistic and multi-problem approach, clearly invoking the 'network of local structures' as a systemic action towards the social inclusion of disabled persons. Significantly, Article 14 of this law introduces the disabled person's right to an 'individualised project'. In order to achieve the full integration of disabled persons (as outlined in Article 3 of Law 104 of 5 February 1992) in family and social life, along with their integration in schools, professional training programmes and the labour market, municipalities are to prepare an 'individualised project' (as defined in Clause 2) at the request of the person concerned. This project is to be prepared in consultation with local healthcare services. However, disabled people are still at a significant disadvantage in the labour market in all the Italian regions covered by the Italia project. In this context, the research we have carried out demonstrates that the pilot project of transferring the ICF's language and methodology to local territories, along with the growing discourse on the notion of a 'personalised project' has initiated a de-medicalisation of the job placement process for disabled persons. It has also created a new kind of network, made up of more integrated and less top-downward procedures (Corbisiero, 2013). Through these ICF pilot projects, Italy is engaging with the process of job placement for disabled persons using a cutting-edge international approach. Policies and services for job placement of disabled persons must be based both on the integration between all actors involved and on adapting the workplace environment to the disabled worker's needs. This environmental adaptation can be achieved through the use of technical and methodological tools that recent research has made available. In this light, the use of SNA methodology has proved to be very effective for assessing the implementation of targeted employment at the procedural level. As the case study of Teramo has demonstrated, the regulatory structure of Law 68/99 is insufficient for the implementation of 'network' models. Many local governments in Italy have interpreted its legal implication, and in part that of the ICF itself, as 'forms to fill in' rather than as potential tools of local governance. The Italian pilot projects showcase the potential inherent in networking and provide stakeholders with new tools for organising the supply chain of targeted employment, such as the ICF and the personalised project. Although mentioned in Law 68/99, systemic actions are, other things being equal, the result of processes and procedures carried out at a local level. In conclusion, we could say that a reform of the system of job placement of persons with disabilities requires a restructuring of the targeted employment programme. The co-existence of both forms of national and local governments creates a dilemma: Who really is responsible for job placement and policy interventions of people with disabilities? The Italian trial that we have shown and the social network analysis method suggested that local networks are still far away from the networks that Law 68/99 requires. Monitoring these processes in a systematic and continuous way could be an effective method to implement the job placement of people with disabilities in Italy.

Notes

1 In this analysis the attribution of signs does not indicate the weight of a relationship but rather its function.
2 In SNA, the index of centrality measures the degree of prestige that each node acquires within a social network. In this particular case, the degree represents the number of recommendations received within the network by each participating actor.
3 As mentioned, the aim of our analysis was to use SNA to describe the organizational-relational models of the 11 territories involved in the ICF pilot project, not the assessment of the effects these models have on actual job placement. Furthermore, historical analysis of job placement statistics is complicated both by the grim economic circumstances of the last five years and by unreliable Italian statistics on job placement for disabled persons at local and national level.

References

Brandt, E.N and Pope, A.M. (eds). 1997. Disability in America: assessing the role of rehabilitation science and engineering, Washington DC: National Academy Press.

Barnes, C. 1999. A Working Social Model? Disability and Work in the 21st Century, Paper presented at the Disability Studies Conference and Seminar, Apex International Hotel, Edinburgh, 9 December.

Barnes, C. 2012. Rethinking Disability, Work and Welfare *Sociology Compass*, 6(6): 472–484.

Borgatti S., Everett M. and Freeman L. 2002. Ucinet 6.0 per windows: Software for social network analysis, Harvard, MA: Analytic Technologies.

Brandt, E.N. and Pope, A.M. 1997. *Disability in America: Assessing the Role of Rehabilitation Science and Engineering*, Washington, DC: National Academy Press.

Corbisiero, F. 2013. Oltre l'ICF. L'inserimento lavorativo delle persone disabili attraverso l'implementazione di azioni e strategie di rete. In Valerio, P., Striano, M., and Oliverio, S. (eds) *Nessuno escluso*, Napoli: Liguori Ed.

Crow, L. 1996. *Including All of Our lives: Renewing the social model of disability*. In Barnes, C. and Mercer, G. Exploring the Divide, Leeds: The Disability Press, pp. 55–72.

European Commission. 2007. *Situation of Disabled People in the European Union: the European Action Plan 2008–9* COM(2007)738 final (accessed 4 November 2014).

European Commission. 2010. *Europa 2020. Una strategia per una crescita intelligente, sostenibile e inclusiva*, COM(2010) 2020.

Ferrucci, F. (ed.). 2005. Disabilità e politiche sociali. Sociologia e politiche sociali 8: 24–29.

Griffo, F. (ed.). 2007. L'inclusione come strumento dei diritti umani. In Mascia, M. (ed.), Dialogo interculturale, diritti umani e cittadinanza, Padova: Marsilio, pp. 167–182.

Heymann, J., Ashley Stein, M. and Moreno G. 2014. *Disability and Equity at Work*, Oxford: Oxford University Press.

Hoogeveen, J.C. 2005. Poverty and disability in Uganda, *Journal of African Economies*, 14 (4), 603–631.

Imrie, M. 2004. Disability, embodiment and the meaning of home, *Housing Studies*, 19(5): 745–763.

Loeb, M. and Eide, A.H. 2004. *Living Conditions among People with Activity Limitations in Malawi. A national representative study*, Oslo: Sintef Health Research.

Ministero del lavoro e della previdenza sociale. 2006. Terza relazione al Parlamento sullo stato di attuazione della legge 12 marzo 1999, n. 68 'Norme per il diritto al lavoro dei disabili. Anni 2004–2005, Roma.

Nordenfelt, L. 2003. Disability, action theory and ICF. *Newsletter on the World Health Organization Family of International Classifications*, 1(1):13–15.

Oliver, M. 1990. *The Politics of Disablement*, Basingstoke: Macmillan.

Parlamento Italiano 1999. *Legge 12 marzo 1999, n. 68. Norme per il Diritto al Lavoro dei Disabili, Gazzetta Ufficiale n. 68*.

Prinz, C. 2002. Towards a coherent policy mix. Paper presented at Active Labour Market Policies for People with Disabilities, Brussels: OECD July 2002.

Sen, A. 1985. *Commodities and Capabilities*, Amsterdam: North–Holland.

Simmel, G. 1890. *Über soziale Differenzierung: sociologische und psychologische Untersuchungen, (On Social Differentiation. Sociological and Psychological Investigations)*. Leipzig: Duncker & Humblot.

UN. 2006. *Convention on the Rights of Persons with Disabilities*. New York: United Nations.

U.S. Census Bureau. 2008. Facts for features. Americans with Disabilities Act: July 26. http: www.census.gov./PressRealease (accessed 4 November 2014).

Wasserman, S. and Faust, K. 1994. *Social Network Analysis: method and applications*, Cambridge: Cambridge University Press.

WHO. 1980. International Classification of Impairments, Disabilities and Handicaps. A manual of classification relating to the consequences of disease, Geneva: CH.

WHO. 1999. ICIDH-2: International classification of functioning and disability. Beta-2 draft, short version, Geneva: CH.

WHO. 2001. International Classification of Functioning, Disability and Health, Geneva: CH.

WHO. 2013. World Health Statistics, Geneva: CH.

5

SITES OF OPPRESSION

Dominant ideologies and women with disabilities in India

Nandini Ghosh

Introduction

Violence against women and girls is one of the most pervasive forms of human rights violations in the world. It is present in every country, cutting across national, cultural, economic, social and political boundaries. It takes many forms and its causes are located in a complex interweaving of political, cultural and social factors that both stem from and lead to unequal power relations between men and women.

The *United Nations Declaration on Elimination of Violence against Women* (1993) has defined *violence against women* as 'any act of gender-based violence that results in, or is likely to result in, physical, sexual or psychological harm or suffering to a woman, including threats of such acts, coercion or arbitrary deprivations of liberty, whether occurring in public or private life.' Violence against women includes, but is not limited to, (a) physical, sexual and psychological violence occurring in the family, including battering, sexual abuse of female children in the household, dowry-related violence, marital rape, female genital mutilation and other traditional practices harmful to women, non-spousal violence and violence related to exploitation, (b) physical, sexual and psychological violence occurring within the general community, including rape, sexual abuse, sexual harassment and intimidation at work, in educational institutions and elsewhere, trafficking of women and forced prostitution and (c) physical, sexual and psychological violence perpetrated or condoned by the state, wherever it occurs.

The United Nations considers that violence against women is a manifestation of historically unequal power relations between men and women, which have led to the domination over and discrimination against women by men and to the prevention of their full advancement, and that violence against women is one of the crucial mechanisms by which women are forced into a subordinate position with men. However state response to violence against women continues to frame it as either an 'intimate' problem between two partners or as a rare crime committed by a deviant man, a law and order frame being now dominant in our society (Boucher 2007, Martin 2005). Thus the focus shifts to punishing the perpetrators rather than focusing on the systemic roots of violence.

Violence experienced by disabled women can often be the same in many ways as that perpetrated against non-disabled women. All the barriers that women in Indian society experience are there for women with disabilities, along with the social and political marginalization they face as people with disabilities. The simultaneous oppression faced by women with disabilities as women and disabled people compounds their life situation and makes them more vulnerable to abuse and violence. This violence is often covert and sometimes apparent, perpetrated by multiple players and continues for longer periods of time. It is the social implications of that disability that provokes their vulnerability to abuse. Socio-cultural ideologies that construct women with disabilities as weak, dependent, asexual or highly sexed due to repression, unproductive and incapable of giving birth to or mothering children etc., initiate a process of violence in lives of disabled women from childhood to adulthood and beyond. Lacking knowledge, education and the confidence to confront perpetrators, disabled women often become entrenched in a cycle of violence within families, communities and in workspaces.

This chapter seeks to explore the ways in which socio-cultural ideas regarding gender and disability perpetrate violence against women with disabilities in India. This violence is experienced by disabled women latently in their daily lives through everyday practices and cultural behaviour as well as in openly brutal cases of assault within their own communities and in society in general. In order to understand the operation of violence in lives of disabled women, this chapter draws on data from two sources: one, from primary data collected by the author between 2008 and 2010 from women with disabilities living in West Bengal as part of a larger study on gender; the other is secondary data collated from news reports, media reports and case reports prepared by feminist groups in India on increasing violence against women especially disabled women. The seven women who participated in the study on gender and disability are representative of disabled women living both in urban and rural areas of Bengal and mirror the situation of many disabled women living in India. All names used in this chapter are pseudonyms given by the author to conceal their identity.

Covert forms of violence

According to Bagchi (1995), Indian womanhood is based on a multi-layered accretion of myths that serves patriarchy in both its global and local manifestations. Bengali society has been largely patrilineal with the household being patrilocal and women have little status or place as an individual in orthodox Bengali society (Urquhart 1927, Engels 1996). For women in Bengal, all relationships centre around the men in their families: their fathers, brothers and later their husbands. Women's lives can be divided into three phases: daughter, wife and mother –

the first is supposed to be brief with more importance given to the latter roles. Hence the bodies that women experience are always mediated by constructions, associations and images which most patriarchal socio-cultural formations accept and endorse (Dube 1989, Bagchi 1995, Thapan 1995). Socio-cultural ideologies of gender and disability deem disabled women to be unfit to be a homemaker, wife and mother because of their assumed functional limitations (Begum 1992, Morris 1993). Such ideologies are often linked to ideas regarding acceptable and productive bodies, and hence disabled women often find themselves left out of gendered representations and the symbolic order within traditional patriarchal communities.

Violence is embedded in the ways in which the authority assumed by the state and the patriarchal medical and social system are all aimed at normalizing the disabled female body (Meekosha 1998, Silvers 1998). Disabled girls and their families, socialized into accepting that impaired bodies are imperfect, focus on presenting a semblance of femininity to the outside world. Agatha underwent a series of operations and at the age of four years, was able to walk with the help of crutches and callipers. Parents hoped that reducing the visual impact of the disability would give a semblance of normalcy and would also enable their daughter to be able to fulfil her designated roles within the family set-up. On the other hand, women with mild degrees of disability find that parents are afraid of medical or surgical interventions, fearing a worsening of their condition. Jahanara's father was thankful that

> at least I could walk and as a girl who would have to be married off, I needed to be as normal as possible.

Aparna's father refused to take her for surgery, as he was afraid that surgery would take away the little strength she had in her disabled leg.

Disabled women report a continuous process of de-sexing through language, symbols and practices that ensure that both disabled women and society in general negate their sexuality. From their adolescence girls are given subtle messages regarding repression of her sexual needs. While families rarely tell the girl directly, subtle messages are used to condition the young disabled girl to accept her 'fate' by comparing her to the sons of the family who never have to leave their natal home. Asha's grandmother would tell her,

> You stay in this house like a son. Other girls will get married and leave but you will stay here always.

The de-sexing of girls is evident in the analogy of the disabled girl being like a son, denying her femininity and sexuality and at the same time underlining the fact that she would never be married off like her other sisters. Rita recalls that the women in their neighbourhood would repeat, 'Non-disabled girls can expect a lot of things and have lots of desires, which is not allowed for disabled girls.'

Disabled women reveal that they had received messages from society, especially the women around them, all through their childhood and adolescence telling them that they are unattractive because of their impairments. Denial of sexuality often begins at home and gendered socialization ensures that disabled girls themselves come to fear both the reputation of a loose woman as well as the shame associated with a disabled woman having sexual urges. This kind of fear of social shame and ostracism, however, is more visible in girls living in rural areas, as these are relatively closed communities, where every action is noticed and commented upon. Sandhya revealed that she has consciously never allowed any man to get close to her. Although she talks to other men in the neighbourhood or in the village, she maintains a distance so that people around them will never get a chance to gossip about her:

> How can I? Just imagine, people would say, 'she is like that and look, how she is flirting with boys.'

Asha confirmed that she felt scared whenever she talked to men and boys, because rumours about her liaisons with men would ruin her reputation in the village.

Despite the denial of their sexuality, disabled women fear repercussions, both physical and social, over any sexual attention that they might receive. From early adolescence, mothers have warned their disabled daughters to avoid male attention in order to protect their reputation as the onus was on the disabled women, as single women, to guard against getting an unsavoury reputation. Asha's mother felt,

> If some boy forces his attention on her, everyone will say, she couldn't control herself.

Sulekha's mother urged Sulekha not to incite or excite the local boys, who used to heckle her.

> *Ma* says ignore what they are saying. I know it is my fate and I have to listen to such things.

On the other hand, families often consider their disabled daughter is less at risk in terms of sexual advances as compared to the non-disabled ones. Asha's mother is less afraid for her older (disabled) daughter than for her younger daughter as she is sure that nothing untoward would happen to Asha. She feels safe enough to leave Asha alone at home till late at night, but worries about her younger daughter in similar circumstances.

The threat of defamation as a loose, highly sexed woman becomes the strategic tool of gendered ideologies in India that seek to control and restrain all women in general and disabled women in particular. Anita, working as casual labour in the cement factory near her house, was not allowed to continue there for long, as the other villagers were envious of her contacts in the factory and started spreading rumours about her 'liaisons' inside.

> The villagers talked about how I was granting the factory people sexual favours in order to get the work. They were angry that a dwarf like me was able to find work so easily.

Anita left the work as she did not want to be discredited and tagged as a 'loose' immoral woman, leaving her vulnerable to advances of men in the village. Similarly Mita, working as supervisor of the kitchen in a disabled children's residential institution, had to bear the reprisals from the entire group of staff, who taunted her for being *khoda/langda* (lame/crippled) and cast aspersions on her femininity.

> As I was unmarried and without children, they even called me barren and incapable of understanding because I had never borne children.

The gender/ability ideologies that deny women without children recognition as women, was used by junior staff as a weapon to discredit and devalue Mita, both on grounds of her disability and because she was a woman. Similarly, when the management wanted her to quit the job, they resorted to maligning Mita's reputation as a 'good' woman by insinuating that she was having an affair with one of her married colleagues. The speculation about her relationship and fear of loss of her reputation compelled Mita to leave her job, thereby reinforcing patriarchal controls over her morality and character as a woman and abilist ideologies about a disabled person as a capable worker.

Disabled women face both a denial of their sexuality as well as sexual abuse in the public domain. Men in public spaces often treat these women as available for not only ridicule and pity but also for sexual favours. The ideology that deems these women as sexually unattractive works in the favour of men who treat disabled women as objects of pleasure without fear of repercussions, as 'who would ever think of doing anything to a girl like her?' Anita feels that her sexuality is denied by men who deem her unfit for marriage, while making sexually suggestive comments when they meet her in social situations. Even some of her *gyati* (blood-kin) men and brothers-in-law tease her with sexually loaded comments and invite her alone to watch movies or go out for a pleasure trip. Anita feels they think that because she is short, she also must be less intelligent:

> Some jokingly offer to marry me, and others refer to me as their '*choto bou*' (younger wife with the connotation of short wife). I feel sad, because I know they would never dare to crack such jokes with other women, yet they laugh loudly at me.

Anita knows that if she complains, very few people would believe that she had been treated as a sexual object while others would feel that she invited the comments in some way.

Overt expressions of violence

The Crime in India Report 2012 published by the National Crime Records Bureau, has listed rape as the fastest growing crime in India, which has increased by 902 per cent from 1971 to 2012. However there are almost no figures on the number of rapes of disabled women as this category has not been disaggregated from the total data, even though data on other groups of women like women from scheduled castes and scheduled tribes is disaggregated from within the rape statistics. Waxman (1991) asserts that the aim of violence towards disabled women is not merely to preserve male supremacy but also to preserve non-disabled superiority. Sexual abuse has more to do with oppressive use of power and is related to issues of control and power. Research worldwide has sought to reveal that socio-cultural gender ideologies tend to regard women with disabilities as asexual (Asch and Fine 1988, Shaul, Dowling and Laden 1985, Waxman 1989). However women with disabilities are at a much greater risk of being sexually abused than other women (Musick 1984, Senn 1988). Others report that women in institutions are at a much greater risk of being sexually abused than other women with disabilities (Musick 1984, Stefan, 1987). It may seem like a contradiction that women with disabilities are not seen as sexual beings and at the same time they are at a much greater risk of being sexually abused.

Sexual violence against disabled women is rampant, both within the supposedly safe zone of the 'home' – be it familial or custodial – and without (Sengupta and Mandal 2013). Research studies conducted by several organizations (Swabhiman 2005, Aaina 2008, AWWD 2008) in different states of India reveal that the disabled are most at risk within their homes, not just because of their disability but because of gendered/abilist ideologies that consider them to be asexual and family members would rather deny and hide such instances rather than highlight them. Swabhiman, an NGO in Odisha, undertook a survey in 2005 in 12 districts and found that more than 12 per cent of the physically-challenged women have been raped and 15 per cent molested while the count is 25 per cent and 19 per cent respectively for the intellectually challenged women.

In the last few years, there has been a marked increase in incidence of sexual violence towards women with disabilities in India, with cases of violations being reported from all over the country. What is striking is the rise in the number of violations, across types of disabilities and in different locations and positions of powerlessness. While one section of the critics ascribe this rise to greater reporting due to awareness raising, the other groups entrenched in socio-cultural ideologies prefer to attribute this increase to the heightened sexuality of disabled women who after seeking sexual favours, cry rape against the men. Sengupta and Mandal (2013) report the existence of a stereotypical view of disabled women that considers them to be unable to control their sexual urges. In 2001, in a case where a speech-and-hearing-impaired girl was raped by two policemen inside a prison van in Kolkata, the officer-in-charge had said it was common knowledge that disabled girls were 'sex starved' and it was the girl who had in fact attacked the policemen. More recently, during the course of an enquiry into the sexual assault on a female inmate by a male staff at a Kolkata mental health institution in April 2012, the superintendent of the institution said that he himself was scared of going inside the female ward for fear of being 'molested'. Such attitudes are prevalent within mainstream society and among service providers and people entrusted with the care and protection of disabled women.

There have been at least 35 cases of rape, sexual molestation and violence documented in different newspapers of India from 2008 to 2014. Analysing such reported cases of sexual violence against disabled women, there is a distinct trend. Most of the cases were reported by women with hearing and speech impairments followed by mentally-challenged women, women with locomotor and multiple impairments. There are a few cases of sexual assault on women with mental illness and visual impairments also. A significant proportion of disabled girls were children and also below the age of consent, with the ages of the survivors ranging from nine years to 45 years. There are very few cases of rape or molestation reported by the family members or close relatives, negating the findings of the small-scale studies conducted in India. Looking at the violence of the assault, it is very clear that the sexual violence of disabled women follows the trend for all women in India: while around 60 per cent of the cases were by single perpetrators, there were a significant number of violations by multiple perpetrators. The perpetrators are both known and unknown people for these women, with neighbours, distant relatives, people living in the neighbourhood, service providers, etc., constituting the former and passers-by, strangers and protectors like security guards and policemen comprising the latter. These cases have been reported both from rural and urban areas, where either the disabled women were lulled into a sense of security and then violated or forcibly dragged away to secluded places and assaulted.

While 55 per cent of the cases highlight a single instance of violence, there are 45 per cent of cases where the sexual abuse was carried on over an extended period of time. This is also because many of these women were in protective custody, either within families or in institutions. In almost 30 per cent of the cases, the violation was revealed only when the disabled woman started exhibiting signs of pregnancy. In most of these cases, disabled women turned to their families for preliminary support. However what is a very disturbing trend is the increasing number of cases being reported from various institutions, government and non-government, where most of these women have sought refuge either for education, medical and other treatment, vocational training or shelter. As an example, the most gruesome report came from a shelter run by a non-government organization, where women in protective custody of the state were housed in West Bengal.

Case 1

At the government funded non-government shelter home for destitute women in the Hooghly district of West Bengal, there were a total of 87 residents – 46 women at the short-stay home, 16 at the home for the mentally-challenged and 25 at a cottage home. In early July 2012, some of the inmates of the home sent messages out to the nearby villagers about the mysterious death and surreptitious burial of Guria, a 32-year-old deaf inmate of the home. Guria had been rescued from the streets by Bankura police on 22 May and sent to the home under state protection. According to the authorities of the institution, Guria was killed on 1 July when a ceiling fan fell on her head. After obtaining the death certificate, the authorities buried the body within the premises of the institution without police permission. On 3 July, the authorities handed police a 'death certificate' stating the speech-and-hearing-impaired woman had died of cardio-respiratory failure. Despite the two-day gap, police did not verify their statement.

The District Social Welfare Officer, Hooghly, under whose custody Guria had been placed, initiated a police enquiry which led to the recovery of Guria's dead body and dead bodies of two more persons namely Ranjana Debi and Sumita Paswan, buried within the premises of the home near the banks of the river Damodar. There were injuries all over the bodies, including wounds on the head. It has been revealed that the women living in the institution, some for more than 20 years, were tortured physically and sexually by the secretary of the home along with other associates. The caretaker of the centre allowed outsiders to enter, who sexually abused the inmates in the evening. After the news of the incident spread, the West Bengal government revoked the licence of the institution, moved the residents of the home thereafter to another shelter home run by an NGO and police arrested the secretary of the home and his aide, who have been remanded in police custody.

There have been a series of cases reported from state-run hospitals and mental institutions, where women with psycho-social disabilities and who are challenged mentally have been sexually violated by the male staff of the facility. Most of these women are in a doubly helpless situation – on one hand they are in custody of the state, as they are considered to be incapable of taking care of themselves yet on the other hand, the social perception of their disability renders them incapable of registering complaints against their custodians. The state denies agency to these women and systemically deprives them of opportunities to express their sexuality and sexual rights. The same state system then exploits these women entrusted in their care, emboldened by a social ideology that questions the mental capacities of these women.

What this case and other similar instances have revealed clearly is the state apathy on the one hand with regard to dealing with issues of violence against disabled women and the covert sanction of sexual exploitation of disabled women on the other hand by the authorities who are meant to provide security and protection. The state, which had responsibility for protecting the women with disabilities, took perfunctory interest in them after releasing them into the custody of government and privately run institutions. State custody of such women with disabilities also is without a plan for rehabilitation, which is clearly evident from the fact that some of the residents have been there for more than 20 years and have not been trained in any skills for independent living. On the other hand, the open and continued sexual exploitation of disabled women within the institution remains unabated, perpetrated by people responsible for the protection. Social norms that negate the sexual needs of women with disabilities become the shield behind which such acts of sexual violence are propagated by greedy authorities seeking to make more money by selling sexual access to these women. Being disabled, many of them with communication difficulties and others with mental illness and challenges, the authorities assumed that these women would be unable to complain, and even if they did so, there would be few who believed them. Further, the power of the authorities to make decisions on their behalf and to dispose of their mortal remains rendered the women even more powerless, and gave the authorities a sense of control over the lives and deaths of these women.

Case 2

Savita, a 19-year-old intellectually disabled woman, was living in a government run shelter institution in Chandigarh in early 2009. An orphan, Savita was repeatedly raped allegedly by more than one security guard of the institution. Once her pregnancy was detected, she was moved to another government run institute on 18 May 2009, from where a complaint was registered with the police after Savita informed medical and social workers about the incident. The district administration and the social welfare department which was in charge of Savita's custody sought to terminate her pregnancy on grounds of her limited intellectual capacity and supposed inability to care for the child. A three-member board comprising a psychiatrist, a clinical psychologist and a special educator recommended medical termination of pregnancy, which was then ordered by the Punjab and Haryana High Court. The debate raged by professionals in the disability sector and lawyers in full media glare sought to problematize the maternal rights and responsibilities of a 'mentally retarded' girl with an 'IQ of a nine-year-old'. When Savita pleaded to continue the pregnancy, the Supreme Court of India was forced to step in to allow Savita to bear her child. Sections of civil society and the media were surprised at the judgment and expressed concern about the mental condition and indeed the future of the child.

The battle over Savita was fought more over her right to give birth to the child and ability to rear him/her rather than about the perpetrators who were actually supposed to protect her. The debate and the controversy over her right to give birth completely shielded the rest of the criminal proceedings, which were actually against the state mechanisms of protection. The judge observed that the case was an eye-opener and showed the state of affairs in institutions that were meant for the welfare of the destitute. The court also reminded the state that it was its responsibility to take care of the child, more so because it was the state's employees who were responsible for the situation.

In a sense, Savita's case is example of the high-handed way in which state government, administration and society in general considers the reproductive rights of women with disabilities, especially those with intellectual impairments and mental illness. In the 1990s in Maharashtra, 17 mentally-challenged girls below 18 were made to undergo hysterectomies. The state chose to control the girls' reproductive rights by deploying extreme measures. The professionals involved in that decision neither denied that hysterectomies were done, nor did they perceive them as a violation. They justified them as having been done in the best interests of the girls. In both these cases, the focus is more on controlling the reproductive rights of the woman perceived to be mentally 'slow', rather than focusing on the systematic sexual violence that is perpetrated by society, state actors and institutions devised to protect the interests of women with disabilities. By churning the debate on the right to be a mother on the part of a woman with intellectual disabilities, the state itself raised the question of a fit and thus unfit mother. What this dialogue between the state, civil society and feminist organizations also did was to shift attention away from the state's failure to protect the rights of women, especially disabled women, in the custody of the state.

Case 3

In February 2012, a deaf young girl, Rajni was raped by a junior doctor in a government hospital in the Bankura district of West Bengal. Rajni, who had been admitted to hospital with chest pains the day before and was in the female ward with her mother, was taken by one of the junior doctors to another room on the pretext of conducting some medical tests. After some time, when her mother became worried about the prolonged examination and went to investigate, she found the 19-year-old Rajni lying naked and unconscious. Rajni's mother raised a cry over the state of her daughter and was threatened by other medical personnel about registering a formal complaint. A police complaint could be lodged only with the help of the family members of one of the women occupying the adjacent bed. Even before any enquiry had been conducted the Superintendent of Police pointed out the difficulties in carrying out any investigation because Rajni was deaf and needed an interpreter. Rajni was subjected to a medical examination in Bankura and then was taken by police personnel to Kolkata for a second one. Her clothes and bed sheets were taken for forensic examination. The first medical report of Rajni confirmed she was raped. The doctor accused of raping Rajni was arrested on the hospital premises a week after the incident and appeared before a district court and was remanded in police custody.

The hospital constituted a three-member committee to look into the allegations, which were declared to be false. The medical doctors' associations closed ranks along with the government medical personnel to defend the doctor and accuse Rajni of false allegations for petty benefit. Overnight the room where Rajni had been taken for examination and then violated sexually was turned into a store room and the door was dismantled to give the impression that both she and her mother were lying about the incident. Other inmates of the female ward and their relatives were threatened with non-treatment or negligence if they gave evidence. The nurses and other medical staff on duty refused to discuss the issue, implying foul play against medical personnel. The roster records were changed to show that the accused doctor had not been on duty that night and an alibi was created for him at a well-known club in town. The unspoken assumption in this case voiced by some junior medical personnel was that there was no reason why an educated upper-middle class doctor would even look at a deaf girl from a poor family living in a village.

For a poor family from a remote rural village with very little education, the state mechanisms which included the medical fraternity, the police and the judicial system seemed like a formidable barrier that sought to render them powerless by demonstrating the might of the established and accepted state structures. The family stood accused not just of falsely implicating the doctor but also of making demands for money and marriage to the family of the doctor, which strengthened the argument against them. The medical doctors, police personnel and political leaders on the other hand used media and their power to influence them and public opinion about the falseness of the case, thereby reinforcing the powerlessness of the poor and marginalized in front of the might of the state and its representatives. The issue of the sexual violence perpetrated against a deaf girl was subverted into the case of class politics and superiority of the state mechanisms over individual resistance.

Case 4

There have been a large number of reports of sexual violence against women with disabilities in the Hooghly district, which is close to Kolkata in West Bengal. At least seven cases of rape and assault have been registered with the police and are awaiting trial, especially with the help of a local NGO that has assisted families with the legal processes. However, most of the cases are still in the judicial courts, without any justice meted out to the women involved. Of the oldest reported cases in 2004–5, two of the women, one with multiple disabilities and the other deaf, have proceeded with their lives abandoning their legal cases as they were taking too much time and bringing too much community attention to their situation. While one of the girls' families went for a financial settlement and support, the other girl dropped the case when she got a government job and got married.

Of the later cases, one concerns Mina, 23 years, a tribal deaf girl, who lives with her mother in a hut and both work as agricultural labourers in the local fields. Two years ago, when Mina was returning home from work alone, three men forcibly dragged her away and raped her. When her mother became worried about her delayed return, she was found in a disoriented condition and bleeding badly. A police case was registered on the same day, and Mina was taken for medical examination and the accused were arrested. The case is now being tried at a fast-track court in the area. Seema, a 13-year-old girl with cerebral palsy was alone at home in June 2013 as her parents were out selling sweets for a living. A neighbour came in and carried her away to some bushes beside a nearby pond and raped her and left her there. In the evening, her parents found her with injury marks all over her body and without any clothes. Her father immediately registered a case with the police and at present Seema's case is being tried. But Seema was unable to bear the trauma of the sexual assault and died after a severe epileptic fit in December 2013.

Rachana, an 18-year-old mentally-challenged woman was sexually violated by her neighbour's 19-year-old son on a regular basis when her mother used to go every morning to sell flowers. The incident came to light when she was discovered to be around three months pregnant. After the mother lodged the police complaint Rachana was able to identify the perpetrator and he was subsequently arrested. However, the state medical examination of Rachana did not identify any use of force and neglected to mention that she was pregnant. Hence the NGO had to conduct a separate medical examination in order to establish her pregnancy and to offer a complete medical report to the judges. In the meantime, the father of the perpetrator tried all strategies to ensure that the case did not reach the courts, from offering financial support to using threats and political intimidation even for the NGO and finally offering marriage with his son. However the mother of Rachana has stood up against such intimidation and is quite determined to carry on the fight for justice for her daughter.

From all the above cases, one point that becomes obvious is the need for training police officers regarding the correct procedure, especially if the person who is sexually assaulted is a disabled girl and a child too. Most of the police officers, though sympathetic, are not aware of the protocols to be observed while interrogating and seeking information from the disabled girls/women. While the police do not usually delay in sending the woman for a medical checkup, there are often gaps in their investigation and filing of the cases in the courts of justice. In the judicial courts, the lawyers obfuscate the process of justice by asking for fresh dates and wasting time on mundane matters. On the other side is the state machinery, where provisions for compensation and rehabilitation of the women have been completely ignored for lack of a government order. The district administration has been unable to take up the rehabilitation process of any of these women or make provisions for financial compensation that is guaranteed by state schemes because they have no order from their higher authorities.

Case 5

Shabana, 25 years old, is a deaf athlete who has represented the state of West Bengal in different national games competitions. Besides winning the State Role Model Prize in 2011, she had won awards in various track and field events from

2003 to 2011 at state level. In June 2012 when she was returning home after practice in district headquarters at Raigunj she got off at the local bus stand in North Dinajpur district and boarded a shared auto-rickshaw to her home. The driver, who apparently realized that she was disabled, reportedly asked other passengers to get off, saying it would not be possible for him to drive in the rain. Then he asked Shabana to come to his place at Baruibari till the rain subsided. When she agreed he took her to his place where he allegedly raped her through the night again. In the morning, when the girl could finally leave Das's place, neighbours suspected foul play and asked her what the problem was. She somehow conveyed to them everything and was helped to go home. Shabana went home and along with her mother put in a written complaint against the driver, who was arrested the next day. He appeared in court and was sent to jail custody for 14 days.

Different political parties came up with new campaigns every day, claiming to provide support for the victim. The perpetrator's allegiance to the ruling party stoked a controversy after he was sent to jail. Opposition parties cried foul over the attitude of the police and said he should have been remanded in police custody. The opposition organized a rally at Hemtabad and demanded exemplary punishment for the accused. They also met the Hemtabad BDO and demanded the accused be taken in police custody. After nearly 18 months a fast-track court judge convicted the auto-rickshaw driver, and sentenced him to ten years rigorous imprisonment for raping Shabana. He was also instructed to pay a fine of Rs. 5000 to her or suffer detention for another three months.

The only difference between all the previous cases and the case of Shabana is the fact that she was already a well-known figure in national athletics and she had the benefit of education. Shabana was able to produce a written statement in acceptable language which could be used as evidence against the perpetrator. Her status as a star athlete also served to bring not only media attention but also political patronage of all colours, which helped in the path of seeking justice. In India it is estimated that only about 5 per cent of the cases of sexual violence against disabled women are reported – the reasons for not reporting such cases lie as much in the socio-cultural ideologies as in an aversion for the long drawn-out legal processes. Most of the disabled women who experience sexual assault and violence are kept wondering if seeking justice is at all possible for them. Patriarchal socio-cultural ideologies deem sexual violation as more damning for the women who are violated than the men who are the perpetrators. When a disabled woman is sexually assaulted, then all blame is pinned on the woman, for being sexually repressed, for not being able to resist, for offering provocation and finally for daring to reveal the crime. Hence under-reporting of such instances influenced by such ideologies is crushed by the legal procedure and the continued sexual abuse of the violated woman, who has to again and again confront not only the perpetrators but a state system that is biased towards the male perpetrators and against the disabled woman whose sexuality is brought to the forefront.

Despite proactive laws, the state mechanisms and socio-cultural ideologies regarding women with disabilities still influence the ways in which sexual violence is institutionalized, propagated and in a way legitimized in Indian society. Of the cases of sexual assault/violence registered by disabled women with the state agencies, there are no statistics available about the rate of conviction in these cases. One of the reasons for this is that the testimonies of girls and women with disabilities are often fractured owing to physical or mental impairment and hence are usually not given due importance by the police or the courts. In a case in 2009 in Rajasthan, where two persons had raped a deaf girl, the judicial magistrate acquitted the accused as the girl was unable to speak and hence unable to identify the accused, and declared the girl to be of unsound mind. The attitudes of police officers, at local police stations, who are dealing with these cases, are alarming. From making sarcastic or snide remarks, to acting late on the cases, to not having women officers deal with the cases, the local police stations show an ineptness, ignorance and a total blindness to dealing with issues of rape sensitively which may even amount to criminal negligence on their part.

Conclusion

Feminists have always identified the source of male power and domination over women in the socio-economic and ideological structures of society, which guarantee and legitimize the unequal power relations between men and women. Power is constituted by, develops, and is exercised through the interconnection of sexuality, aggression, violence and masculinity, all of which compromise women's bodily and sexual freedom. Women with disabilities in India are rendered powerless in a social order that does not want to acknowledge the self-hood of such women, stemming mainly from a fear and abhorrence of disability and cultural ideologies about women. Thus disabled women face violence in society which ranges from hidden forms of violence through socialization and social control through ideologies and institutional policies to open expressions of aggression ranging from sexual assault, molestation to rape.

Gender/ability ideologies generate violence in the lives of disabled women in India through the social construction of disabled people as asexual and the repression of women's sexuality. The socio-cultural ideologies that negate disabled women's sexuality, thereby creating a veneer of untouchability, become the very basis of exploitation of these women within the patriarchal social order. The powerlessness of disabled women is constructed through socialization processes that ingrain in these women contradictory ideas regarding their undesirability on the one hand and the fear of stigmatization as a sexually hyperactive woman on the other. However this denial of the sexuality of disabled women is the precise cause of their being more vulnerable to sexual abuse, as they are unprepared to recognize violence, exploitation and domination and yet submit to and yearn for it, as it becomes their means of being recognized as women. On the contrary, families and state endorse such repression of sexuality in the form of sterilization, which removes the stigma of undesirable pregnancy but fails in providing protection from sexual abuse.

The disempowerment of disabled women is further reinforced by state mechanisms, which guided by dominant social constructions, legitimize and yet ignore the systematic and systemic violence meted out to disabled women, either in custodial protection, as users of state-provided services or within family and community contexts. The stigma attached to both sexuality and disability ensure most often that voices remain silent or are silenced not only by patriarchal socio-cultural ideologies but also by overt state responses to such crimes against disabled women. Thus the present state of affairs may be addressed through simultaneous processes of sensitizing state services to respond to the issues raised by disabled women in the area of violence and abuse, and state promotion of positive images of disabled people and women, fostered through proactive programmes and policies that on one hand build capabilities and self-confidence of disabled women and on the other hand, promote inclusion and appreciation of their abilities within families, communities and in society.

References

Aaina (2008) Women with Disabilities Status Report – an analysis of data collected from 8 districts. Unpublished report, Aaina, Bhubaneswar Orissa.

Asch, A. and Fine, M. (1988) Introduction: beyond pedestals. In M. Fine and A. Asch (eds) *Women with Disabilities: Essays in Psychology, Culture and Politics*, Philadelphia, PA: Temple University Press.

AWWD (2008) *Attitude and policy towards woman with disabilities by the key actors in development. A study on the status of Women with disabilities in five states of Eastern part of India*, Kolkata: AWWD.

Bacquer, A. and Sharma, A. (1997) *Disability: Challenges Vs Responses*, New Delhi: Concerned Action Now.

Bagchi, J. (ed.) (1995) *Indian Women: Myth and Reality*, Kolkata: Sangam Books.

Begum, N. (1992) Disabled women and the feminist agenda, *Feminist Review* 40: 70–84.

Boucher, L. M. (2007) Naming the problem: feminists frame violence against women. Unpublished Doctoral Thesis, York University. www.brescia.uwo.ca/iwil/events/conferences/lisa_mae_boucher.pdf> (Accessed 10/01/2014).

Bunch, C. (1992) *Gender Violence: A development and human rights issue*, Dublin: Attic Press.

Dube, L. (1989) On the construction of gender: Hindu girls in patrilineal India. In K. Chanana (ed.), *Socialisation, Education and Women: Explorations in Gender Identity*, New Delhi: Orient Longman.

Dube, L. (1997) *Women and Kinship: comparative perspectives on Gender in South and South East Asia*, Delhi: Vistaar.

Engels, D. (1996) *Beyond Purdah? Women in Bengal 1890–1939*, Delhi: Oxford University Press.

Gochenour C. and Longo, R. E. (1981) Sexual assault of handicapped individuals, *Journal of Rehabilitation*, 47, 3: 24–27.

Hillyer, B. (1993) *Feminism and Disability*, Norman, OK: University of Oklahoma Press.

Lonsdale, S. (1990) *Women and Disability*, London: Macmillan.

Maqbool, S. (2003) The situation of disabled women in South Asia. In A. Hans and A. Patri (eds) *Women, Disability and Identity,* New Delhi: Sage.

Martin, P. Y. (2005) *Rape Work: Victims, Gender and Emotions in Organizational and Community Context,* New York: Routledge.

Meekosha, H. (1998) Body battles: bodies, gender and disability. In T. Shakespeare (ed.) *The Disability Studies Reader: social science perspectives,* London: Cassell.

Morris, J. (1993) Gender and disability. In J. Swain, V. Finkelstein, S. French and M. Oliver (eds) *Disabling Barriers – enabling environments,* London: Sage.

Musick, J. L. (1984) Patterns of institutional sexual abuse, *Response to Violence in the Family and Sexual Assault,* 7, 3: 1–11.

National Crime Records Bureau (2012) Crime in India Report 2012, New Delhi, National Crime Records Bureau, Ministry of Home Affairs, Government of India. http://ncrb.gov.in/CD-CII2012/Statistics2012.pdf (Accessed on 10.2.2014).

Sengupta, S. and Mandal, S. (2013) Not a 'safe' issue: disabled women and sexual violence, *Infochange News & Features,* March.

Senn, C. Y. (1988) *Vulnerable: sexual abuse and people with an intellectual handicap,* Toronto: Roeher Institute.

Shaul, S., Dowling, P. J. and Laden, B. F. (1985) Like other women: perspectives of mothers with physical disabilities. In M. J. Deegan and N. A. Brooks (eds), *Women and disability: the double handicap,* New Brunswick, NJ: Transaction Books.

Silvers, A. (1998) Women and disability. In Jaggar, A. and Young, I.M. (eds.), *Blackwell's Companion to Feminist Philosophy,* pp. 330–340, Oxford: Basil Blackwell Ltd.

Silvers, A., Wasserman D., Mahowald M. B. and Becker, L.C. (1999) *Disability, Difference, Discrimination: Perspectives on justice in bioethics and public policy,* Lanham, MD: Rowman & Littlefield.

Stefan, S. (1987) Women in the mental health system, *The Mental Health Law Project,* 6(4/5), 4–5.

Swabhiman (2005) *Report on Abuse and Activity Limitation: a study on domestic violence against disabled women and girl children in Odisha, India,* Swabhiman, Bhubaneswar Odisha.

Thapan, M. (1995) Gender, body and everyday life, *Social Scientist* July–September, 23 (7–9), 32–58.

United Nations (1993) *United Nations Declaration on Elimination of Violence against Women,* New York: United Nations.

Urquhart, M. M. (1927) *Women of Bengal – A study of the Hindu Pardanashins of Calcutta,* Calcutta: Association Press (YMCA).

Wadley, S. S. (1999) Women and the Hindu tradition. In D.Jacobsen and S. S. Wadley (eds) *Women In India: Two Perspectives,* New Delhi: Manohar Publishers.

Waxman, B. F. (1989) The politics of sex and disability, *Disability Studies Quarterly,* 9(3), 1–5.

Waxman, B. F. (1991) Hatred: the unacknowledged dimension in violence against disabled people, *Sexuality and Disability,* 9 (3), 185–198.

6

HOW TO UNDERSTAND VIOLENCE AGAINST DISABLED PEOPLE

Halvor Hanisch

Introduction

The issue of violence against disabled people has recently moved onto center stage in disability studies. The purpose of this chapter is to outline how this violence should be understood, but not primarily in order to support certain understandings as opposed to certain others. The *how to* in the title relates to the processes through which we develop our understandings of violence against disabled people. The specific understandings belong to specific knowledge trajectories; and the workings – and possible reworkings – of these trajectories that is the subject of this chapter.

The chapter makes a four-stage argument: (1) the disturbing strength of the empirical findings raises an obligation to give violence a central place in disability studies *thinking*, (2) most disability scholars, nevertheless, expand their perspectives to *include* violence, rather than letting the insights on violence engender theoretical development, (3) there are rudiments, in available research, suggesting otherwise (4) the knowledge of violence against the disabled can also shape disability studies perspectives on other issues.

Since "violence" is increasingly used on a variety of social phenomena, a note is needed on how the term is applied in this chapter. Unless otherwise defined, this chapter relies on Robert Audi's now classical definition of interpersonal violence as "The physical attack upon, or the vigorous physical abuse of, or the vigorous physical struggle against, a person" (1971: 61). Although Audi reserves his notion of intentionally violent acts, the arguments in this chapter pertain to intentional and unintentional acts alike. It is also necessary with a note on the use of the term "disabled people" in this chapter: While this term denotes the general group – thereby explicating a social perspective on life with an impairment – the expression "people with" is reserved for specific impairment groups.

Empirical findings: victimization

We should base our understanding of violence against disabled people on significant findings from empirical research. To point out such crucial findings is not easy: there is still a lack of robust empirical research, in particular from low-income and middle-income countries, and different operationalizations and measurements make it difficult to compare or combine research in this area.

However, the World Health Organization has recently conducted two systematic reviews. Examining research on violence against disabled adults and children published in the period 2001–2011, they investigated prevalence and risk factors (Jones et al. 2012, Hughes et al. 2012). Since these reviews have fairly strict exclusion criteria, and the adult review only with past-year experiences of violence rather than violence throughout the life-course, findings from those reviews must be combined with evidence from other research. When combined, available research on victimization gives at least five clues for further thinking.

Violence against people with disabilities is disproportionately prevalent (compared to violence against people in general). On the one hand, this finding is only provisional: the WHO reviews conclude that the research is scarce and employs different measurements and research instruments. The included studies defined both disability and violence differently, and some were limited to specific forms of violence such as sexual abuse. This variance gave, not surprisingly, differing and uncertain prevalence estimates. On the other hand, the conclusion seems robust, and cuts across almost every available study: the prevalence estimates remain comparatively disproportionate, even if they vary in size.

The disproportionate prevalence cuts across gender differences. The WHO review concerning adults demonstrates that disabled women are at a greater risk than disabled men (Hughes *et al.* 2012: 1628). On the other hand, the review also underlines that violence is disproportionate among both men and women. Specific research with disabled men also confirms that disabled men are more likely to experience violence than non-disabled women (Mitra & Mouradian 2014).

While the WHO review regarding children and adolescents does not address gender, another recent review found "a complicated and inconsistent pattern" (Stalker & McArthur 2012). On the one hand, Stalker and McArthur show that the disproportion connected with disability is not only strong and fairly independent of gender, but perhaps even so powerful that it reverses the otherwise very strong association between gender and violence: while non-disabled girls are at considerably greater risk than non-disabled boys, this is not necessarily the case for disabled children. On the other hand, a recent prevalence study found that "after controlling for other risk factors, physical disability was a significant predictor of contact and non-contact SV [sexual victimization] for boys, but not for girls" (Mueller-Johnson *et al.* 2014).

The disproportionate prevalence cuts across many different forms of violence, including sexual violence and threats of violence (Jones *et al.* 2012: 904, Hughes *et al.* 2012: 1626). Multiple literature reviews also demonstrate that related forms of aggression, such as bullying, neglect, sexual harassment and psychological abuse, are disproportionately prevalent (Rose *et al.* 2010, Horner-Johnson & Drum 2006: 63, Jones *et al.* 2012: 905).

Violence is disproportionate in many different groups of disabled people. Although disabled people are at hightened risk in general, the risk is particularly high for people with learning disabilities and people with psychiatric conditions. Moreover, the WHO reviews calculated more disproportionate pooled prevalence estimates (for combined measures of violence) for children than for adults. The most crucial finding – that people with disabilities are more often subjected to violence than their non-disabled peers – is nevertheless confirmed across diagnoses. With regard to children with cerebral palsy, people of old age and people with restricted growth, for instance, researchers have also found high prevalence of abuse and violence (Govindshenoy & Spencer 2007, Collins 2006, Shakespeare *et al.*, 2010). The disproportion cuts across these subgroups, even if their prevalence estimates differ. Although it is useful to disaggregate some of the issues, the disproportion in victimization is a broad phenomenon presumably intertwined with broad disabling processes.

The disproportionate prevalence seems somewhat independent of social context. Violence against disabled people is best known from the public space or institutional settings. However, the prevalence is also disproportionate – and, in some research, even more disproportionate – in family settings (Jones *et al.* 2012, Hughes *et al.* 2012). Disabled people are not only disproportionately likely to be harmed in public space, they are also disproportionately likely to be harmed by their loved ones.

Empirical findings: perpetration

How common is it – for a non-disabled person – to perpetrate violence against a disabled person? While this question is rarely addressed directly in research, the findings above can shed light on that question if it is rephrased as a metastatistical question of *probability* To demonstrate this possibility, I have applied a Bayesian inferential technique to the estimates in the WHO review on violence against disabled adults.

In order to produce a rough estimate for the 12-month incidence of violent actions against disabled people within the non-disabled population, the Bayesian procedure departs from pooled estimates for victimization. The WHO review concerning disabled adults estimates that 6.1 percent of people with learning disabilities, 24.3 percent of people with serious mental illness and 3.2 percent of those with other ("non-specific") impairments, have been subjected to violence within the last 12 months.

Moving on from these estimates, one must also calculate the probability of being a non-disabled adult. I define this overall probability as the average of the two WHO prevalence estimates found in *Global Burden of Disease* and the *World Health Survey* (17.5 percent). With regard to the 12-month prevalence of serious mental illness – which is the relevant prevalence – I rely on the findings from the WHO *World Mental Health Surveys*. There, the average between the two crucial estimates, for low- and middle-income countries and for high-income countries, respectively, is 3.7 percent (Kessler (The WHO Mental Health Survey Consortium) 2004). The prevalence of learning disabilities is defined with reference to a recent systematic review on the prevalence of "intellectual disability," where meta-analysis gave the prevalence of 1.1 percent (Maulik *et al.* 2011). These estimates imply, when combined, that the non-specific group can be estimated at 12.7 percent.

These figures suggest that the general probability of violence against a disabled person in the past 12 months, is 1.37 percent. However, systematic literature reviews suggest that people with severe mental illness are approximately four times more likely to perpetrate violent acts, regardless of victim characteristics: "approximately 2 percent of persons without a mental disorder perpetrated violence in the past year compared with 7 percent to 8 percent of persons with severe mental illness" (Choe *et al.* 2008: 6). Second, reviews on perpetrators with learning disabilities also suggest a similar disproportion; individuals in this group are approximately twice as likely to perpetrate such acts (Craig *et al.* 2006). For the heterogeneous "non-specific" group, no such assumptions should be made.

By combining the probability of being non-disabled (as we have defined it) with this disproportion, we can calculate that the probability of being disabled (given that one has committed a violent act within the last 12 months) is 15.2 percent. Given a 1:1 ratio – although some perpetrators might have more than one victim – we can calculate that 84.8 percent of a certain type of acts (violence against a disabled person in the past 12 months) is committed by an individual from an 82.5 percent group in the population (non-disabled people).

In summary, based on the reasoning above, we assumed that the probability of someone not being disabled, given the fact that they have committed a violent act against a disabled person, is about 84.8 percent. Meanwhile, the probability of having any of the listed, relevant disabilities (see above) was 17.5 percent and the probability of anyone committing an act of violence against a disabled person was 1.37 percent. Using the Bayes equation, we were able to estimate that 1.408 *percent of the non-disabled population has committed violence against a disabled person within the last 12 months.*

Importantly, this estimate assumed that there was no significant overlap between the impairment groups (i.e. prevalence of learning disabilities, mental illness and non-specific disability). It is likely that this assumption is not true. However, this assumption allows us to produce a probabilistic range for our estimate. If, on the contrary, we were to assume *complete* overlaps between our estimates for impairment groups, then the prevalence of our disabilities becomes equal to the largest impairment group (12.7 percent). As a consequence, our estimate falls to 1.331 percent. So, the 12-month incidence of non-disabled acts of violence against disabled people is somewhere between 1.331 percent and 1.408 percent. Neither 1.331 percent nor 1.408 percent is likely to be a correct estimate. Nevertheless, it is probable, that is, likely, that the true number lies in between.

Knowledge trajectories

How is violence understood in disability studies at present? To answer that question, this chapter relies on the metaphilosophical concepts of analytical, ontological and epistemological priority. Martin K. Davies defines the three concepts thus:

> To say that the notion of X is *analytically prior* to the notion of Y is to say that Y can be analyzed or elucidated in terms of X, while the analysis or elucidation of X itself does not have to advert to Y. [...] To say that X is ontologically *prior* to Y is to say that X can exist without Y, although Y cannot exist without X. [...] To say that the notion of X is *epistemologically prior* to the notion of Y is to say that it is possible to find out about X without having to proceed via knowledge about Y, whereas finding out about Y has to go by way of finding out about X.
>
> (Davies 2003: 96–97)

Here, "priority" must not be confused with prioritization. Instead, Davies' perspectives suggest that knowledge can be analyzed by how it is organized, that is, in terms of "the order of philosophical analysis or elucidation" (2003: 96). Davies' work also suggests that knowledge can be analyzed in terms of three movements or *trajectories*.

First, a phenomenon X (say, violence against disabled people) is often to a varying extent described in terms derived from knowledge of phenomenon Y (say, barriers to social participation). If so, violence is analyzed *by way of* or *with the aid of* knowledge of such barriers, giving another understanding of violence than we otherwise would have had. If that connection, then, leaves the knowledge of those barriers unchanged, violence is analytically posterior to those barriers.

Second, different perspectives also place social phenomena in different *ontological* trajectories. To the extent that we analyze the violence against disabled people as *effects* – alternatively by way of "production," "construction," "exclusion" or other transitive terms – we are inadvertently claiming that certain social processes or conditions pre-exist the disproportionate violence against disabled people. At least if this claim is not followed by some discussion of effects of violence on those other processes, they are positioned as ontologically prior to violence.

Third, violence is often approached through data which is related to the actual violence indirectly. Certain data (say, personal narratives) are used to describe another social phenomenon (the experience of victimization), a description that finally gives access to the analytical object (the social practice of violence against disabled people). If the knowledge bears witness to, or depends upon, such an epistemological trajectory, the violence is epistemologically posterior.

Available research on violence against disabled people falls largely into three traditions. First, there is a considerable body of research associated with the UK social model of disability. Second, a more "cultural" tradition has a strong and growing presence, primarily in North America, and more recently also in Europe. Third, there is also a growing body of research around the notion of "hate crime." This rough typology corresponds largely to Dan Goodley's typology of a "social," a "cultural" and a "minority" model of disability, respectively (2010: 10–15). These three traditions imply different knowledge trajectories, analytically, ontologically and epistemologically.

Analytical trajectories

UK research on violence against disabled people is often characterized by a more or less strict adherence to the UK social model of disability. While Andrea Hollomotz's theoretically ambitious work "adopts a social model approach" (2009: 84, 2013: 478), the first national UK study of domestic violence against disabled women explicitly "uses the social model of disability" (Hague *et al.* 2011: 117).

The shape of this adherence varies. While Hague, Thiara and Mullender refer to a general version of the model, others depart from "debates around the social model(s)," and argue that these debates provide "innovative tools for disability research" or call for theoretical development (Nixon 2009: 84). Jennifer Mays, for instance, argues that "feminist structural interpretations (material feminism) and disability theory should be integrated and used as an additional analytical tool to inform the understandings of domestic violence experienced by women with a disability" (2006:149).

It is worth noting that these scholars investigate violence in the context of pre-existing debates, theories or ways of interpretation, that themselves are left unchanged by the issue of violence. Moreover, a possible integration of materialist feminism and the UK social model – the development of perspectives that Mays suggests – also seems to pre-exist research on violence: they should be integrated and *then* "used." Finally, the perspective we would finally achieve is not said to affect or supplement the pre-existing perspectives, but should remain an area-specific *addition* to those perspectives.

In research on violence, the poststructuralist tradition is perhaps best represented in the work of Dan Goodley and Katherine Runswick-Cole. In one sense, violence becomes analytically prior in their work. Instead of describing interpersonal violence in well-known UK social model terms, they re-frame well-known issues as systemic, psycho-emotional and cultural violence. However, their analytical path seems to turn away from empirical knowledge:

> We follow Zizek's (2008: 1) advice to *step back* from the obvious signals of violence to 'perceive the contours of the background which generates such outbursts'. [...] Violent acts against disabled people can only be

understood by reflecting on the wider circulating practices of a disablist culture.

(2011: 607)

However, it is not possible to analyze violent agency in the light of *all* wider social relations ("wider circulating practices"). A social phenomenon such as physical interpersonal violence), is viewed in the light of certain social practices, on the condition that one chooses not to view it in light of others. Therefore – in contrast, perhaps, to the UK social model tradition – Goodley and Runswick-Cole view interpersonal violence in light of *semantic* structures, "a trenchant dimension of culture [...] the dominant culture of disablism" (2011: 604). It seems clear, therefore, that they position cultural (or semantic) phenomena as analytically prior to interpersonal violence.

The hate crime tradition explores violent acts as forms of – or, sometimes, expressions of – hatred. On the one hand, this leads to an emphasis on attitudes, such as "a pernicious de-valuing of disabled people" that "indicates a disdain for their equality as human beings" (Sin 2014: 106). While the notion of "hatred" is rarely explicated, it seems clear that this hatred or "disdain" is more active than, say, notions of cultural violence. In their *Dictionary of Psychology*, Reber, Allen and Reber argue that hatred is a strong subjective experience, characterized by a desire for destruction and inflicting of pain:

A deep, enduring, intense emotion expressing animosity, anger, and hostility toward a person, group, or object. Hatred is usually assumed to be characterized by (a) the desire to harm or cause pain to the object of the emotion and (b) feelings of pleasure from the object's misfortunes.

(1985: 330)

The hate crime tradition's specific analytical contribution is threefold. First, it points out the severity in disability-related hostility, which clearly goes beyond prejudice. Second, analytical categories such as "disablist hate motivated events" (Roulstone *et al.* 2011: 355) make it possible to emphasize perpetrator agency in a way that is difficult within structurally oriented traditions such as the UK social model tradition. Third, it makes it possible to discern a specific, and highly disturbing motivation for at least some of the violence against disabled people: pleasure from a disabled peer's misfortune.

All three traditions seem to analyze violence against disabled people by way of notions derived from other investigations; investigations of barriers to social participation (the UK social model tradition), investigations of cultural discourses (the poststructuralist tradition) and investigations of explicated hatred and hostility (the hate crime model). We can also conclude that all three traditions seem to argue that "their" decisive findings should be prominent in other areas of investigation, without suggesting that findings on violence could be given a similar prominence in other areas.

Ontological trajectories

How does the disproportionate violence come about? UK disability studies has, at least for the last four decades, been embedded in historical materialism. Hence, most UK research on violence against disabled people sees the material and economic structure as the ontological basis of society. Andrea Hollomotz, for instance, provides "a brief overview of macro forces, which highlighted how social structures act to systematically oppress and violate disabled people" (2013: 488). Within the UK social model tradition, violent acts against disabled people (and, not least, the disproportion in such acts) are mainly said to be produced by material macro factors.

Just as social model scholars position socio-material structures as *sources* or *causes* of this violence, so poststructuralist scholars position violence as effects of cultural structures. Reaching the end of their argument, Goodley and Runswick-Cole conclude that:

> We have now come to *the roots of the violence* of disablism already described in this article. Underpinning the real, psycho-emotional and systemic acts of violence against disabled children is the cultural violence of disablism.
>
> (2011: 609, my emphasis)

The crucial theoretical metaphor here is, of course, the notion of *roots*. This notion includes not only a causal relation (that cultural violence in some sense produces the disproportion in physical violence, rather than the other way around). It also presupposes some kind of *temporality:* discursive or cultural structures are assumed to pre-exist the relation between disability and violence. The disproportion in violence, then, is essentially "produced" or "engendered" by cultural or linguistic structures.

This positioning of language, culture or semantics is bound up with Goodley and Runswick-Cole's explicitly Lacanian path. Not only do Goodley and Runswick-Cole "appropriate" their term for physical violence ("real violence") "from psychoanalysis, specifically Lacanian theory" (2011: 606), Goodley has also recently focused on developing a notion of "psychoanalytic disability studies," which he himself sums up as "Jacques Lacan and Paul Hunt" (Goodley 2012). Their analysis of violence against people with disabilities echoes Lacan's analysis of narcissism, more precisely Lacan's analysis of "an aggressiveness linked to the narcissistic relationship and to the structure of systematic misrecognition and objectification that characterize ego formation" (2002: 94). In ontological terms, Goodley and Runswick-Cole seem to explain violence against disabled people as an "outburst" from the ego formation within an ableist language.

The hate crime model views violence as ontologically posterior to (or *caused by*) hatred. Macro-level explanations often resemble poststructuralist explanations such as Goodley and Runswick-Cole's rooting of violence in "circulating practices." In Pam Thomas' account, for instance, the incidence of hate crime depends on a "dominant culture": "there is the context of a culture that creates and maintains structures and practices that disable and exclude people with impairments" (2011: 111, 108).

On a micro level, violent agency is not only explained by a *pleasure* connected to actual misfortune, but also by a *desire* that is present prior to the actions. To the extent that the hate crime model has a specific ontological contribution, the contribution consists of introducing a *mediating* stage in the trajectory (individual motivation, desire to harm). On both levels, the hate crime tradition views violent agency as an effect of social processes, rather than an active force in those processes.

The three major traditions rely on very different explanations of how society *comes about*, and hence explain the disproportionate violence against disabled people in different ways. However, they all share at least one significant point: all three traditions position the violence as *ontologically posterior*. The implicit claim is that violence is produced by different social practices, without itself being decisive to such practices.

This assumption is problematic in at least two ways. First, the sheer severity of the findings – not only about victimization, but also about perpetration – suggest that violence against disabled people is ontologically important to our society. Second, violence against disabled people is often explained by processes that – within the same ways of thinking – produce *all* "structures and practices that disable and exclude." Hence, our understanding of a disabling society is *expanded* rather than *shaped* by the disturbing findings on violence against disabled people.

Epistemological trajectories

To grasp the epistemological trajectories in the UK social model tradition, we can begin by examining those articles which have an empirical basis. While Andrea Hollomotz relies on semi-structured interviews, some of them aided by vignettes, Hague *et al.* combined national survey data with "in-depth and lengthy interviews" which were "analyzed using thematic analysis methods" (2011: 123).

Goodley and Runswick-Cole similarly relied on "accounts of parents of disabled children" collected in open-ended interviews (2011: 605). Their analysis also was guided by ethnographic work in familial settings. In Vera Chouinard's Lacanian analyses, dealing with violence and disability in Guyana, life-history interviews "first coded by substantive events (e.g. types of violence experienced) and then analysed thematically using NVIVO" (2012: 782).

Within the hate crime tradition, several researchers use victim experiences, such as case descriptions from disabled people's organizations (Thomas 2011: 107–108). More commonly, interpretations of "disabled people's experiences and perceptions" are combined with qualitative analyses of "organizational responses" (Roulstone *et al.* 2011: 352–353). Further along that line, some have also analyzed definitions of hate crime within judicial systems and political institutions (Mason-Bish 2013). The notion of hate crime is also increasingly applied in analyses of crime statistics and survey data (Sherry 2010, Emerson & Roulstone 2014). One might assume that this tradition would be particularly interested in perpetration – given the analytical emphasis on *motivations* – but that does not seem to be the case.

These bodies of research shed light on victims' experiences of violence; on conditions for the disproportion in violence; and on how public services respond to this violence. However, none of the scholars discussed above have collected data on the actual violent interactions. Violence remains epistemologically posterior. It is perhaps no coincidence, then, that these analyses produce knowledge in which violence is analytically and ontologically posterior.

Repositioning violence?

The positioning of violence as analytically, ontologically and epistemologically posterior is not in itself problematic. To the contrary, it would be wrong *not* to let this previous knowledge shape our understanding of violence against disabled people. Similarly, it is clear that acts of violence *can* be ontologically dependent upon other social phenomena. Finally, there is no doubt that a plethora of data – including data that only gives indirect access into the phenomenon of violence – can engender insights into this violence.

However, the gravity of the empirical findings constitutes an imperative. The knowledge of violence must also shape those well-known perspectives. If we do not listen to this imperative, we are in fact implying that violence is less important than the phenomena that are now positioned as analytically, ontologically or epistemologically prior to violence.

Luckily, at least two of the major traditions provide rudiments for rethinking some of our fundamental perspectives. Within the UK social model tradition, Andrea Hollomotz's work provides an interesting point for rethinking violence as ontologically prior. Contrary to her explicit adherence to the UK social model, her notions of a continuum of violence may tear apart several well-known analytical trajectories. While the social model tradition "has *social oppression* as [its] analytical signature" (Thomas 2007: 178), Hollomotz conceptualizes a continuum:

> This broad approach takes account of subtle and mundane incidents of oppression and intrusion. It ranges from structural inequalities, exclusion, imbalanced personal relationships and restricted autonomy, to the ratification of disablist attitudes and a higher tolerance for violence, to emotional, physical and sexual violence in the private sphere and targeted attacks in public. There is no hierarchy.
>
> (2013: 490)

On the one hand, Hollomotz includes violence within an established framework, while the framework itself remains untouched. While the processes are defined as mutually *re-enforcing*, it is not clear if they are mutually *enforced*: Hollomotz still seems to imply that socio-material structures pre-exist, and engender the disabling processes of our society.

On the other hand, there is a potential in Hollomotz' account: her illustration of the continuum includes both material dimensions ("structural inequality") and immaterial dimensions ("hostility"), and both social structures ("social exclusion") and social actions ("physical and sexual assault") (2013: 489). It appears likely, given her theoretical framework, that she often views material dimensions (and other social structures) as ontologically prior to acts of violence. When she nevertheless emphasizes that oppression and violence define a continuum, and explicitly rejects hierarchical thinking, her approach implies an interesting possibility: Other disabling processes can be reconceptualized, perhaps even against the backdrop of the UK social model tradition. Even if some would dismiss a strong reconceptualization, "violence is ontologically prior to disabling process X," they could perhaps view violence as fundamental in the *sustaining* of other disabling processes.

Within the poststructuralist tradition, Goodley and Runswick-Cole' s term "violence of disablism" provides the most important rudiment. Their four "types of violence" are not only an attempt to include interpersonal violence into the agenda. They are also re-framing well-known issues in disability studies, such as barriers to social participation and negative stereotypes as forms of violence. Hence, their work demonstrates that violence could become analytically prior. However, their Lacanian reasoning seems to *divert* them from this potential. Although "violence" is a key term, they frame interpersonal violence with categories and analytical terms derived from the study of language acquisition and linguistic systems.

Emerging data also suggest potential for epistemological priority. Crime statistics are beginning to register the health/disability status of victims. This development could perhaps – if victim and perpetrator characteristics were linked at the individual level – allow us to accumulate specific data on perpetrators of violence against disabled people.

There are also several unexplored sources of qualitative data. In the well-known case of David Askew, for instance, the actual perpetration was documented by surveillance cameras (Shakespeare 2010). An increasing number of perpetrators of violence are also filming their behaviour, and then posting it on YouTube or other websites. These recordings, together with surveillance recordings from institutional settings, could provide data for very valuable video analysis. Similarly, these perpetrators could potentially be important informants. For instance, the experiences and narratives of the so-called "feral boys" Craig Dodd and Ryan Palin – known for harassing and finally killing Raymond Atherton – would provide the basis for disturbing but truly necessary analysis.

These rudiments demonstrate that the issue of violence *can* take center stage in our thinking. They nevertheless remain rudiments, and violence remains analytically, ontologically and epistemologically posterior even if other opportunities are implied. To some extent, that is a matter of reasonable caution. First, there is a risk a wider use of "violence" may "dilute the concept" and make it harder to "identify the extreme forms of violence" (Shakespeare 2014: 224). Second, there is also a risk that an over-emphasis on violence may hamper our insight into (other) disabling structures. Even if violence research somewhat "reshapes" disability studies perspectives, this must not obscure insights developed within earlier "shapes" of those perspectives. This caution, however, does not relieve us from the imperative presented by the empirical findings: even if there are considerable difficulties and risks, the knowledge of violence must be allowed to change and shape "the order of [...] analysis or elucidation" in disability studies.

Research possibilities: violence and larger agendas in disability studies

We have seen that pre-existing disability studies perspectives are often applied *to* the issue of violence. Those pre-existing perspectives undoubtedly grew out of specific bits of evidence. The findings on violence are as significant, or as disturbing, as many of those bits of evidence. Hence, disability studies would be more sensitive to its knowledge base if perspectives were developed *from* research on violence. Other disabling processes would, perhaps, be even better understood if the existing perspectives were supplemented by perspectives in which violence holds analytical, ontological or epistemological priority. The remainder of the chapter tries to outline three such possibilities; (1) that violence could be given analytical priority in our understanding of psycho-emotional disablement; (2) that violence could be given ontological priority in our understanding of how disabled people are culturally "othered"; (3) that violence could be given epistemological priority in the study of neglect and insufficient care.

A possible analytical trajectory: seeing psycho-emotional processes in the light of violence

The notion of psycho-emotionally disabling processes – sometimes termed *barriers to being* – is perhaps best known through Carol Thomas' work. In recent years, that notion is an increasingly important point of reference, particularly in analyses of qualitative interviews (Connors & Stalker 2007, Burns *et al.* 2013). In Thomas' perspective, disabled people are not only people whose bodies have functional problems, or have reduced or different cognition. They are also people whose bodies are *harmed* by social exclusion, or people whose cognitive development is hindered by inadequate education or interpersonal hostility. The *hurting* in "the intended or unintended 'hurtful' words and social actions of non-disabled people [...] in inter-personal engagements" is not only about negative experiences and lowered well-being (Thomas 2007: 72). Psycho-emotional disablism also leads to increased impairment or increased impairment effects. It is therefore important to separate this pain of disablism from "the pain of impairment" (1999: 72–73).

In Thomas' social-relational perspective, the bodies of disabled people (as well as all other bodies) are affected by social processes. This has interesting implications for how the agency involved should be understood. If "words and actions of non-disabled people," as well as the presence of other processes such as barriers to social participation, lead to pain and increased impairment, these actions fit the WHO definition of violent agency: action "that either results in or has a high likelihood of resulting in injury, death, psychological harm, maldevelopment, or deprivation."

If violence was positioned as analytically prior, the *hurting* in "pain of disablism," and not only the *hurt* experienced by disabled people would be even better understood. If the analytical notion were drawn from analyses of violence, we would enrich not only our understanding of the agency involved, but also our understanding of psycho-emotional disablism as a bit more chaotic than what we normally think of as barriers.

A possible ontological trajectory: is the normate built on violence?

Just as violence can become analytically prior, thereby changing analytical concepts and categories, this knowledge can also change the explanations (causality claims) in disability studies. I believe it is necessary to ask an unpleasant question. Could our current society, at least to some degree, be structured and shaped as it is *because of* disproportionate violence against disabled people?

Since the notion of psycho-emotional processes is primarily bound up with the UK social model tradition, the potential is perhaps best illustrated with an issue that is particularly important within the poststructuralist tradition and the hate crime tradition: the identity category of non-disability. This category is sometimes called "the normate," a term coined by Rosemarie Garland-Thomson:

> This neologism names the veiled subject position of the cultural self, [...] the social figure through which people can represent themselves as definitive human beings.
>
> (1997: 8)

While she emphasizes how aesthetic representations "deploy disabled figures" (1997: 9), her argument also resembles less aesthetically oriented arguments, such as Tom Shakespeare's argument that people with disabilities are "fetishized" as "dustbins for disavowal" (Shakespeare 1994).

In Garland-Thomson's perspective, "representational systems" (particularly "the ability/disability system") hold ontological priority, and it is these "circulations" that produce and reproduce the normate (Garland-Thomson 2002: 3). To the extent that micro-level agency is present in her analysis, she mostly refers to the production of representations or classifications: "standardization, mass production and mass culture *produced* the notion of an unmarked, normative body as the dominant subject of democracy" (1997: 78, my emphasis).

Interestingly, these representational systems are not only ontologically prior to the normate. She also emphasizes that "bodies marked and selected by such [representational] systems are targeted for elimination" in the form of a plethora of violence: "infanticide, suicide, lynching, bride burning, honor killings, forced conversion, coercive rehabilitation, domestic violence, genocide, normalizing surgical procedures, racial profiling, and neglect" (2002: 9). It is worth noting that this "elimination" affects women, and sexual and ethnic minorities, in addition to disabled people.

This link to violence against women raises an interesting theoretical parallel. The concept of the normate parallels – both analytically and historically – important gender studies concepts such as Raewynn Connell's concept of "hegemonic masculinity" (1995). Connell has argued that men's violence against women is more than an "expression" of power. She also views violence as ontologically active – that is, decisive – in the engendering and sustaining of hegemonic masculinity:

> violence often arises in the construction of masculinities, as part of the practice *by which* particular men or groups of men claim respect, intimidate rivals, or try to gain material advantages. Violence is not a 'privilege', but it is very often a means of claiming or defending privilege, asserting superiority or taking an advantage.
>
> (2002: 95, my emphasis)

The theoretical resemblance suggests that the active harming of impaired bodies may play a similar role. This parallel is also supported by empirical research. The metastatistical analyses above suggested that every year, somewhere between 1.331 percent and 1.408 percent of non-disabled people perpetrate violence against disabled people. Interestingly, that prevalence is clearly comparable to the prevalence of domestic violence against women. The 2002 UN *World Report on Violence and Health* reviewed ten population-based studies from high-income countries. To the extent that the studies measured recent violence (past 12 months), and excluded violence by other perpetrators, all studies reported prevalence of below 3 percent, one American study even as low as 1.3 percent (WHO 2002: 91).

Violence against disabled people might in itself be a building-block in the construction of the normate. The disproportionate violence against disabled people occurs on the basis of certain cultural frameworks, most notably against the backdrop of a seemingly neutral normate to which all other positions are subordinate and unnecessary. However, violence can also be a part of fundamental processes *by which* the normate emerges, or at least an ontologically important "means" in the sustaining of the normate.

A possible epistemological trajectory: approaching inadequate care through data on violence

Disability scholars *can* explore or analyze violence-specific data such as the violent agency of non-disabled peers. And they should do so: to describe the actual acts, and gain hermeneutic knowledge of *what it is like,* could also open up for insights into the workings of other disabling processes.

As an example of such opportunities, it is useful to look at a disturbingly "consistent picture": the fact that health care services for people with learning disabilities are often inadequate (Kerr 2004: 200). The UK social model tradition has often approached this problem via qualitative interviews with people with learning disabilities who have experienced poor services or neglect (Conroy 2012, Redley *et al.* 2012). A number of researchers have also analyzed policy documents and/or evaluation reports (Redley 2009, Hough 2012). Finally, research has also been conducted with professionals, particularly with regard to care quality improvement (Williams & Heslop 2005).

Research within the poststructuralist tradition has often investigated how certain discourses are "woven into the fabric of social care" (Finlay *et al.* 2008: 358). While most of the research investigates macro-level data such as documents and scientific literature (Gilbert 2005), Finlay and colleagues rely on meso-level ethnographic data. There is also a considerable body of micro-level research, for example case studies investigating how inadequate care is bound up with "social, cultural and personal abjection" (Hall 2012: 48).

These analyses shed light on experiences *of* inadequate care, conditions *for* inadequate care, or responses *to* inadequate care. Data are collected from victims, policy-makers, or general samples of professionals, but never from professionals who themselves are perpetrators of severely inadequate care, neglect or abuse. It is perhaps no surprise, then, that the analyses end up illuminating "barriers to providing high-quality care," rather than the actual practice of inadequate care (Brown & Kalaitzidis 2013: 945).

While data on "ordinary" carework can shed light on inadequate care, so can data on violence. That potential is disturbing, but far from coincidental. Inadequate care may – as, for instance, in the recent case of Connor Sparrowhawk ("LB") – be a form of potentially life-threatening violence. In terms of data, one could, for instance, analyze footage from Winterbourne View, or interviews by ex-carers with a history of inadequate carework.

Analyses of violence could be especially valuable for understanding agency in inadequate care. Just as violence is an embodied action leading to bodily harm, so carework is both physical and often very intimate work. It is more than likely, therefore, that data on *active harming* of disabled people would shed light on what actually happens when care is (or becomes) inadequate. Perhaps this approach may be considered ethically problematic – there is a risk of shaming individual care-workers. However, a bit of shaming is perhaps deserved, or at least morally defensible.

Conclusion

Knowledge on interpersonal violence should become decisive – that is, analytically, ontologically and epistemologically prior – in at least some knowledge trajectories in disability studies. In this chapter I have tried to argue that such a turn is *necessary* because of the disturbing empirical findings, *possible* if we rethink some of our analytical categories and epistemological approaches, and finally *fruitful* – both for research on violence and other areas of research.

If these opportunities could prove so fruitful, why do researchers hesitate to re-position violence in knowledge trajectories? In my view, this hesitation is not only academic but also deeply personal. It is difficult to *bring ourselves* to realize the severity of the issue: we "[don't] want to believe that human beings could be so vile" (Shakespeare 2010). It is less painful to imagine the agency of non-disabled peers as indirectly harmful – for instance, via the imposition of disabling barriers – than to imagine active harming of people's bodies.

The strength of the empirical findings suggests that insights into violence against disabled people could re-open our eyes to "the underlying barbarism of civilization" (Goodley & Runswick-Cole 2011: 611). Such an eye-opener may increase the *trouble* in doing disability studies. However, those troublesome paths are worth pursuing. Troubles (both one's own and those of others) often engender fruitful examples of critical thinking.

Acknowledgements

I would like to thank Jan Grue, Ted Hanisch and Tom Shakespeare for being excellent readers, and Reid Offringa for excellent support with metastatistical analyses.

References

Audi, R. (1971) On the meaning and justification of violence, in J. Schaffer (ed.) *Violence*. New York: McKay.

Brown, S. and Kalaitzidis, E. (2013) Barriers preventing high-quality nursing care of people with disability within acute settings: a thematic literature review, *Disability & Society*, 28(7), 937–954.

Burns, N., Watson, N., & Paterson, K. (2013) Risky bodies in risky spaces: disabled people's pursuit of outdoor leisure. *Disability & Society*, 28(8), 1059–1073.

Choe, J. Y., Teplin, L. A., & Abram, K. A. (2008) Perpetration of violence, violent victimization and severe mental illness: balancing public health concerns. *Psychiatric Services*, 59(2), 153–164.

Chouinard, V. (2012) Pushing the boundaries of our understanding of violence and disability: voices from the Global South (Guyana), *Disability & Society*, 27(6), 777–792.

Collins, K. A. (2006) Elder maltreatment, *Violence against Women*, 130(9), 805–822.

Connell, R. W. (1995) *Masculinities*, Berkeley, CA: University of California Press.

Connell, R. W. (2002) On hegemonic masculinity and violence. Response to Jefferson and Hall. *Theoretical Criminology*, 6(1), 89–99.

Connors, C. & Stalker, K. (2007) Children's experiences of disability: pointers to a social model of childhood disability, *Disability & Society*, 22(1), 19–33.

Conroy, P. (2012) No safety net for disabled children in residential institutions in Ireland, *Disability & Society*, 27(6), 809–822.

Craig, L. A., Stringer, I., & Moss, T. (2006) Treating sexual offenders with learning disabilities in the community. A critical review, *International Journal of Offender Therapy and Comparative Criminology*, 50(4), 369–390.

Davies, M. (2003) Philosophy of language, in N. Bunnin (ed.). *The Blackwell Companion to Philosophy*, Oxford: Blackwell.

Emerson, E. & Roulstone, A. (2014) Developing an evidence base for violent and disablist hate crime in Britain. Findings from the Life Opportunities Survey, *Journal of Interpersonal Violence*, doi:10.1177/0886260514534524.

Finlay, W. M. L., Antaki, C., & Walton, C. (2008) Saying no to the staff: an analysis of refusals in a home for people with severe communication difficulties, *Sociology of Health and Illness*, 30(1), 55–75.

Garland-Thomson, R. (1997) *Extraordinary Bodies: Figuring Physical Disability in American Culture and Literature*, New York: Columbia University Press.

Garland-Thomson, R. (2002) Integrating disability, transforming feminist theory, *NWSA Journal*, 14(3), 1–32.

Gilbert, T. P. (2005) Trust and managerialism: exploring discourses of care, *Journal of Advanced Nursing*, 52(4), 454–463.

Goodley, D. (2010) *Disability Studies. An Interdisciplinary Introduction*, London: Sage.

Goodley, D. (2012). Jacques Lacan + Paul Hunt = Psychoanalytic disability studies, in D. Goodley, B. Hughes, & L. Davis (eds) *Disability and social theory. New developments and directions*. London: Sage.

Goodley, D. & Runswick-Cole K. (2011) The violence of disablism, *Sociology of Health and Illness*, doi: 10.1111/j.1467–9566.2010.01302.x.

Govindshenoy, M. & Spencer, N. (2007) Abuse of the disabled child: a systematic review of population-based studies, *Child: Care, Health and Development*, 23(1), 41–52.

Hague, G., Thiara, R., & Mullender, A. (2011) Disabled women and domestic violence. Making the links, a national UK study. *Psychiatry, Psychology and Law*, 18(1), 117–136.

Hall, E. (2012) Spaces of social inclusion and belonging for people with intellectual disabilities, *Journal of Intellectual Disabilities Research*, 4(supp. 1), 48–57.

Hollomotz, A. (2009) Beyond 'vulnerability': an ecological model approach to conceptualizing risk of sexual violence against people with learning difficulties. *The British Journal of Social Work*, 39(1), 99–112.

Hollomotz, A. (2012) Disability and the continuum of violence, in A. Roulstone & H. Mason-Bish (eds) *Disability, Hate Crime and Violence*, New York: Routledge.

Hollomotz, A. (2013). Disability, oppression and violence: toward a sociological explanation, *Sociology*, 47(3), 477–493.

Horner-Johnson, W. & Drum, C. E. (2006) Prevalence of maltreatment of people with intellectual disabilities. A review of recently published research, *Mental Retardation and Developmental Disabilities Research Reviews*, 33(5), 552–558.

Hough, R. E. (2012) Adult protection and 'intimate citizenship' for people with learning disabilities: empowering and protecting in light of the No Secrets review, *Disability & Society*, 27(1), 131–144.

Hughes, K., Bellis, M. A., Jones, L., Wood, S., Bates, G., Eckley, L., McCoy, E., Mikton, C., Shakespeare, T. and Officer, A. (2012) Prevalence and risk of violence against adults with disabilities: a systematic review and meta-analysis of observational studies. *The Lancet*, 379(9826), 1621–1629.

Jones, L., Bellis, M. A., Wood, S., Hughes, K., McCoy, E., Eckley, L., Bates, G., Mikton, C., Shakespeare, T. and Officer, A. (2012) Prevalence and risk of violence against children with disabilities: a systematic review and meta-analysis of observational studies. *The Lancet*, 380(9845), 899–907.

Kerr, M. (2004) Improving the general health of people with learning disabilities. *Advances in Psychiatric Treatment*, 10, 200–206.

Kessler, R. (The WHO Mental Health Survey Consortium) (2004) Prevalence, severity and unmet needs for treatment of mental disorders in the World Health Organization World Mental Health Surveys. *JAMA*, 291(21), 2581–2590.

Krug, E. G., Dahlberg, L. L., Mercy, J. A., Zwi, A. B. and Lozano, R. (eds.) (2002) *World Report on Violence and Health*. Geneva: World Health Organization.

Lacan, J. (2002) *Écrits*, London: Norton.

Mason-Bish, H. (2013) Conceptual issues in the construction of disability hate crime, in A. Roulstone & H. Mason-Bish, *Disability, Hate Crime and Violence*. New York: Routledge.

Maulik, P. K., Mascarenhas, M. N., Mathers, C. D., Dua, T. & Saxena, S. (2011) Prevalence of intellectual disability: a meta-analysis of population-based studies. *Research in Developmental Disabilities*, 32(2), 419–436.

Mays, J. M. (2006) Feminist disability theory: domestic violence against women with a disability. *Disability & Society*, 21(2), 147–158.

Mitra, M. & Mouradian, V. E. (2014) Intimate partner violence in the relationships of men with disabilities in the United States. *Journal of Interpersonal Violence*, doi:10886260514534526.

Mueller-Johnson, K., Eisner, M. P. & Obsuth, I. (2014) Sexual victimization of youth with a physical disability. An examination of prevalence rates and risk and protective factors. *Journal of Interpersonal violence*, doi:10.1177/0886260514534526.

Nixon, J. (2009) Domestic violence and women with disabilities: locating the issue in the periphery of social movements. *Disability & Society*, 24(1), 77–89.

Redley, M. (2009) Understanding the social exclusion and stalled welfare of citizens with learning disabilities. *Disability & Society*, 24(4), 489–501.

Redley, M., Banks, C., Foody, K., & Holland, A. (2012) Healthcare for men and women with learning disabilities: understanding inequalities in access, *Disability & Society*, 27(6), 747–759.

Rose, C. A., Monda-Amaya, L. E., & Espelage, D. L. (2010) Bullying perpetration and victimization in special education: a review of the literature, *Remedial and Special Education*, 32(2), 114–130.

Roulstone, A. & Mason-Bish, H. (2013) *Disability, Hate Crime and Violence*. New York: Routledge.

Roulstone, A., Thomas, P., & Balderston, S. (2011) Between hate and vulnerability: unpacking the British criminal justice system's construction of disablist hate crime, *Disability & Society*, 26(3), 351–364.

Shakespeare, T. (1994) Cultural representations of disabled people: dustbins for disavowal, *Disability & Society*, 9(3), 283–299.

Shakespeare, T. (2010) The cruel toll of disability hate crime, *The Guardian*, 12.03.2010.

Shakespeare, T. (2014) *Disability Rights and Wrongs Revisited*, London: Routledge.

Shakespeare, T., Thompson, S. & Wright, M. (2010) No laughing matter: medical and social experiences of restricted growth, *Scandinavian Journal of Disability Research*, 12(1), 19–31.

Sherry, M. (2010) *Disability Hate Crimes: Does Anyone Really Hate Disabled People?*, Farnham: Ashgate.

Sin, C. H. (2014) Using a 'layers of influence' model to understand the interaction of research, policy and practice in response to disablist hate crime, in N. Chakraborti & J. Garland (eds) *Responding to Hate Crime*, Bristol: Policy Press.

Stalker, K. & McArthur, K. (2012) Child abuse, child protection and disabled children: A review of recent research, *Child Abuse Review*, 21(1), 24–40.

Thomas, C. (1999) *Female Forms: Experiencing and Understanding Disability*, Buckingham: Open University Press.

Thomas, C. (2007) *Sociologies of Disability and Illness. Contested Ideas in Disability Studies and Medical Sociology*, Basingstoke: Palgrave Macmillan.

Thomas, P. (2011) 'Mate crime': ridicule, hostility and targeted attacks against disabled people, *Disability & Society*, 26(1), 107–111.

Williams, V. & Heslop, P. (2005) Mental health support needs of people with a learning difficulty: a medical or a social model? *Disability & Society*, 20(3), 231–245.

7

'THE INVISIBLES'

Conceptualising the intersectional relationships between dyslexia, social exclusion and homelessness

Stephen J. Macdonald

Introduction

The chapter discusses the relationship between disability, impairment and homelessness within a social context. As there is a general lack of literature examining a relationship between specific learning difficulties and homelessness, the chapter predominantly draws on literature which links mental health/learning disabilities to risk factors for becoming homeless. The study applies a quantitative methodology, drawing on primary data from the *Multiple Exclusion Homelessness Across the United Kingdom Survey*. Therefore, this study takes a structural approach to understanding the intersections between social exclusion, disability and key life events for homeless people with dyslexia.

This chapter analyses quantitative data on key domains of social exclusion for adults with dyslexia who have experienced homelessness. A comparison is made between adults with (n=68) and without dyslexia (n=375) who have experienced homelessness in the United Kingdom (UK). This is to investigate whether there are any statistically significant relationships relating to homelessness and dyslexia that can be conceptualised sociologically. While the chapter discusses different global approaches to defining homelessness, it focuses on UK definitions and policy responses.

The data reveals that people with dyslexia are over-represented within the survey population, and that there is an increase in addiction problems and mental health issues for this particular group. In particular, dyslexic participants are more susceptible to self-harm and increased suicide attempts. Although it might be expected that dyslexic people do not access health and social services, this study shows an increased engagement with particular professionals. I will conclude by suggesting that health and social services need to acknowledge conditions like dyslexia in order to improve support for this particular group of people that have experienced homelessness. The implication is that disabling barriers arising from childhood trauma, addiction issues, unemployment and a lack of services significantly reduce the life chances of homeless people with dyslexia.

Defining homelessness

Public and media perceptions of homelessness predominantly portray individuals who do not have access to housing and sleep 'rough' on the streets of towns and cities (Lee *et al.* 2010). Yet this is only one group of a larger population of people who are defined in legislation as 'homeless'. Farrugia (2011: 763) gives the following definition of homelessness:

> Homelessness describes any form of accommodation which does not meet the prevailing cultural standard in terms of facilities or security of tenure. This includes rough sleeping or squatting, 'couch surfing' with a variety of friends, or stays in refuges and other forms of accommodation service.

The United Nations distinguishes the category of 'primary homelessness', which refers to people without shelter, living on streets and considered 'roofless' (United Nations Economic and Social Council 2009: 3), from a significantly greater group of people who fall into the 'secondary homeless' category. This refers to individuals who do not have a permanent residence and fluctuate between temporary living conditions (i.e. temporary living with family/friends; housed in a shelter/hotel; squatting, etc.) (United Nations Economic and Social Council 2009). Globally, it is estimated that 500 million people can be defined as not having a home, i.e. experiencing secondary homelessness, whereas 100 million people have no housing whatsoever, i.e. primary homelessness.

Global research literature is dominated by studies that have been conducted in the United States, particularly from a social justice viewpoint (Hore 2013). Three per cent of American citizens can be classified as homeless and a further 1.6 million Americans either are living in shelters or are in transitional housing (USHUD 2009, Lee *et al.* 2010). This US literature expands the UN's 'primary' and 'secondary' definitions of homelessness: for example, Lee *et al.* (2010) suggest that patterns of homelessness fall into three clear categories which are defined as transitional, episodic and chronic. The first group refers to a temporary and brief homeless period where people move in with family or friends which can be described as a once-in-a-lifetime experience, with many not defining their own experience as a state of homelessness. People in the episodic category experience temporary re-occurring cycles of homelessness over short periods of time. This is a group which is often overlooked within the research because they are less visible than people living on the streets of towns and cities. Finally, chronic refers to individuals who experience long periods or permanent states of homelessness (Culhane *et al.* 2007, Lee *et al.* 2010). It is this group that usually shapes the social perception of homelessness, as these individuals are often visible, living on the streets of our major cities. Lee *et al.* (2010) suggest that although chronic homelessness is over-represented in social research in the US, this is actually the smallest homeless population of the three categories.

UK policy on homelessness

In the UK, the vast majority of the 600,000 people defined as homeless are individuals living in temporary or transitional accommodation with no permanent living residence (DCLG 2014). The UK concept of homelessness was defined in policy in the Housing (Homeless Persons) Act (1977) which stated that homelessness is when a person has no accommodation or has had access to their accommodation restricted or withdrawn.

The 1977 Act set out criteria which defined 'priority need groups' that could be considered at risk of becoming homeless in England and Wales (Lund 2011). Support was predominantly aimed at families/single parents with dependent children, or families experiencing homelessness through emergency flooding, fire or other disasters. Furthermore, there was recognition of certain social groups who were considered vulnerable as a result of mental and learning disabilities, physical disabilities and old age (Lund 2011). Hence, local housing authorities had a duty to provide temporary accommodation for these priority need groups. This policy was amended in the Housing Act (1996), which gave local authorities a legal responsibility to house the *'priority need groups'* within their local areas. Hence it was local authorities who were held accountable to prevent homelessness in their regions.

The list of at-risk groups was extended further in the Homelessness Act (2002), where 'vulnerability' was expanded to include young adults aged between 16 and 17, care leavers between 18 and 20, victims of domestic violence, people leaving the Armed Forces and offenders having served a custodial sentence. Furthermore, local authorities can no longer justify just offering short-hold tenancies to people experiencing homelessness. The 2002 Act also states that individuals outside the 'at-risk groups' must also be eligible to receive support to eradicate homelessness within England and Wales. Local authorities now have a legal duty to give 24-hour advice and support for people who are experiencing, or are at risk of experiencing homelessness.

While the Act made it clear that any individual at risk of becoming homeless must receive support, this only refers to individuals with national legal status within the UK, creating a new distinction between 'statutory homelessness' and 'non-statutory homelessness'. For statutory homeless people access to services within a 24-hour period is legally enshrined into policy, yet for the non-statutory group, consisting of illegal immigrants and intentional homeless people, access to services and support is denied. Although the Homelessness Act (2002) was aimed at eradicating homelessness and protecting vulnerable members of the community from becoming homeless, this protection only extends to UK and European citizens, resulting in a two-tier system of support in the UK.

Homelessness, risky pathologies and disability

A number of studies in the UK and US have revealed a link between disability and homelessness. For example, Basu and Stuckler (2012) have suggested that homeless people experience increased physical and mental health problems and disability issues compared with communities that live in permanent residence. Their research reports that people who experience chronic homelessness die on average 40 years earlier than people living in permanent residence. Basu and Stuckler (2012: 127) suggest people with rising debt experience an increase of stress, anxiety and depression and often cut back on food and medicine in order to prevent the onset of homelessness.

Although there has been a growing body of research within the UK which has attempted to analyse the qualitative and quantitative experiences of disabled people who have experienced homelessness, this research has been somewhat dominated by the concept of risk management and the promotion of psychological 'treatments' (Taylor at al. 2006; Farrell 2012; Hore 2013). From a risk perspective, particular groups are vulnerable to the experience of homelessness, such as people with mental health difficulties, young people and people who have experienced traumatic events within childhood, or in the case of ex-military in adulthood. Therefore, the majority of homeless research has been framed from a mental health perspective. This type of research attempts to identify risk factors in order to target appropriate health services and where necessary give access to medical and psycho-medical treatments (Wormer 2004; Pluck et al. 2011; Taylor at al. 2006; Farrell 2012).

For example, a study by Taylor at al. (2006) analyses the health practices of young homeless people. This research suggests that housing people is not enough to prevent the onset of episodic and chronic homelessness in the UK. Analysing data from 150 young participants aged between 16 and 25 years the authors report that there is a strong link between homelessness and mental health problems. The entire group of young people reported having multiple needs relating to experiences of self-harm, suicide, and drug and alcohol problems. It was reported that participants had a range of mental health problems which could be defined as mild to severe, ranging from stress and anxiety, depression to more severe signs of post-traumatic stress and psychosis. The study recognised a complex psychosocial component to the experiences of these young people, as the entire group reported some level of physical and sexual abuse during their childhood. The authors conclude that mental health issues play a significant role into pathways into homelessness and need to be confronted first in order to prevent homelessness.

Similar research in the US by Berk-Clark and McGuire (2013) investigated ex-veterans' experiences of chronic homelessness. Comparable to Taylor et al. (2006), their analysis illustrates the impact of traumatic events and the onset of mental health conditions that make people vulnerable to homelessness; however this trauma was predominantly experienced in adulthood when serving in the military rather than through childhood abuse. This study particularly illustrates a link between mental illness and substance abuse by these ex-veterans. Hence, addiction issues and psychosis were considered a key risk factor into chronic and episodic homelessness for ex-veterans.

Links between traumatic life events and the onset of mental 'illness' have also been reported as a significant risk factor for people with learning difficulties who have experienced homelessness. Yet, some of these studies demonstrate the tendency to over-pathologise the behaviours of this community, for example research by Pluck et al. (2011), investigating a link between homelessness and learning disabilities. They examined the impact that traumatic childhood events have on the developmental process of cognitive function (low IQ). This study suggested that three-quarters of participants could be clinically defined as having a neuro-behavioural impairment, as the group's cognitive function was below an average IQ of 88. Although abuse and neglect during a participant's life could be significantly related to the experiences of homelessness, the trauma did not significantly impact on the cognitive development (IQ) of participants. This study applied a biomedical methodology, but rather than suggesting that homelessness is a result of IQ limitations, it stated the key risk factors were mental health and addiction problems. Similarly to previous studies discussed, it was not symptoms of learning difficulties that made individuals vulnerable to becoming homeless but those of mental health and addiction problems.

Applying an epidemiological approach, Mercier and Picard (2011), when studying learning difficulties and homelessness, suggested that a statistical correlation exists between issues of abuse and childhood trauma which results in an increased vulnerability to homelessness. Again, they note that people with learning difficulties showed significant symptoms of mental health and addiction problems. They report that 90 per cent of this group described having an addiction problem and all reported experiencing extreme poverty. Interestingly they also recognise the gender differences of participants, as women tended to keep some form of family ties, which they suggested reduced their periods of homelessness compared with their male counterparts. This study suggests that once individuals with learning difficulties gained access to services this significantly improved their chances of acquiring permanent residence.

Yet, although these studies are useful from an individual perspective, as Hore (2013) notes this type of research somewhat pathologises homelessness through symptoms of underlying personality or mental health problems. She suggests that when homeless people come into contact with health services, signs and symptoms relating to mental health come to dominate discourses around individuals' homeless experiences. Hore (2013) argues that studies examining homelessness must move beyond pathology, in order to conceptualise pathways into homelessness from a structural and social justice perspective. From a social justice perspective, Burns (2009) highlights the strong relationship between social inequalities and exclusion which results in people with mental health and learning difficulties being over-represented in marginalised groups and experiencing situations like homelessness. Hence, the association between homelessness and mental health/intellectual disabilities derives not through vulnerability caused by biomedical symptoms but rather that homelessness results from structural discrimination.

Homelessness and social exclusion

From a sociological perspective, Farrugia (2011) suggests that a focus on individual experiences and risk factors alone has the effect of neglecting the structural elements to homelessness. Farrugia (2011) applied a biographical approach to analysing homeless people's life stories, but rather than focus on issues such as self-harm, drug use, or depression, he highlights issues of poverty, unemployment and unstable housing. He suggests that for young people from a working-class background, job markets are often temporary, low paid and unstable. For the young people within his study, it was reliance on unstable housing such as privately rented accommodation which resulted in them being easily evicted (Farrugia 2011). Hence, it was these issues that led to pathways into homelessness, rather than issues of pathology. Similarly, research by Basu and Stuckler (2012), demonstrates the structural nature of homelessness by statistically linking homelessness to the current economic global crisis. Basu and Stuckler (2012) compare the different responses to the economic crisis implemented by New Labour and the Conservative-led government between 2007 and 2012 in the UK. Due to the economic and banking crisis, home repossession rose from 25,900 to 48,000 between 2007–2010.

Surprisingly, due to New Labour housing policy although there was a significant rise in repossessed houses the total number of homeless families fell from '63,170 families in 2007 to 40,020 families in 2009' (Basu and Stuckler 2012: 149). Unfortunately, in 2010 once the Labour government was replaced by a Conservative-led coalition, the social housing initiatives developed by New Labour were dramatically cut. As Basu and Stuckler (2012) illustrate, because of these political choices which preferred austerity over stimulus 10,000 households were pushed into a state of homelessness. Hence the key issue is not about individuals being vulnerable to homelessness due to personal problems but that economic mismanagement and political ideology is at the heart of the current rise in homelessness within the UK. It should be noted that Basu and Stuckler (2012) recognise that since 2010 there has been an increase in mental health and addiction problems in the UK, but they attribute this rise to rising social stress and anxieties caused by the economic crisis and the dismantling of UK welfare support.

If Basu and Stuckler (2012) are correct and homelessness is as a result of economic policy rather than risk factors relating to mental health and addiction problems, then access to affordable housing becomes the central factor. In

Lee *et al*.'s (2010) review of US homeless policy, they suggest that the traditional US approach of supporting someone that has experienced chronic homelessness would have primarily emphasised the need for health services. This would have dealt with an individual's addiction issues, mental and physical health needs and given a person access to temporary resettlement. Once 'treatment' had been successful this would have been followed by access to a permanent residence. Hence, the 'housing readiness' model is driven by a health ideology which implies that a person who is homeless is 'broken' and must be repaired before individuals can be trusted with a permanent residence (Lee *et al*. 2010).

Lee *et al*. (2010) suggest that the 'housing readiness' strategy of treatment first, and social and economic support second, is misguided. They advocate a 'housing first model' where the primary concern is getting a homeless person access to a permanent residence. Once a permanent residence with clear economic support has been accessed then this is reinforced by health and social care support. Therefore from this perspective the first step is to access stable permanent housing, followed by risk management strategies in order to confront addiction and health related issues. They suggest that housing first followed by health and welfare support will prevent the re-occurrence of primary and secondary episodic and chronic homelessness. This housing first model has been adopted by the Obama government in the US, but had not been implemented across the UK at the time of writing.

Dyslexia and homelessness

As discussed, studies that conceptualise disability within the homeless literature are to a certain degree dominated by the notion of mental health; as a result very few studies have investigated links between dyslexia and homelessness. An early example of such a study was conducted by Barwick and Siegel (1996) in the US, and suggested that there was an increase of people with reading or writing disabilities in the homeless population. As with studies into mental health and learning disabilities, this study pathologises the link between dyslexia and homelessness by explaining the increased population due to risk factors relating to dyslexic symptoms. Within their research, Barwick and Siegel (1996) suggest that 52 per cent of their sample of homeless young people showed symptoms of specific learning difficulties. They indicate that this prevalence is significantly higher than the 4 per cent to 10 per cent of people with dyslexia in the general population (Semple and Smyth 2013). However, their research dismissed an association between poor school attendance and pathways into homelessness. They found no statistical association between poor school attendances for people with dyslexia in comparison with that of poor school attendance in the non-dyslexic population. They report:

> given the high prevalence of learning difficulties in our sample, it is possible that learning difficulties and underlying processing deficits

placed certain individuals at risk and may even have contributed to the dysfunctional experiences that precipitated their homelessness.

(Barwick and Siegel 1996: 664)

Although they dismissed educational disengagement as a risk factor for the dyslexic population, they suggested there may be a link between the defects of dyslexia and homelessness. Yet a review of the research literature by Markos and Strawser (2004) disputes Barwick and Siegel's research findings. They suggest that homelessness for people with dyslexia was not due to symptoms of dyslexia but caused by social disadvantage. For Markos and Strawser (2004) the key factors leading to an increase of people with dyslexia in the homeless population were unemployment and poverty. They suggest that people with dyslexia are particularly vulnerable to unemployment, especially if they are from a lower socio-economic background. Hence, homelessness for people with specific learning difficulties results from poor educational provision and other aspects of social disadvantage, such as abuse or addiction problems.

Research with UK homeless people conducted for the Thames Reach Action Group also discovered high levels of poor literacy. Olisa *et al.* (2010) found that 55 per cent of participants had significant difficulties in filling in forms and 46 per cent had significant general literacy problems. They suggest that poor literacy had undermined relationships for their homeless service users, as 20 per cent reported it affected their self-esteem. A further 17 per cent reported this made it more difficult for them to keep in contact with family and friends because of their inability to write letters (Olisa *et al.* 2010). Although this study could not make a direct link between dyslexia and homelessness due to problems with diagnosis, the authors highlight the prevalence of literacy difficulties within their research participants. Their research highlighted how education could itself generate barriers, on the basis of adult literacy classes which excluded rather than included dyslexic learners: these classes were accessed by homeless service users, yet were not equipped to deal with adults with complex literacy needs (Olisa *et al.* 2010).

In support of this claim, Markos and Strawser (2004) argue that it is educational discrimination that results in poor literacy skills for this group. Therefore, inferior educational experiences lead to low self-esteem and for some people develop into severe issues of stress, anxiety, depression and substance misuse. Markos and Strawser (2004) point out that over the past 30 years, social and health services have been developed aimed at the needs of homeless people with mental health or intellectual disabilities. However, this is not the case for people with dyslexia, as there are almost no specific interventions developed to target homeless individuals with specific learning difficulties. Therefore, Markos and Strawser (2004) advocate a need for integrated educational services, accessed through social services, in order to prevent people with dyslexia from increasingly becoming part of the chronic and episodic homeless population.

Methodology

Over recent years criticisms have been made of disability studies due to its lack of engagement with quantitative research methods (Shakespeare 2006). To confront some of these criticisms, this study has attempted to assess quantitatively the relationship between dyslexia and the increased likelihood of a person becoming homeless. The data in this study was obtained from the *Multiple Exclusion Homelessness Across the United Kingdom Survey* accessed through the Data Archives UK Service (Fitzpatrick *et al.* 2010). The fieldwork was comprised of a questionnaire survey and extended interviews which were conducted in 2010 by York University (Fitzpatrick *et al.* 2010).

In this study, the research compared two groups of participants that have experienced homelessness and used them as the independent variable. The first group consisted of participants (N=68) who have experienced homelessness and who have dyslexia. The second group consisted of individuals (N=375) without dyslexia who have also experienced homelessness. The data was collected by Fitzpatrick *et al.* (2010) who worked in partnership with organisations such as street outreach teams, drop in services, day centres, direct access accommodation, soup runs, etc. From these groups, six services were randomly selected from different geographical locations (Leeds, Belfast, Birmingham, Bristol, Cardiff, Glasgow, and London) to obtain a population sample. Information was collected in this survey on participants' dyslexia diagnosis by means of self-reporting. The author acknowledges the limitations to this method when collecting data on disability and in particular dyslexia.

In the following analysis, descriptive statistics have been used in the form of cross-tabulation and One-way-ANOVA tests to examine distribution of cases when examining the correlation between two or more variables. Two or more variable frequency distributions were analysed to discover if variables (i.e. dyslexia = homelessness × traumatic life events × social conditions = increased/decreased chance of homelessness) are statistically independent or if they are associated (De Vaus 2002). The data from this survey was subsequently analysed and only data was used which was calculated to be of significance ($P<.05$). The data was analysed using SPSS in the form of single variable analysis (univariate), and where data was calculated to be of significance ($P<.05$), bivariate analysis was also applied (De Vaus 2002).

It should be noted that within the social demographics at the multivariate stage of analysis, dyslexia did not have a significant impact on the population variables concerning sex, age or ethnicity. Hence, there was no ratio difference between the dyslexic and non-dyslexic groups in relation to sex, age and ethnicity populations. In both groups, males were over-represented compared with females (males = 79.4 per cent and females = 20.6 per cent). In both groups age demographics reveal a steady increase in homelessness between 16 to 34 years which peaks at the 45 year age group (16–34= 38.3 per cent; 35–54=50.4 per cent; 55+ = 11.3 per cent). After this age group, homelessness steadily decreases dramatically in the 55 year plus category. In relation to ethnicity for each group, 94 per cent were UK or European citizens and only 6 per cent reported having been born outside of Europe (UK citizens = 78.3 per cent; European = 15.3 per cent; non-European = 6.4 per cent). Therefore this indicates that within this study the vast majority of participants had 'statutory status' and could access homeless support under the current Homelessness Act (2002).

In the bivariate data analysis a number of significant themes (P<.05) emerged including history of episodic and chronic homelessness, victimisation, criminality, mental health and addiction issues, and welfare support. This research is influenced by a critical realist approach to disability and impairment, and this article applies a 'social relational model of disability' to the data analysis (Reindal 2008). Therefore, the author recognises the interactional elements of disability and impairment at the molecular, biological, psychological and sociological levels (Danermark 2007). In this approach, impairment is acknowledged, as the research uses it as a framework of analysis (dyslexia diagnosis). Hence, rather than automatically rejecting the psycho-medical models, this research views these models as useful when commenting on issues of impairment (symptoms and neurological structures). Such models only become oppressive when they attempt to explain social issues (such as homelessness) within a medical context (Macdonald 2010).

Homelessness is a social condition, because it is society that constructs social and cultural norms, maintained by housing policy and living conditions. The route into homelessness is not determined by biological neurological 'weaknesses' but rather by structural and environmental issues. If people with dyslexia are more likely to become homeless, from a social relational model perspective this could be due to both 'personal' social restrictions *and* 'imposed' social restrictions. The social relational model still allows a possible distinction between 'disability' as disabling structural barriers and 'impairment' as biological/neurological variations, but acknowledges that one cannot exist without the other (Reindal 2008). Thus, limitations are due to a significant neurological variation (i.e. dyslexia), the failures of an educational system to identify and adequately support children with dyslexia resulting in psychological implications (alienation), and disabling barriers in the form of structural exclusion in education, health/social services and job markets, etc. (Reindal 2008; Shakespeare 2013). It is suggested that all of these factors interact and feedback at each level resulting in an increased risk of social exclusion (Shakespeare 2013).

Findings: social demographics and dyslexia

As discussed, previous research conducted by Barwick and Siegel (1996) and Olisa et al. (2010) indicated that people with specific learning difficulties were significantly over-represented in their sample of homeless people. Yet

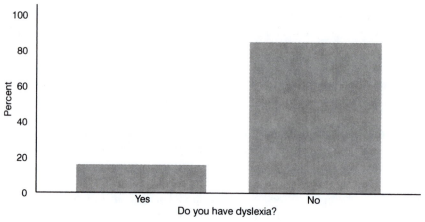

FIGURE 7.1   Dyslexia in this sample

in this study, only 15.3 per cent of participants reported having dyslexia. This figure is significantly lower than these previous studies suggesting the dyslexia prevalence for the homeless population is at 52 per cent (Barwick and Siegel 1996) and 46 per cent (Olisa *et al.* 2010). This figure is also slightly lower than the population of dyslexic offenders within the prison system at 20 per cent (DI 2005; Macdonald 2013). Nonetheless, 15 per cent is significantly higher by comparison with the general population in the UK, where it is estimated at 4 per cent (Semple and Smyth 2013), showing the overrepresentation of people with dyslexia among this study's homeless population.

Homelessness and childhood trauma

As discussed, there was general consensus in the literature that childhood trauma leaves individuals vulnerable to pathways into homelessness, particularly chronic homelessness (Taylor *et al.* 2006; Lee *et al.* 2010; Mercier and Picard 2011). In this study, participants with dyslexia reported an increased experience of childhood neglect and abuse. In Table 7.1, 27.9 per cent of the dyslexic group reported experiences of neglect, 35.3 per cent reported physical abuse and 37.9 per cent sexual abuse. This is compared with the non-dyslexic group that reported experiences of neglect at 15.7 per cent, physical abuse at 19.7 per cent and sexual abuse at 20.2 per cent. These findings reveal that participants with dyslexia described a significant (P≤.02) increase in traumatic experiences of abuse in childhood compared with the general homeless population.

In Table 7.1, the findings also reveal that participants with dyslexia experienced an increased likelihood of being thrown out by a parent/carer as a child. As we can see the data reveals that 57.4 per cent of participants with dyslexia, compared with 32.3 per cent without dyslexia, were made homeless by their parent/carer. Furthermore, 57.4 per cent of the dyslexic group reported

TABLE 7.1 Homeless people's reports of childhood neglect

History of homelessness		Yes (%)	No (%)	Sig
Reported neglect	Dyslexic	27.9	72.1	P=0.01
	Non-dyslexic	15.7	84.3	
Reported child abuse (physical)	Dyslexic	35.3	64.7	P=0.00
	Non-dyslexic	19.7	80.3	
Reported child abuse (sexual)	Dyslexic	37.9	58.6	P=0.02
	Non-dyslexic	20.2	76.0	
Were thrown out by parents/carers	Dyslexic	57.4	42.6	P=0.00
	Non-dyslexic	32.3	67.7	
Ran away from home as a child (more than 1 night)	Dyslexic	57.4	42.6	P=0.00
	Non-dyslexic	30.7	69.3	

having actively run away from their childhood home compared to 30.7 per cent of the non-dyslexic group. This seems to indicate evidence that there is a steady progression into homelessness, starting in childhood which advances into adulthood, for many participants with dyslexia.

Adult homelessness

When examining the experiences of adult homelessness, a number of significant differences (P≤.01) appeared within the data analysis. The findings in Table 7.2 suggest that the dyslexic group experienced episodic or chronic homelessness earlier in their lives compared with the non-dyslexic group. This claim seems to be supported as on average people with dyslexia first stayed in a hostel/shelter at the age of 26 years, compared to the non-dyslexic population who reported their first stay in a hostel was at 30 years. Furthermore, the dyslexic population reported first sleeping rough on average at the age of 22 compared with that of 29 years for the general homeless population.

TABLE 7.2 Differences in experiences of adult homelessness

Age first stayed in hotel/hostel refuge/night shelter	Dyslexic Non-dyslexic	Mean =	26 years 30 years	P=0.01
Age when sleeping rough	Dyslexic Non-dyslexic	Mean =	22% 29.2%	P=0.00
Number of times person has been homeless	Dyslexic Non-dyslexic	Mean =	11.1 9.5	P=0.00
Years spent sleping rough	Dyslexic Non-dyslexic	Mean =	5.1 years 3.5 years	P=0.05

Participants with dyslexia also indicated that they had become homeless more times compared with the general homeless population. The dyslexic group reported experiencing homelessness on average 11 times compared with the non-dyslexic group who on average experienced homelessness nine times. A significant difference also appeared in relation to the amount of time people slept rough over their lifetimes. The dyslexic group reported sleeping rough on average for five years compared with the non-dyslexic group indicating 3.5 years. In general, these findings seem to imply that people with dyslexia are at an increased risk of becoming either episodic or chronic homeless compared to the general homeless population.

Education and employment

As discussed, studies that have linked dyslexia and homelessness suggest education plays a significant role in the social exclusion of this group (Markos and Strawser 2004; Olisa *et al.* 2010). However, in this study both groups reported obtaining very few formal qualifications. Only 20 per cent of participants had acquired GCSEs, 14.9 per cent achieved A-levels and 11.6 per cent have graduated with a degree. There was no significant data (P>.05) to suggest that the dyslexic group achieved fewer qualifications compared with the non-dyslexic group. Nonetheless, Kirk and Reid (2001) and Macdonald (2012), when studying offenders, indicate that it is educational disengagement which leads to social exclusion rather than just qualifications.

There was some evidence of this when examining issues relating to truancy and school bullying. As we can see in Table 7.3, 41.2 per cent of participants with dyslexia reported being bullied, compared with only 21.9 per cent of the non-dyslexic group. Although both groups reported fairly high levels of truancy it was the dyslexic group who reported slightly higher levels at 67.6 per cent compared with 46.7 per cent. There was also a slight difference between groups when reporting on the age that individuals left school. As we can see from Table 7.3 the average age of school leavers for the non-dyslexic group was 16 years; this is compared with only 15 years for the dyslexic group. Therefore, this presents some evidence that participants with dyslexia had an increased chance of being bullied, were more likely to truant from school and on average left school before the UK's legal age. This data illustrates some evidence that the dyslexic group had disengaged with education before becoming homeless.

In the data findings unemployment rates were considerably high for both groups in this study (P≤.05). However, although educational qualifications were at a similar level, it is the dyslexic group which reported the highest unemployment rates. As we can see from Table 7.3, 100 per cent of participants with dyslexia were claiming benefits and only 1.5 per cent had been paid for work in the previous month. When comparing this to the general homeless population, 79.7 per cent were claiming benefits and only 8.8 per cent reported receiving money for paid work. Furthermore, there was a significant difference

TABLE 7.3 Dyslexia, education and employment

Education and employment		Yes (%)	No (%)	Sig
Truanted from school	Dyslexic	67.6	32.4	P=0.00
	Non-dyslexic	46.7	5.3	
Badly bullied at school	Dyslexic	41.2	58.8	P=0.00
	Non-dyslexic	21.9	78.1	
Age of school graduation	Dyslexic	Mean =	15 years	P=0.05
	Non-dyslexic	Mean =	16 years	
(UK) benefits in the past month	Dyslexic	100	0	P=0.00
	Non-dyslexic	79.7	20.3	
Paid work in the past month	Dyslexic	1.5	98.5	P=0.03
	Non-dyslexic	8.8	91.2	
Begged (asked passers-by for money in public place)	Dyslexic	45.6	54.4	P=0.03
	Non-dyslexic	32.0	68	

between groups when examining activities like begging in order to obtain money. As we can see from Table 7.3, 45.6 per cent of participants with dyslexia reported begging in a public place for money. In relation to the non-dyslexic group, only 32 per cent reported engaging in this activity for financial gain. Hence this analysis suggests that homeless people with dyslexia were increasingly excluded from work and more dependent on benefits and begging than homeless people who were not dyslexic.

Crime and drug use

Since the 1960s there has been a wealth of research which has linked dyslexia to an increase in criminality (Critchley 1968; Morgan 1996; Kirk and Reid 2001; Selenius et al. 2006). In Table 7.4 there is evidence to suggest that there is a significant (P≤ .03) increase in class-A drug consumption by participants with dyslexia. However, although the dyslexic group is significantly higher, both groups score relatively high in this category. In Table 7.4 participants with dyslexia reported an increased use of heroin at 55.9 per cent compared to the non-dyslexic group at 41.6 per cent. As Taylor et al. (2006) and Mercier and Picard (2011) suggest, drug use features significantly in the experiences of homeless people with mental health conditions and intellectual disabilities. Therefore, Table 7.4 reveals this is also the case for homeless people with dyslexia. Yet, it is the dyslexic group who appear to be more likely to engage in health services to overcome their addiction problems compared to the non-dyslexic group. As we can see, 50 per cent of the dyslexic group have engaged

TABLE 7.4 Crime and dyslexia

Crime		Yes (%)	No (%)	Sig
Used hard drugs	Dyslexic	55.9	44.1	P=0.02
	Non-dyslexic	41.6	58.4	
Used methadone drug in the past month	Dyslexic	50.0	50.0	P=0.03
	Non-dyslexic	30.2	69.8	
Shoplifted	Dyslexic	55.9	44.1	P=0.01
	Non-dyslexic	39.2	60.8	
Charged with a violent criminal offence (i.e. robbery, rape, murder)	Dyslexic	33.8	63.1	P=0.03
	Non-dyslexic	24.5	74.2	

in the methadone programme over the past month. This is compared with only 30.2 per cent of the non-dyslexic group.

Within this study, the data findings reveal that there was a significant (P≤ .03) increase in economic and violent crimes committed by the dyslexic group. As we can see participants with dyslexia were more likely at 55.9 per cent to shoplift compared with the non-dyslexic group at 39.2 per cent. Although there was a significant relationship between shoplifting and the use of hard drugs (P= .03), there was not a significant difference between dyslexia, hard drug use and shoplifting. The dyslexic group also reported having been involved in more serious offences relating to robbery, rape, or murder. As Table 7.4 illustrates, 33.8 per cent of dyslexic participants have been charged with a violent offence compared with 24 per cent of the non-dyslexic group. There has been much debate around the causal factors relating to dyslexia and crime (Rice 1998; Kirk and Reid 2001; Samuelsson et al. 2003; Selenius et al. 2006). Research by Macdonald (2012, 2013) implies that people with dyslexia are over-represented in the criminal justice system, not because of dyslexic symptoms, but due to educational barriers which negatively impact on adult life with reference to employability. By referring to Tables 7.3 and 7.4, this study's findings might support the educational exclusion hypothesis.

Mental health

There have been a number of studies which suggest an intersectional relationship between learning impairments, mental health issues and homelessness (Markos and Strawser 2004; Olisa et al., 2010 and Mercier and Picard, 2011). Within this study there was clear evidence of an intersectional relationship between people with specific learning difficulties and that of mild to moderate forms of mental health problems. It should be noted that mental health problems were

TABLE 7.5   Mental health and dyslexia

Mental health		Yes (%)	No (%)	Sig
Anxiety, depression or bad nerves, psychiatric problem	Dyslexic	66.2	33.8	P=0.00
	Non-dyslexic	48.5	51.5	
Self-harm	Dyslexic	55.4	40.0	P=0.00
	Non-dyslexic	29.4	67.9	
Attempted to commit suicide	Dyslexic	56.9	32.3	P=0.00
	Non-dyslexic	41.2	56.9	
Times of attempts at suicide	Dyslexic	Mean =	4.5 times	P=0.01
	Non-dyslexic	Mean =	2.8 times	
Admitted to mental health hospital	Dyslexic	47.1	52.9	P=0.00
	Non-dyslexic	28.5	71.5	

particularly high in both groups of participants that experienced homelessness, however for individuals with dyslexia there were significantly higher levels of mental health problems within this group ($P \leq .01$). In Table 7.5, 66.2 per cent of individuals with dyslexia reported having anxiety and depression which was 17.7 per cent higher than the non-dyslexic group (at 48.5 per cent). The act of self-harm also seemed to be a particular problem for people with dyslexia, as 55.4 per cent engaged in this ritual compared to 29.4 per cent of the non-dyslexic group.

Equally worrying was an increase in suicide attempts for dyslexic participants. Fifty-six point nine per cent of people with dyslexia reported that they had attempted to commit suicide compared to 41.2 per cent of non-dyslexic participants. Furthermore, for participants that had attempted to commit suicide, the dyslexic group had attempted this on average 4.5 times compared to 2.8 times for the non-dyslexic group. Furthermore, 47.1 per cent of participants with dyslexia (an increase of 18.6 per cent) had been admitted to a mental health hospital compared to the non-dyslexic group (at 28.5 per cent). This final piece of analysis may highlight poor transitional support by mental health services from hospital to community care for people that have become homeless in this study.

Access to services

Within the data analysis there were a number of significant differences ($P \leq .05$) in relation to how people accessed health and social services. As we can see from Table 7.6, 50 per cent of participants with dyslexia had access to a social worker compared with only 36 per cent of the non-dyslexic group. Forty-seven point one per cent of participants with dyslexia received support from a drugs worker compared to 30.4 per cent of the non-dyslexic group. Furthermore,

TABLE 7.6   Health and social services

Assessment of services		Yes (%)	No (%)	Sig
Social worker	Dyslexic	50.0	50.0	P=0.02
	Non-dyslexic	36.0	64.0	
Drug worker	Dyslexic	47.1	52.9	P=0.00
	Non-dyslexic	30.4	69.6	
Probation officers	Dyslexic	44.1	55.9	P=0.03
	Non-dyslexic	31.2	68.8	
Community psychiatric nurse,	Dyslexic	38.2	61.8	P=0.05
psychologist/psychiatrist	Non-dyslexic	26.9	73.1	

44.1 per cent of participants with dyslexia have contact with a probation worker and 38.2 per cent a psychiatric professional. This is compared to 31.2 per cent of the non-dyslexic group with access to a probation worker and 26.9 per cent of non-dyslexic participants having contact with a psychiatric professional. Tables 7.1 to 7.4 in this study suggest reasons why the dyslexic group might have increased access to these professionals: dyslexic participants had increased drug and alcohol problems, increased experience of childhood abuse and increased likelihood of being arrested compared with the non-dyslexic group.

Yet, although dyslexic participants had increased access to social and health professionals this does not seem to have impacted on reducing pathways into homelessness. Unfortunately for the dyslexic group, the vast majority of participants still reported having addiction problems, were more likely to experience chronic homelessness and reported higher levels of mental health problems than the non-dyslexic group. This data seems to suggest multiple lost opportunities in order to confront the intersectional experiences of inequality and abuse for this group. This might support Olisa *et al.*'s (2010) suggestion that although dyslexic participants often engage in services, because services do not adjust their practices with reference to dyslexia, this leads to many participants disengaging with the support on offer by these practitioners.

Conclusion

This chapter has presented evidence that people with dyslexia are over-represented within the homeless population in the UK. This does not suggest that other factors like age, social class, mental health or gender are not equally important and significant when studying pathways into homelessness. But due to the substantial number of statistically significant relationships that have appeared within the data findings, this study suggests that dyslexia also needs to be recognised as a key risk factor alongside these other variables when conceptualising pathways into homelessness. Hence, in this study, individuals with dyslexia reported experiencing increased levels of neglect and child abuse. Participants with dyslexia were more likely to have addiction problems, commit crime and were less likely to be employed compared with the general homeless population. Furthermore, participants with dyslexia were more likely to self-harm and attempt suicide than their non-dyslexic counterparts. What this study demonstrates is the existence of significant intersectional barriers between dyslexia, unemployment, homelessness and mental health problems. These findings seem to suggest that there is a clear link between early experiences of abuse in childhood and the progression of mental health problems in adulthood for homeless people with dyslexia.

Yet as Hore (2013) indicates, many studies that offer similar explanations unintentionally pathologise the experience of homelessness by suggesting that it is caused by symptoms of mental health issues. As Farrugia (2011) states, homelessness is as a result of low paid, temporary job markets, unemployment and unstable housing rather than pathologies. As highlighted in the work of Basu and Stuckler (2012), the increase in homelessness is because of a direct result of the political decision-making of governments rather than due to public health alone. However, for participants with dyslexia once they become homeless, the data in this study seems to suggest that they have an increased probability of spiralling into the episodic and chronic homeless population.

In my opinion, these findings do not endorse the health-based 'housing readiness model' of treatment followed by permanent housing but that of the 'housing first model'. As demonstrated in research by Lee *et al.* (2010) the 'housing first model' deals with homelessness first, by offering permanent residence, followed by health and economic support. However, this approach will only work if people have access to intensive health, social and economic support, which will prevent the recurrence of homelessness for this group. A package of support needs to offer financial stability, appropriate drug and alcohol services, mental health support to deal with trauma, access to educational support and to career and guidance services. As Taylor *et al.* (2006) suggest, current services are over reliant on charities which do not have the expertise to deal with the complexities of homelessness. For the 'housing first model' to succeed, professionals working in partnership with one another need to specialise in supporting people that have experienced homelessness and have a multitude of additional needs.

The need for specialist support is demonstrated in the findings, as despite participants having access to health and social welfare services, this did not lead to a reduction in drug use, unemployment or access to permanent residence for participants with dyslexia. Therefore, this analysis suggests that there have been numerous missed opportunities by practitioners in order to help people with dyslexia out of homelessness. The data indicates that contemporary services must broaden their scope beyond mental health support in order to include specific issues that affect people with dyslexia and other learning difficulties (Markos and Strawser 2004; Olisa *et al.* 2010). To coincide with Markos and Strawser's (2004) proposal, specific educational support must be integrated into current housing, health and social welfare strategies to help this group break the cycle of homelessness. I conclude by endorsing the 'housing first model' with integrated multi-layered services including economic, health, social welfare and educational support. By doing this, homeless services have a chance to effectively deal with the multiple problems experienced by people with dyslexia that have become homeless in the UK. Yet in order to achieve this, the UK government must increase rather than decrease public spending which seems unlikely in the current economic climate.

References

Barwick, M.A. and Siegel, L.S. (1996) Learning difficulties in adolescent clients of a shelter for runaway and homeless street youths. *Journal of Research on Adolescence*, 6, 649–670.

Berk-Clark, C.V. and McGuire, J. (2013) Elderly homeless veterans in Los Angeles: chronicity and precipitants of homelessness. *American Journal of Public Health*, 103 (2), 232–238.

Basu, S. and Stuckler, D. (2012) *The Body Economic, Why Austerity Kills*, London, Penguin.

Burns, J.K. (2009) Mental health and inequity: a human rights approach to inequality, discrimination, and mental disability. *Health and Human Rights,* 11 (2), 19–31.

Critchley, M. (1968) Reading retardation, dyslexia and delinquency. *The British Journal of Psychiatry*, 114, 1537–1547.

Culhane, D.P., Metraux, S., Park, J.M., Schretzman, M., & Valente, J. (2007) Testing a typology of family homelessness based on patterns of public shelter utilization in four U.S. jurisdictions: Implications for policy and program planning. *Housing Policy Debate*, 18:1–28.

Danermark, B. (2007) Interdisciplinary research and critical realism: the example of disability research. *Journal of Critical Realism*, 5 (1), 56–64.

DCLG (2014) *Homelessness Statistics*. London, Department for Communities and Local Government.

De Vaus, D.A. (2002) *Surveys in Social Research*, London, UCL Press.

Dyslexia Action (2005) *The Incidence of Hidden Disabilities in the Prison Population: Yorkshire and Humberside Research Report*. Egham, The Dyslexia Institute.

Farrell, D. (2012) Understanding the psychodynamics of chronic homelessness from a self-psychological perspective. *Journal of Clinical Social Work*, 40, 337–347.

Farrugia, D. (2011) Youth homelessness and individualised subjectivity. *Journal of Youth Studies* 14, (7), 761–775.

Fitzpatrick, S., Johnsen, S. and Braml, G. (2010) *Multiple Exclusion Homelessness Across the United Kingdom,* [computer file]. Colchester, Essex: UK Data Archive [distributor], December 2011. SN: 6899, http://dx.doi.org/UKDA-SN-6899-1.

Gustavsson, A. (2004) The role of theory in disability research – springboard or strait-jacket? *Scandinavian Journal of Disability Research*, 6(1), 55–70.

Hore, B. (2013) Is homelessness a matter of social justice for counselling psychologists in the UK? *Counselling Psychology Review*, 28, (2), 17–29.

Kirk, J. and Reid, G. (2001) An examination of the relationship between dyslexia and offending in young people and the implications for the training system, *Dyslexia*, 7, 77–84.

Lee, B.A., Tyler, K.A. and Wright, J.D. (2010) The new homelessness revisited. *Annual Review of Sociology*, 36 (1), 501–521.

Lund, B. (2011) *Understanding Housing Policy* (second edition), Bristol, Policy Press.

Macdonald, S.J. (2010) Towards a social reality of dyslexia. *British Journal of Learning Disabilities*, 38(1), 21–30.

Macdonald, S.J. (2012) Biographical pathways into criminality: understanding the relationship between dyslexia and educational disengagement. *Disability and Society*, 27 (3), 427–440.

Macdonald, S.J. (2013) The right to be labelled: from risk to rights for pupils with dyslexia in 'special needs' education, in Donovan, C. and Kearney, J. (eds) *Constructing Risky Identities: Consequences for Policy and Practice*, London, Palgrave.

Markos, P.A. and Strawser S. (2004) The relationship between learning disabilities and homelessness in adults. *Guidance and Counselling*, 19, (2), 1–24.

Means, R. (2007) Safe as houses? Ageing in place and vulnerable older people in the UK. *Social Policy and Administration*, 41 (1), 65–85.

Mercier, C. and Picard, S. (2011) Intellectual disability and homelessness. *Journal of Intellectual Disability Research*, 55 (4), 441–449.

Morgan, W. (1996) London offender study: creating criminals – why are so many criminals dyslexic? PhD dissertation. University of London.

Olisa, J., Patterson, J. and F. Wright, (2010) *Homeless Literacy Report*, London, A Thames Reach Action Research Report.

Parsell, C. and Marston, G. (2012) Beyond the 'at risk' individual: housing and the eradication of poverty to prevent homelessness, *Australian Journal of Public Administration*, 71, (1), 33–44.

Pluck, G., Lee, K., David, R., Macleod, D.C., Spence, S.A. and Parks, R.W. (2011) Neurobehavioural and cognitive function is linked to childhood trauma in homeless adults. *British Journal of Clinical Psychology*, 50, 33–45.

Reindal, S.M. (2008) A social relational model of disability: a theoretical framework for special needs education? *European Journal of Special Needs Education*, 23 (2), 135–146.

Rice, M. (1998) Dyslexia and crime: some notes on the Dyspel claim. Unpublished article, Institute of Criminology, UK, Cambridge, University of Cambridge.

Samuelsson, S., Herkner, B. and Lundberg, I. (2003) Reading and writing difficulties among prison inmates: a matter of experiential factors rather than dyslexic problems. *Scientific Studies of Reading* 7 (1), 53–73.

Selenius, H., Daderman, A.M., Meurling, S.W. and Levander, S. (2006) Assessment of dyslexia in a group of male offenders with immigrant backgrounds undergoing a forensic psychiatric investigation. *Journal of Forensic Psychiatry and Psychology*, 17 (1), 1–22.

Semple, D. and Smyth, R. (2013) *Oxford Handbook of Psychiatry* (3rd edition). Oxford: Oxford Press.

Shakespeare, T. (2006; 2013). *Disability Rights and Wrongs*, London, Routledge.

Taylor, H., Stuttaford, M., Broad, B. and Vostanis, P. (2006) Why a 'roof' is not enough: the characteristics of young homeless people referred to a designated Mental Health Service. *Journal of Mental Health*, 15 (4), 491–501.

Wormer, R.V. (2004) Homelessness among older adults with severe mental illness: a biologically based developmental perspective. *Journal of Human Behavior in the Social Environment*, 10 (4), 39–49.

United Nations Economic and Social Council (2009) *Economic Commission for Europe: Counting Homeless People in the 2010 Census Round: Use Of Enumeration and Register-Based Methods*, Geneva, Conference of European Statisticians.

United States Department of Housing Urban Development. (USHUD) (2009) Annual Homeless Assessment Report to Congress, Washington, DC., U.S. Congress.

PART III
Care and control

8

SPACES OF INDIFFERENCE

Bureaucratic governance and disability rights in Iceland

James Rice, Kristín Björnsdóttir and Eiríkur Smith

Introduction

The purpose of this chapter is to explore the power relations that mediate the circumstances and daily experiences of disabled people in Iceland who live in group homes and supported housing arrangements. We focus specifically on the experiences of two individuals whose applications for direct payment contracts have been rejected and therefore do not have access to independent living arrangements. Our analysis of power is sympathetic to Michel Foucault's contention that once individuals are made 'visible' by power they could then be made knowable and governable (Foucault, 1977). The people whose lives are the focus of this chapter are unique individuals with specific interesting stories to tell, but many elements of their narratives reflect power relations that mirror the situation faced by many other disabled people in Iceland. As engaged researchers, we aim to illuminate the extent and disproportionate nature of these power relations for disabled people who live in group homes and supported housing environments, in order to build a case for direct payments and independent living arrangements. However, this chapter also highlights our findings which suggest another perspective to consider – that of practices of indifference – in which civil rights, notions of equality and comparable standards of living barely register as a concern on the part of the authorities beyond the provision of services which meet only the basic level of existence, and what this may mean for strategies to counter these kinds of power relations.

Power can indeed manifest as a repressive force that sometimes simply says 'no' and constrains choices. The 'no' in response to requests for direct payments, independent living and choice of residence was articulated to our research participants in a variety of ways by the responsible authorities.

This included basic negative replies that referred to an external authority for legitimation, such as budgetary restrictions or the regulations that governed service provision; service arrangement offers that simply could not be accepted due to their limited scale, even though the service needs of individuals were well known; and requests that simply went unanswered and ignored. However, we also suggest that our research participants sometimes needed to be 'seen' by the state, or seen in particular ways, in order to receive the assistance and support they required and were entitled to rather than being ignored or marginalized by the educational, support and therapeutic services they interacted with over the course of their lives. Within the critical social sciences, to be made 'visible' by the state is often interpreted as inherently negative, as being made knowable and thus governable, even if this visibility is at times difficult to detect, as noted in Michel Foucault's well-known interpretation of Jeremy Bentham's Panopticon (Foucault, 1977). Yet individuals also draw upon parallel technologies of legibility to 'compel the state to see them' (Street, 2012: 2). What our research participants often experienced was not being seen, forgotten about and attitudes of indifference. The anthropologist Michael Herzfeld (Herzfeld, 1992) argued in his study of bureaucratic power that indifference 'is the rejection of common humanity. It is the denial of identity, of selfhood' (Herzfeld, 1992: 1). Herzfeld sought to explore the question as to why it is that political entities, such as states, local governments and their institutions, officially celebrate individual and group rights, yet are often very selective in applying these rights. One conclusion he draws is that we need to pay attention to the broader cultural values that legislators, officials and bureaucrats share as citizens, rather than simplistic notions of petty tyrants behind desks. He writes, 'The roots of official intolerance and indifference lie in popular attitudes, upon which official discourse builds to make its own case' (Herzfeld, 1992: 49).

We fear that the entrenched values and methods of service provision that exist in Iceland, which support and reinforce the 'right' of various authorities to govern the lives of disabled people (or ignore them or trivialize their needs), will prevent the progressive spirit of much recent legislative work and action plans from being meaningfully translated into practice. Certainly counter-action needs to occur in the legislative-legal sphere, but Herzfeld's point about the roots of indifference is suggestive of the need for activists to engage with the cultural views and value systems within bureaucratic organizations and the larger society in which they are embedded. The Independent Living Movement in Iceland was formally founded on 17 June 2009 and is therefore a relatively new ideology compared to the neighbouring countries. A year later, in June 2010, the Icelandic parliament adopted the resolution on the implementation of personalized, user-led services (NPA) in Iceland (Jóhannsdóttir et al., 2009). Since this time, little has been accomplished and only a select few have been granted direct payments. According to a report produced by the Icelandic Association of Local Authorities (2014), as of September 2013 a total of 47 individuals have made user-controlled personalized agreements with their local service area, including an additional

17 contracts between the municipality and a personal representative. However, not all individuals who wish to make such service arrangements have been able to do so, or do so in a satisfactory way, and not all municipalities in Iceland currently offer such arrangements. It would appear that much still remains to be done to convince service personnel, officials and the general public of the unjustness of the existing arrangements and that it is not acceptable that people have limited control over their lives, have to live with people not of their choosing, and are not able to access the services and opportunities that others take for granted, because of their impairments.

This chapter is written from the perspective of disability studies which privileges knowledge derived from the experiences of disabled people and identifies disability 'as a social problem that should be addressed by socio-political interventions' (Goodley, 2011: 3). We choose to avoid the 'models' approach which has been characteristic of disability research for some time and favour instead a 'critical realist' approach which 'gives weight to different causal levels in the complex disability experience' (Shakespeare, 2013: 73). Despite the growing body of critical disability research in Iceland (Traustadóttir et al., 2013), it is possible that the general public fails to appreciate the disempowering situations that many disabled people face in their daily lives, particularly in regard to housing and service provision. Disability service provision appears to be constructed as technical solutions to providing basic needs that are generally not predicated on the notion of human rights, choice, or even a vision of the need for living a life that approximates the basic expectations of the non-disabled population. Services are executed in a generally de-politicized manner, as rational, objective and logical solutions to providing individuals with needed support. It has been argued that this de-politicization of outcomes is an essential feature of bureaucratic governance in general, which masks the strengthening of bureaucratic power and stifles criticism (Ferguson, 1994). Service provision is not neutral and devoid of power relations. While the 'total institution' that Goffman (1961) analysed appears to be largely a thing of the past in Iceland in the context of disability, and does not approximate the living situations of our particular research participants, many of the more subtle everyday acts of disempowerment still persist within group homes and supported living environments. This ranges from the inability to choose where one lives, and with whom, waking, bathing, and eating schedules that have to accommodate service providers and others who may be sharing services, to ongoing practices of monitoring and surveillance. There is still a basic need in disability research to communicate the subjective experiences of these daily acts of disempowerment and affronts to dignity not only to service providers but the general public in order to build support for change. Oppression need not exist in the extreme in order to be felt as oppression. As long as services remain in the control of others, just and dignified support arrangements will remain elusive.

Our analysis of the narratives of our research participants will focus in three areas. First, the significant transition age from teenage years to adulthood, in which the desire for further education became increasingly constrained and living arrangements outside of the immediate family were decided. Second, their experiences of life within quasi-institutional settings, in which it became apparent that a long-standing pattern of lowered expectations on the part of educators, service professionals and even family members resulted in, essentially, an 'optimal' outcome as an individual adjusted to life within such a setting and with little expectations for a normative life course as expected on the part of non-disabled people. Lastly, we will focus on their experiences as they resisted these expectations and power relations through their efforts to lobby for independent living arrangements. The final part of this story, however, is yet to be written.

Methods

This chapter offers a collective case study based on two participants whose applications for independent living (IL) contracts were rejected. Many of their experiences seemed to us to parallel common patterns in Iceland. According to Yin (2003: 13), case study research 'investigates a contemporary phenomenon within its real-life context, especially when the boundaries between phenomenon and context are not clearly evident'. A collective case study is based on two or more cases and enables the researcher to explore differences within and between cases (Yin, 2003).

Using a purposive sampling approach, we selected two disabled participants, a man and a woman, who had applied at least once for IL contracts or direct payments but had been rejected by their municipalities and therefore currently live in assisted living facilities organized by their local welfare services and share staff and assistance with other disabled people. 'Anna' is a woman in her late thirties with physical impairments who needs round-the-clock assistance. She lives with her partner in her own apartment but receives services from the municipality that are shared with other disabled people in the same apartment building. Anna dropped out of upper-secondary school and is currently unemployed but has previously worked in the open labour market and a sheltered workshop. 'Jón' is a man in his early thirties with a physical impairment and progressive muscle weakness for which he requires 24-hour assistance. He lives in a group home with three other disabled men. He completed upper-secondary school, but he has been frustrated in his attempts to go to university. The municipality in which he lives does not support his transportation needs for attending university, and he is unable to move closer to the university as his request to receive services in that municipality was denied.

Each case was constructed based on data collected through a series of semi-structured, open-ended interviews with the aim of getting the research participant to describe with his or her own words their perspectives, values, and life-experiences (Kvale, 1996). The interviews took place at the participants' homes. The interviews were transcribed and coded by using axial coding in order to identify core categories, relationships between them and their context

(Creswell, 2012). The interviews were undertaken in Icelandic and all direct quotations translated by the authors of this chapter. However, we encountered difficulties in directly translating certain words, phrases and colloquialisms from Icelandic into English and so we relied to a greater degree on paraphrasing the material rather than direct quotations as we would have done in Icelandic. Given the small size of Iceland and its dense social networks, both names and certain identifying details have been changed to ensure confidentiality.

Findings

We divide this part of the chapter into three sections. First, we describe the transition years of the participants and the support they received before leaving the care of their parents. Then we explore the power relations within their homes, and finally we discuss their quest for independent living and lobbying for control.

Transition years

Mark Priestley (2003) and others (e.g. Hughes *et al.*, 2005) have argued that tensions and contradictions emerge during the transition years faced by disabled youth. Young people in general are conceived of by the state and its organs as potential human capital. Such a perspective warrants investment in young people in their formal education and training as well as preparation for adulthood as workers, consumers and future parents. Yet practices by the state, particularly in the educational arena, continue to deny these capacities and potentialities on the part of disabled youth and young adults (Björnsdóttir, 2014). The narratives of our research participants suggest that even from a young age their futures were perceived as constrained and limited in comparison with their non-disabled peers. Given the lack of support they experienced, this has in effect become a self-fulfilling prophecy about their futures, and prophecies they have continued to resist into adulthood.

Jón was born in the early 1980s in a town outside of Reykjavík. Since the age of five he had various diagnoses which sought to explain his stumbling and increasing mobility issues and was finally diagnosed with a form of muscular dystrophy when he was seven years of age. It is not clear how aware the municipality was of the family's need for support. As a working-class family of meagre means, Jón's father worked extensive shifts while his mother took most of the responsibility for the increasing caring duties. Jón noted that a rift appeared to be growing between his father and his mother. Jón recalled being unsure sometimes if he would be assisted after his mother said that she was 'no longer going to do the job alone' and wanted his father to do more in the home. He says he was not mistreated as such, but felt insecure and distressed during this time. It was not until Jón was 15 years old that the family received any governmental assistance, and even that was limited to nights and only on weekdays.

A similar situation appeared to hold for Jón in grammar school. The assistance he received was not based on any particular vision of his needs or future, but a rather *ad hoc*, after-the-fact solution to particular problems that arose as his mobility deteriorated. In the fourth grade Jón needed a wheelchair, but aside from a computer donated by the philanthropic Lion's Club organization received no particular support. When he needed assistance, it was provided by staff or peers. Later he was able to receive assistance from the *skólaliði* (paraprofessional), an assistant in most grammar schools who functions as a quasi-caretaker and hall monitor. In a way, the paraprofessional became his de facto personal assistant throughout his grammar school years (which extends to 16 in Iceland).

Anna is nearly ten years older than Jón, but her situation in grammar school was parallel in many ways even though she lived in Reykjavík. Because of her need for physical assistance, she did not go to the neighbourhood school like her non-disabled peers but instead was driven to a school in a different neighbourhood that specialized in teaching students with physical impairments. She spent part of her time in a class with non-disabled students, and for the rest was segregated in a special education classroom. She described her grammar school education as lacking any vision of her needs or potential future. For example, unlike her non-disabled peers, she did not study any languages or sciences and her dyslexia diagnosis was always secondary to her mobility issues and physical impairment. The quality of her grammar school education made it impossible for her to complete her A-levels and she was forced to drop out of school. Anna has never been provided with any explanation as to why she was excluded from certain subjects, and as far as we know there is no documentation of who decided that she would not follow the national curriculum. Simons and Masschelein (2005) claim that 'This exclusion from normal education is not regarded as a kind of exclusion in an ethical or political sense, however; to the contrary, this exclusion is regarded as a necessary condition for offering an adapted form of treatment' (p. 213). The struggle for basic education, either in terms of physical access or limited quality, has profound implications for post-compulsory education and adulthood. This is particularly so in terms of 'special programmes' which 'reduces the marketable value of the competences acquired, and reinforces young disabled people's status as devalued human capital' (Priestley, 2003: 109).

This lack of vision for students who had significant physical impairments but no intellectual impairment became even more pronounced when Jón attempted to enter upper-secondary school (Icelandic: *framhaldsskóli*) which is the transitionary phase between grammar school and university for ages 16 to 20. Here, the barriers he faced became even more pronounced. These schools are operated by the state, rather than municipality, and some do operate a special educational programme (Icelandic: *starfsbraut*); however these programmes are generally for those with learning difficulties who are not able to meet the requirements of the national examinations. However, since Jón was always part of the mainstream programme and had completed all of the necessary examinations he remained part of the mainstream school but had to contend with all of its inaccessible features, as there was simply no other option at the time. The type of paraprofessional who Jón had relied upon during his grammar school years was unavailable at upper-secondary level. Jón was therefore forced to rely on the voluntary assistance of staff and peers for basic assistance needs as the school was unable to financially provide a personal assistant. This caused him to become less and less interested in school activities – it was continually tiring, challenging and limiting to ask for assistance. But he persevered, though it took him ten years to complete upper-secondary school as opposed to the usual four.

It is very difficult to see much evidence of governmental rationality at work in Jón's case during his school years in terms of his situation. Changing laws and the shift to municipal rather than state responsibility for the grammar school system in 1995 did have effects, but the more significant actions seemed to be the result of happenstance rather than a careful consideration of his needs. The system appeared to be rather uninterested in 'looking at him', whereas, ironically, he would have benefited from being 'seen by the state' (Street, 2012) in order to receive the assistance he required. The notion of personalized, user-led assistance was generally not on the radar, in a manner of speaking, in the Icelandic disability policy context in the 1990s.

Once Jón's domestic situation came to the attention of the local municipality, some actions followed, and careful attention needs to be paid to the different ways in which different governmental systems may respond, or not. By the mid-90s, the local authorities became aware of the family's need: within a few years the authorities acted to purchase a shell of a newly built house and render it accessible, as the family was unable to afford new housing on their own. Jón was grateful for this help, and as such the potentially positive implications of governmental assistance need to be acknowledged, though this aid still remained out of the control and management of either Jón or his parents. The family was not consulted when it came to the design and fittings of their new home: for instance, the question of who was going to sleep where was all in the hands of occupational therapists and other experts.

However, support in the home remained insufficient. The progressive nature of Jón's impairment created more and more demands on his mother: she had to turn him over during the nights and do all the traditional work at home as well. His father devoted himself more and more to work, and the relationship started to crumble. Fearful of the ability of his mother to provide the care he needed, and about the deteriorating state of things within the home, Jón had no choice but to call the regional office responsible for disability matters and ask for more assistance. They reacted quite speedily and offered the family eight-hour night shifts on weekdays. Despite this, shortly afterwards his parents' relationship broke down and his father moved out. In order for Jón to get full service, based on the existing law which governed disability matters in Iceland, he would have to live in a group home or any designated service apartment with an organized night shift. Since there was no room available in the region's institutions for a

man using an electric wheelchair, the decision was made very early to change his house into a group home. It was most likely the case that no other option was possible, since personalized user-led services were not, and still are not, available in his area. This meant that Jón's mother and sister had to move out and be replaced by group home residents, together with all of the additional staff, management and bureaucratic modes of operation.

Jón had no say when it came to this 'reconstruction'. The former family home was rented and remained municipal property, as was the now newly created group home. The responsible authorities implemented their standard institutional procedures and structures. Staff were hired in order to secure services for the whole day and refurnish the house. The manager took over Jón's personal matters, such as his finances and medical issues. Decisions about who would move into the home were also entirely in the hands of the local authorities. Jón recalled for us his memories of the two women who moved in that he found particularly difficult to live with: one with mental health issues woke up during the nights, ran around the house and knocked on everyone's window, as well as taking food out of the fridge and throwing it in the garbage; the other was a teenage girl who was dealing with a lot of emotional issues at the time and found it hard to be separated from her family. What struck us most was Jón's calm recollection of events which would have been unsettling if not traumatic for many.

Life within the home

When we compared the two case studies on which this chapter is based, we realized that although the participants' living circumstances were different – Jón lives in a group home and Anna lives in her own apartment with assistance – both of them had to conform their lives to a schedule over which they had little or no control. Anna and Jón were relatively young, in their late teens, to be no longer living with their parents. Anna was not involved in the decision-making process but, as with Jón, in order to receive full services under Icelandic law at the time she could no longer live with her parents. Icelandic research suggests that this is a common theme (Björnsdóttir, 2009; Broddadóttir, 2010). The 'offices', or local authorities, decide when disabled individuals are ready to move out into a group home or other supported living arrangement. Their readiness is decided and defined by the governing bureaucracy and its experts, rather than by the feelings or wishes of the individuals themselves. When Anna was 19, her father had become ill and the municipality was looking for a young disabled woman who wanted to move into a small apartment and share services with another disabled woman who also lived in this apartment building. Anna recalls: 'My parents could not care for me any longer because dad had a heart attack. I had never thought about moving away from home. I was just a teenager'. Although Anna was not ready to start living on her own she still had a good deal of control over her life at her home and she was involved in choosing and hiring staff and organizing assistance. This all changed when she bought her own apartment with her partner. The first apartment was too small for two people and they decided to buy an apartment in a large apartment building where the municipality offered shared on-site services for disabled people. These services were controlled by the municipality. As the result of this move, Anna lost control over her home and there were institutional qualities to the services she received, based on hospital-like schedules. Anna explains: 'I get very tired struggling all the time to get the support I need and should get by law'.

The schedules at Anna's and Jón's homes are made and organized by the staff. Unlike those who reside in private domestic spaces, Jón and Anna need to accommodate their lives to a schedule which meets the needs of service providers and is more like the daily routines one would find in a hospital, than the patterns of a private home. Within this space, there are rotating shifts, with staff members and residents who come and go, quite unlike private residences where the inhabitants are either related through kinship or have agreed to cohabit. Jón lives with three other men in a group home, who all need different levels of assistance: staff members need to prioritize who will get assistance first in the morning and who needs to wait.

After Anna moved into her own apartment, she could not decide for herself when she would get assistance with activities of daily living such as bathing. She was assigned assistance for bathing two days a week at a predetermined time with no reference to her wishes. This meant she often had to choose between bathing or social participation. After a long battle with the support system, Anna is now able to choose which day she has a bath but staff members decide the timing, because it has to be synchronized with the needs of six other people receiving assistance in the building. Although she has only partial control over her own life and body, this victory has brought her back a measure of choice about her daily activities.

Jón and Anna are restricted by the need to synchronize themselves to the hospital-like schedule of their homes. It is difficult or even impossible for them to be spontaneous, because all of their actions need to be synchronized to the schedules and service availability linked to their places of residence, let alone other external issues such as transport availability and the accessibility issues within the larger environment. Even within the microenvironment, control and choice are also circumscribed, depending on the vagaries of the individual nature of the management and staff. For example, Anna had specifically requested not to be assisted by male staff members in personal care matters, but was told by the manager at the time that the choice was not hers to make:

> [the manager] told me that I was the only one who did not want to get assisted by male staff members and it was my problem and I had to deal with it. But when she quit and the new manager took over I realized that she had been lying to me and other women in the building had also complained about getting assisted by male staff for personal issues.

The internalization of these schedules as a form of disciplinary power is evident at places in their narratives. For example, Anna has described forgoing meals in deference to staff workloads. She explains: 'I feel sometimes that I am co-dependent to staff. When the manager told me she had so much she needed to do before her shift was over, and it was getting late, and I had not had dinner yet, I agreed to go to bed without eating. This is difficult to deal with'.

It is not only the daily routines and schedules that contribute to the institutional qualities of their homes. For example, Anna wants staff to ring the doorbell before they enter her apartment. Most comply with her wishes but generally do not wait for Anna or her partner to answer the door. They know that someone is entering their apartment but cannot stop them from doing so which limits their privacy and sense of comfort. Many members of the general public may have experienced similar conditions temporarily, when staying in hospitals. But for Anna and Jón this is a constant in their lives. We have observed staff members, residents, and in one case the children of staff members, come and go from Jón's room when we were conducting interviews. Each resident has a private room, but the washroom, living room and dining room are shared spaces. One member of our research team was worried by the fact that the washroom in the group home did not have a lock or any means to prevent entry by another party, while on another occasion the interview was being conducted in Jón's room while a private birthday party was being thrown in the shared space for another resident. These episodes highlight the distinct differences between the patterns and expectations within private domestic spaces versus the living conditions experienced by disabled people who require support, which often remain unquestioned.

Another issue which caught our attention and demonstrates the institutional qualities of their living arrangements was the use of documents. Matthew Hull (2012) argues that documents are not merely objective tools that bureaucratic organizations use in their day-to-day operations but that they are 'constitutive of bureaucratic rules, ideologies, knowledge, practices, subjectivities, objects, outcomes, even the organizations themselves' (Hull, 2012: 251). An analysis of the way in which documents are used in these residential settings was not the primary focus of our research, but observations and interviews revealed their omnipresence. It was not unusual to see bathing schedules, meal planners, or medical charts of the residents posted in plain view. We became aware of how often and when Jón is bathed, whereas for ourselves this information is private. While there are sometimes good reasons for such planning, the casual and relaxed attitudes to what is often very personal information is striking and speaks volumes about the way in which the residents are situated and perceived by the service providers. Such forms of governmentality would be dramatically reformed in the context of personalized, user-led services in which an individual has a say and control over such information, if indeed it needs to be collected at all. This is one of the daily injustices of life in an institutional setting that non-disabled people only ever experience during temporary visits to hospitals.

Lobbying for control

Above we have emphasized the lack of power of our research participants within these spaces and highlighted the institutional qualities of the services or assistance they receive. However these individuals are by no means totally oppressed and powerless in their lives. Jón's living situation remains a complex mix of empowerment and disempowerment, for which a unilinear analysis would be insufficient. Though he has significant mobility issues, he enjoys a certain status that the residents he lives with who have intellectual disabilities do not. As he grew older, he was encouraged to gain more control over his personal matters. He was always heavily involved in decisions relating to his needs and personal life, so the encouragement to do so by the staff was perhaps a way for the professionals to make an attempt at being supportive and understanding. To begin with he was mainly 'given' control over his finances but today he controls most of his personal matters (from buying caring products to communicating with health professionals). Unlike other residents, Jón 'decides' what is for dinner and writes his own reports for the social services.

Nevertheless, Jón experiences numerous limitations because of his residence. The group home is treated as an institution in the system, and services are provided for the house and not for individuals, which hinders his participation outside the home. During a conference in Iceland in 2006, Jón became aware of independent living and after hearing about a number of individuals in Reykjavík who received such arrangements, decided to apply. However, because personalized, user-led services currently have no legal basis in Iceland, it remains up to the individual municipalities to decide whether or not they want to offer these services. In this case, his application was refused because the region in which he resides does not offer this as a service option. Undaunted, he decided to apply to university and the group home manager applied for an additional staff member since, if accepted, Jón's need for assistance would create a shortage for the others. This request was also denied and with no explanation, as was another similar request in 2011. Jón responded to this denial by requesting a transfer to another group home where additional personal assistance was available – in this case he did not even receive an acknowledgement of his letter. He was simply ignored. As Hoag writes,

> while a good deal has been said – and to great effect – about the significance of the statistic ... or of the social life and circulation of the document ..., thinking through prospection and indeterminacy in bureaucratic worlds can help us to understand the implications of that information which goes unmade, or of the effects of documents stagnating in trays, cubbies, and computers.
>
> (Hoag 2011: 87)

Jón's last attempt to move out from the group home and get personalized services took place in the summer of 2012 when it was announced that applications had opened in Reykjavík. He received confirmation of his application four weeks later; another letter four months later that said they were still working on the application but they had been taken by surprise by the amount of applications; and then finally eight months later, more than a year after he sent in his application, he received a letter that stated he was not eligible for such service arrangements in Reykjavík since his legal residence was elsewhere. He had entered the classic space of governmental rationality and logic, a catch-22 situation in which the assistance he needs may be available, but he already needs to be living in that locale to get the assistance. In order to be able to move to that locale to get assistance, he would already need to have assistance. According to a lawyer we consulted, the answer he received is in violation of Icelandic law.

Anna's living situation is no more empowering than that of Jón's group home, despite the fact that her apartment is self-contained and supposedly 'private'. This is partly because she shares services with six other people, but also because the quality of the assistance and the extent of her control over her daily life rest largely upon the characteristics and personalities of service managers and staff. Anna has little opportunity for social participation but receives 24 hours per month for support with external social activities (liðveisla). When Anna learnt of independent living, she became convinced that this type of assistance would improve the quality of her life and make it possible for her to participate in society. She owned her apartment and wanted to be able to hire her own personal assistants and would therefore be free from the synchronization of timetables with other disabled residents in her apartment building. In 2007 she applied for direct payments and was offered a 15-hour contract, despite the fact that all concerned parties were aware that she needed 24-hour assistance: Anna explains: 'We were offered a total 15 hours for both of us [her and her partner who is also disabled]. I need assistance with everything. I cannot do anything on my own. I cannot use my hands. I need 24 hours and cannot share that with him [her partner] because then we are expected to be together all the time. It is obvious that I could not accept this contract'. This raises the question of governmental candour with regard to their commitment to the principles of equality and social justice that too readily fall from the lips of ministry officials. The only explanation Anna received for this inadequate contract was that there was no more funding available – she would either have to make do with 15 hours or continue with the services she was receiving.

Like Jón, Anna applied for personalized services when applications opened in Reykjavík in the summer of 2012. After a long waiting period she was informed by the service office that she had not been chosen for personalized services. No formal letter was sent to her, nor was any explanation forthcoming. She was simply not one of the lucky few who had been chosen for Reykjavík's experimental programme of personalized services. Since this time the local authorities tried to get her to sign a service agreement which detailed that the local social services centre would decide how many hours she would receive.

As a protest, Anna has not signed the contract and she remains very angry about how she has been treated. However, not signing the contract means she is risking not receiving the services she depends upon. But she feels that her refusal to accept their decision is the only way for her to protest.

Concluding comments

Our findings are suggestive of frontline service workers and group home managers who are often, though not always, kind and caring individuals who try to do the best they can with the resources they have and within the bureaucratic context in which they work. However, they operate within a larger institutional framework and broader cultural value system that appears to care very little about the disabled subjects who are governed by Iceland's system of group homes, at least beyond the provision of the basic necessities. Our findings suggest that, past the age of 18, there is little such vision for disabled people with significant impairments. Residence within a supported living environment and access to basic needs is seen as a 'success'. And this is not just about the group home system, but extends to other areas as we have shown, such as education. Whether this is by design, by neglect, due to lack of funding or due to ill-conceived policy, the outcomes are nevertheless evident. Power also involves the power not to look, to be indifferent, to simply not care. Yet as Herzfeld argues, the roots of indifference lies in culture not in legislation, action plans or budgetary tables. The cultural materials on which the legitimacy of bureaucratic power is constructed are also shared by citizens and as such subject to change. With these very same cultural materials, 'citizens find the resources they need to fight back against importunate officials who claim to be doing the bidding of 'the state" (Herzfeld, 1992: 50).

Recent Icelandic disability law revisions and action plans are replete with references to human rights, such as policy alignments made with references to the Convention on the Rights of Persons with Disabilities, or slogans and mantras such as accessibility or equality 'for all'. However, one stumbling block that we encountered during writing this chapter was the depressing fact that our research indicates how little has changed on the ground. The solution is not to make existing services 'better' but to radically re-envision disability support and services, away from the traditional residual model of the bureaucratic provisioning of basic needs, and towards user-controlled personal assistance and direct payments.

References

Björnsdóttir, K. (2009) Resisting the reflection: social participation of young adults with intellectual disabilities, PhD thesis, University of Iceland, Reykjavík.
Björnsdóttir, K. (2014) 'Ég fékk engan stuðning í skólanum': fötlun, kyngervi og stétt ['I didn't get any support in school' disability, gender, and class], in Rúdólfsdóttir, A.G.,

Elísson, G., Jóhannesson, I.Á., and Erlingsdóttir, I. (ed.) *Fléttur 3, Jafnrétti, menning, sam* félag [Equality, culture, society], Reykjavík: University of Iceland Press, pp. 233–257.

Broddadóttir, S. (2010) Að flytja úr foreldrahúsum: upplifun og reynsla ungs fólks með þroskahömlun og foreldra þeirra [Moving out: the experiences of young adults with intellectual disabilities and their parents], MA thesis, University of Iceland, Reykjavík.

Creswell, J. W. (2012) *Educational Research: planning, conducting, and evaluating quantitative and qualitative research*, 4th edition, Boston: Pearson.

Ferguson, J. (1994) *The Anti-Politics Machine: 'development', depoliticization, and bureaucratic power in Lesotho,* Minneapolis, MN: University of Minnesota Press.

Foucault, M. (1977) *Discipline and Punish: the birth of the prison,* New York: Random House, Inc.

Goffman E. (1961) *Asylums. Essays on the Social Situation of Mental patients and Other Inmates,* London: Penguin.

Goodley, D. (2011) *Disability Studies: an interdisciplinary introduction,* London: Sage.

Herzfeld, M. (1992) *The Social Production of Indifference: exploring the symbolic roots of western bureaucracy.* Chicago, IL: University of Chicago Press.

Hoag, C. (2011) Assembling partial perspectives: thoughts on the anthropology of bureaucracy, *PoLAR: Political and Legal Anthropology Review,* vol. 34, no. 1, pp. 81–94.

Hughes, B., Russell, B. and Paterson, R. (2005) Nothing to be had 'off the peg': consumption, identity and the immobilization of young disabled people, *Disability & Society,* vol. 20, no. 1, pp. 3–17.

Hull, M.S. (2012) Documents and bureaucracy, *Annual Review of Anthropology,* vol. 41, no. 1, pp. 251–267.

Icelandic Association of Local Authorities (2014) *Flutningur málefna fatlaðs fólks frá ríki til sveitarfélaga* [Transfer of the affairs of disabled people from state to municipalities]. Reykjavík: SÍS/ Icelandic Association of Local Authorities.

Jóhannsdóttir, V., Haraldsdóttir, F. and Traustadóttir, R. (2009) 'Upphaf notendastýrðar þjónustu á Íslandi' [The beginings of user led services in Iceland], *Research in Social Sciences – Conference Proceedings,* The Social Science Research Institute, University of Iceland, Reykjavík, pp. 295–304.

Kvale, S. (1996) *InterViews: an introduction to qualitative research interviewing,* Thousand Oaks, CA: Sage.

Priestley, M. (2003) *Disability: a life course approach,* Cambridge: Polity Press.

Shakespeare, T. (2014) *Disability Rights and Wrongs Revisited,* 2nd edition, Abingdon: Routledge.

Simons, M. and Masschelein, J. (2005) Inclusive education for exclusive pupils: a critical analysis of the government of the exceptional, in Tremain, S. (ed.) *Foucault and Government of Disability,* Ann Arbor, MI: University of Michigan Press, pp. 208–228.

Street, A. (2012) Seen by the state: bureaucracy, visibility and governmentality in a Papua New Guinean hospital, *The Australian Journal of Anthropology,* vol. 23, no. 1, pp. 1–21.

Traustadóttir, R., Sigurjónsdóttir, H.B. and Egilson, S. (2013) Disability studies in Iceland: past, present and future, *Scandinavian Journal of Disability Research,* vol. 15, Supplement 1, pp. 55–70.

Yin, R. K. (2003) *Case Study Research: design and methods,* 3rd edition, Thousand Oaks, CA: Sage.

9

MENTAL CAPACITY AND THE CONTROL OF SEXUALITY OF PEOPLE WITH INTELLECTUAL DISABILITIES IN ENGLAND AND WALES

Lucy Series

In England and Wales, people with intellectual disabilities have sex in the shadow of two legal regimes. Under the Sexual Offences Act 2003 (SOA), it is a criminal offence to engage in sexual activity 'with a person with a mental disorder impeding choice', defined as lacking the 'capacity' to make a choice about consenting to sex (s30). This modernized older laws prohibiting a man from having extra-marital sex with 'a woman whom he knows to be an idiot or imbecile' (s7 SOA 1956). The intention behind this was to create a law which would permit people with intellectual disabilities to enjoy sexual relationships, whilst retaining a deterrent against sexual exploitation (Law Commission, 2000).

Meanwhile the Mental Capacity Act 2005 (MCA) governs when a person has the 'mental capacity' to give or refuse consent to their care arrangements, including restrictions on their liberty or intrusions into their privacy and bodily integrity. Because sex with a person who lacks 'mental capacity' is a crime, public authorities are required to 'undertake the very closest supervision of that individual to ensure, to such extent as is possible, that the opportunity for sexual relations is removed' (*IM v LM*, 2014: §1). Sometimes these steps amount to a deprivation of their liberty (*D Borough Council v AB*, 2011; *A Council v H*, 2012). The source of this legal obligation to control people has not been made explicit by the Court of Protection, which was established under the MCA. It may be an interpretation of the state's 'positive obligations' under the European Convention on Human Rights to prevent the exploitation of 'vulnerable persons' where it knows, or ought to know, that it might occur (e.g. *Đorđević v Croatia*, 2012: §138). The common law duty of care may place private caregivers under similar obligations (Bartlett, 2010).

The concept of 'mental incapacity' thus plays a twofold gatekeeping role in relation to sex: it invalidates a person's consent, rendering sexual activity with them a criminal act, and it *also* renders lawful restrictions on their liberty and invasions of their privacy to prevent them from engaging in sexual activity. This chapter asks, after Richardson (2013: 90), 'can mental capacity bear the burden placed on it here?'

Background

In the early twentieth century, when eugenic discourses were in the ascendant, the Mental Deficiency Act 1913 introduced guardianship as a way to control people with intellectual disabilities who were living in the community, so that they did not 'procreate'; a policy adopted because of public opposition to sterilization (Fennell, 1992). Today, control over the sexuality of people with intellectual disabilities no longer has an explicit eugenic basis, but is framed in terms of their vulnerability to sexual exploitation, or to harmful social and emotional consequences arising from relationships, pregnancy, or health risks connected with sex.

Many people involved in the lives of people with intellectual disabilities may regard their sexuality with some ambivalence (Aunos and Feldman, 2002). Their families may regard sexual relationships as unacceptably dangerous (Heyman and Huckle, 1995). They may seek their sterilization (Aunos and Feldman, 2002) or long-term use of contraception (McCarthy, 2011). An implicit role of care and support services may be the regulation of sexuality (Brown, 1994). These concerns are not entirely without foundation (Heyman and Huckle, 1995). People with intellectual disabilities are more likely to experience sexual violence than non-disabled people (Hollomotz, 2011). Parents with intellectual disabilities experience an array of barriers to social justice (Jones, 2013). These risks have a complex etiology, arising from an interaction of social and environmental factors with a person's impairment (Hollomotz, 2011; Shakespeare, 2013). The critical question is: what kinds of measures are acceptable to protect people against these risks, and what criteria should we use to determine when they should be applied?

The Mental Capacity Act 2005

Guardianship legislation has undergone significant changes since the twentieth century. The MCA was presented as a law that would 'empower' people, rather than control them (Lord Chancellor's Office, 2007). It is sometimes described as establishing 'rights' for people with disabilities to make their own decisions (e.g. Hollomotz, 2011: 42, 43, 49). Yet in strictly legal terms, the MCA simply sets out the circumstances where a person's ordinary legal rights to make decisions may be denied, on grounds connected with their disability. In contemporary disability rights parlance, this is a denial of 'legal capacity'. A new international treaty – the United Nations Convention on the Rights of Persons with Disabilities ('CRPD', 2006) – has critiqued such laws as a discriminatory denial of legal capacity for people with disabilities (Dhanda, 2012; United Nations Committee on the Rights of Persons with Disabilities, 2014). Only a decade ago the MCA was considered a leading example of legal capacity legislation which complied with contemporaneous international human rights norms. However today it is considered likely to violate them because it stands at odds with a 'new paradigm' of rights articulated in connection with Article 12 CRPD – the right to legal recognition before the law (Bartlett and Sandland, 2013; Richardson, 2013).

This chapter considers critiques of the MCA's empowering credentials by looking at case law concerning the capacity to consent to sex. This is one of the best developed areas of law on mental capacity as it has been the subject of extensive litigation. These cases offer a stark illustration of the issues and tensions in using 'mental capacity' as a gatekeeper to paternalistic interventions.

The MCA's main claim to being progressive and empowering is its 'decision specific' and 'functional' approach to capacity. A person is presumed to have 'mental capacity' until it is demonstrated otherwise (s1(2), see also s2(3)). However, the mental capacity of people with disabilities is more likely to be called into question than for others, so this presumption may subtly shift for them. Unlike earlier 'status' approaches to legal capacity, which would have denied some people with disabilities legal capacity in all areas of their life, the MCA is 'decision specific' and so a person might have legal capacity to make some decisions but not others. Whilst this may afford some people greater autonomy than status-based approaches to capacity, it also means that people's mental capacity to make decisions could be called into question in any area of their decision making, and repeatedly over time. The Official Solicitor – who typically represents the 'best interests' of people 'who lack the capacity to litigate' in the Court of Protection – has argued that this can be burdensome on public authorities and 'will encourage paternalistic attempts to deprive the disabled with capacity of their autonomy' (Pitblado, 2013).

The MCA uses a 'functional test', which defines a person as unable to make a decision if they are unable:

- to understand the information relevant to the decision,
- to retain that information,
- to use or weigh that information as part of the process of making the decision, or
- to communicate his decision (whether by talking, using sign language or any other means) (s3(1)).

This 'functional' approach to mental capacity purports to focus on the *process* by which a person made a decision, not the outcome of that decision – and thus to avoid being hostage to the subjective values of those assessing capacity (Law Commission, 1991). The Act specifies that 'A person is not to be treated as unable to make a decision merely because he makes an unwise decision' (s1(4)). Yet scholars have questioned the MCA's 'value neutrality'.

Freyenhagen and O'Shea (2013: 67) argue that the MCA may inevitably 'smuggle in contentious evaluative commitments without discussion'. Veitch (2006) argues that the supposedly objective test of 'mental capacity' is attractive because it allows us to disavow the value judgments at work in these cases. Unsurprisingly, capacity assessors describe experiencing difficulty disentangling 'unwise' from 'incapacitous' decisions (Williams *et al.*, 2012), and express concern that 'On the same set of facts, two practitioners could come to a completely different view' (House of Lords Select Committee on the Mental Capacity Act 2005).

The MCA contains a 'diagnostic threshold', which requires that any failure of the functional test must be caused by 'an impairment of, or a disturbance in the functioning of, the mind or brain' (s2(1)) to constitute 'mental incapacity'. This requirement appears facially discriminatory as it means adults without disabilities could fail the functional test and yet retain their legal capacity (Bartlett and Sandland, 2013: 198; Dhanda, 2012). Paradoxically though, in some cases it has served to make it *harder* to demonstrate that a person with disabilities 'lacks mental capacity' because although they failed the functional test causation could not be shown (*CYC v PC*, 2013).

Some have questioned how far the functional test does assess an internal 'cognitive' process of deliberation by drawing attention to relational elements and power dynamics of capacity assessments. Stefan (1992–1993: 766–7) observes that:

> the whole focus of a competence inquiry centers on the alleged incompetent person to the exclusion of the powerful side of the dialogue. Therefore, incompetence is seen as the attribute of the less powerful person and all failures of communication are attributed to her.

Morgan and Veitch (2004) argue that capacity assessments do not so much assess how a person makes a decision, but 'whether the person making that decision can construct a convincing case why he or she reaches the standard of the 'ability' that law expects in such circumstances'. This is an important distinction, and it suggests that capacity assessments may often depend upon a person's ability to persuade and articulate, rather than to *decide*.

Article 12(3) CRPD obliges states to give people with disabilities the support they may require in exercising their legal capacity. The MCA takes some steps in this direction, but in contrast with the absolute duty to provide support under the CRPD its requirements are heavily qualified. It merely states that people should not be treated as lacking capacity unless 'all practicable steps' have been taken to help them to make a decision (s1(3), see also s3(2)). It does not specify who should provide this support, nor does it give any legal recognition to the kinds of supports which a person might use in exercising legal capacity, in contrast with other jurisdictions (Then, 2013). In some cases people have been held to 'lack capacity' *because of* their reliance on others for assistance with decision making

(*Verlander v Rahman*, 2012). As Bartlett and Sandland (2013: 180) observe, the Court of Protection sometimes imposes measures on a person against their will on the grounds that it will enhance their mental capacity. This stands at odds with the consensual model of support for the exercise of legal capacity, including supported decision making, proposed in connection with the CRPD (UN Committee on the Rights of Persons with Disabilities, 2014). Bartlett and Sandland also comment that it is a 'rare case' where the Court of Protection does consider whether all steps to support a person to make a decision have been exhausted (p.198).

When people 'lack capacity', third parties may make decisions on their behalf in their 'best interests' (s1(5)). Best interests decision makers must consider the person's past and present wishes, feelings, values and beliefs. They must help the person to participate in the decision 'so far as reasonably practicable', and consult with others engaged in caring for them or with an interest in their welfare (s4). The aim of this approach is 'to consider matters from the patient's point of view'; however these subjective factors are not binding on substitute decision makers (*Aintree University Hospitals NHS Foundation Trust v James*, 2013). Where best interests decisions depart from a person's subjective will and preferences they will constitute 'substitute decisions', which the Committee on the Rights of Persons with Disabilities' (2014) maintains are prohibited by Article 12.

Under the MCA, decision makers must consider the least restrictive course of action (s1(6)), but are not obliged to adopt this course. Neither does the MCA create any pressure to *make available* less restrictive options. Where restraint is used or threatened, or a person's liberty is restricted, it must be a proportionate response to the likelihood of the person suffering harm, and the seriousness of that harm (s6). The MCA also contains a framework for detention in care homes and hospitals – known as the deprivation of liberty safeguards.

The imposition of substitute decisions which conflict with a person's own will and preferences on disability-related grounds is considered by many to be a form of disability discrimination which violates Article 12 CRPD (Dhanda, 2012). The UN Committee on the Rights of Persons with Disabilities (2014) has stated that the CRPD requires states to offer support and to abolish regimes of substitute decision making. This was a highly contentious issue during the negotiations of Article 12 CRPD (Dhanda, 2012). The claim that imposing measures on people with disabilities against their will on disability-related grounds is discriminatory also arises in connection with Article 14 CRPD (the right to liberty), Article 17 CRPD (respect for physical and mental integrity), and other elements of the CRPD. In addition, Article 23 CRPD prohibits discrimination against people with disabilities in matters connected with marriage, family life and relationships. This chapter does not aim to provide a legally 'correct' interpretation of the CRPD, nor offer any alternative legal framework which might satisfy the CRPD, but it does offer some examples of how 'mental capacity' approaches can indeed operate in the discriminatory and oppressive ways that critics maintain.

Case law: issues and tensions

The court cases discussed here bring to the surface tensions between a desire to adopt a low threshold for capacity, in order to safeguard rights to liberty and privacy, and the pull of a higher threshold which would permit a more protective approach.

Minimalist approach

Early cases adopted a low threshold for the capacity to consent to sex, requiring only a 'rudimentary knowledge of what the act comprises and of its sexual character to enable her to decide whether to give or withhold consent' (*X City Council v MB, NB and MAB*, 2006: §74). In *D Borough Council v AB* (2012) Mostyn J[1] commented that 'the Court must tread especially carefully where an organ of the state proposes that a citizen's ability to perform, in a non-abusive way, the sex function should be abrogated or curtailed. It involves very profound aspects of civil liberties and personal autonomy' (§11). Accordingly, Mostyn J took a minimalist approach to the capacity to consent to sex, requiring only an understanding of the following (§42):

- The mechanics of the act
- That there are health risks involved, particularly the acquisition of sexually transmitted and sexually transmissible infections
- That sex between a man and a woman may result in the woman becoming pregnant.

Where homosexual sexual activity was concerned, the third requirement was discounted. In this case, 'Alan'[2] did not attain this low threshold of capacity because his knowledge of the health risks of sex was limited: 'he thought that sex could give you spots or measles' (§44). Mostyn J ordered the council to 'provide Alan with sex education in the hope that he thereby gains that capacity' (§52), so that the restrictions could be lifted.

Alan's case highlights difficulties with even this 'minimalist' approach. Alan failed the test because of his limited understanding of sexual health matters, consequently he was deprived of his liberty until he could demonstrate a better understanding. Yet a legal system that results in deprivation of liberty because a person believes that sex might give you spots or measles, then releases them from detention when they have corrected this false belief, seems arbitrary and absurd. The courts have not spelt out precisely what knowledge a person must demonstrate to pass this element of the test. It is hard to see how they could do so in a way that does not either collapse into vagueness ('there are some health risks'), or place expectations of knowledge on people with disabilities which other members of the population are not required to demonstrate. Many people without disabilities have poor knowledge of sexually transmitted infections

(Samkange-Zeeb *et al.*, 2011), but there is no question of this meaning they cannot give a legally valid consent to sex. The suggestion that those people should be closely supervised and their liberty restricted until they can demonstrate this knowledge would be unthinkable. In this element of the test, there is a clear danger that – despite the express efforts of some judges to avoid this – the 'mental capacity' approach can discriminate against people with disabilities.

In Alan's case, it is also pertinent to ask whether his lack of understanding was caused by a mental impairment – as required by s2(1) MCA – or by inadequate sex education. It is unclear from the judgment whether those assessing Alan's mental capacity took any steps at the time to help correct his false belief that sex could give you spots or measles, as would be required by s1(3) MCA. There is a danger that this element of the test may be neglected by assessors who would prefer an outcome which restricts a person's opportunities to engage in sexual activity.

Mostyn J's minimalist approach makes demands on abilities to articulate knowledge of pregnancy and health risks connected with sexual activity. This will almost inevitably mean that people with serious communication impairments will be found to lack capacity in this regard. Yet it is not inevitable that these people are being sexually exploited if they enjoy sexual relationships where they are able to demonstrate an ability to choose or refuse sexual activity, and benefit from sexual and personal intimacy.

The 'management of monsters'

Sandland (2013) draws on historical case law on sexuality and intellectual disabilities, to argue that beneath the surface of claims to intercede on behalf of the 'vulnerable', one can often discern a deeper concern with managing deviant or 'monstrous' sexuality. Sandland sees Alan's case as a modern example of this preoccupation with dangerousness and monstrosity. It appears that the question of Alan's capacity to consent to sex arose not because there were concerns about potential harm to him – indeed, possible harms to Alan are not discussed anywhere in the judgment – but because of suspicions that he may have behaved sexually inappropriately in front of children when unsupervised in the community.

Unlike the Mental Health Act 1983 (MHA), the MCA only purports to protect the interests of the individual, not the public. Yet there are signs that the MCA is being used to manage 'dangerousness' to others. ZZ had mild intellectual disabilities, and was sexually attracted to children (*Y County Council & ZZ*). 'George' had a string of psychiatric diagnoses, including 'childhood autism, obsessive-compulsive disorder, dissocial personality disorder, mixed anxiety disorder and paedophilia' (*J Council v GU & Ors*, 2012: §5). The MCA was used to deprive them of their liberty on grounds that they lacked the capacity to consent to their care arrangements. In neither case are the findings of incapacity reasoned, as they were not contested. This can occur in Court of Protection cases where 'litigation friends' may conduct litigation in a person's 'best interests', not according to their will (Series, forthcoming). The strip searches, room searches and surveillance to which George was subject were so invasive that Mostyn J queried whether they might not violate his rights to private life, as there was no guidance on using the MCA in this way and the monitoring mechanisms were so weak. Lawyers practising in this area observed 'It is no doubt in the 'best interests' (broadly defined) of any potential sex offender to be kept under such close supervision that no opportunities for offending behaviour arise, but that is not how society functions in respect of those without learning disabilities' (39 Essex St Court of Protection Team, 2013). These cases show how under the MCA a person's disability can form the basis of a regime of preventive detention, which could not be applied to potential sex offenders without disabilities without any criminal conviction, to stop them from committing offences.

Understanding the nature of consent itself

Most researchers writing about sexuality and intellectual disabilities agree that a component of a valid consent to sex is understanding that it is a choice which a person can refuse (McCarthy and Thompson, 2004; Hollomotz, 2011; Centre for Disability Law & Policy, 2012). Yet in Alan's case, Mostyn J had deliberately excluded an understanding of consent from the test of capacity to consent to sex, on the (somewhat bizarre) basis that paedophiles and rapists are regarded as having the capacity to consent to sex despite not – in Mostyn's view – understanding the nature of consent (§39). However, in *A Council v H* (2012), Hedley J held that it was important that a 'highly sexualised' young woman with intellectual disabilities understood 'that they do have a choice and that they can refuse' (§25).

Understanding the consequences?

The MCA requires a person to be able to understand the 'reasonably foreseeable consequences' of making a decision either way (s3(4)); this has given rise to debate over precisely what consequences a person must understand in order to consent to sex. The Court of Protection has generally been reluctant to expand this information beyond a bare minimum.

In *A Council v H*, H's carers were 'perplexed' by her sexuality – she described a history of 'willingness to have sex with anyone who asked her including strangers', sex with groups of much older men, of having had oral and anal sex and 'that she had attempted to have sex with dog' (§9). The council argued that capacity required an understanding of the emotional and moral issues pertaining to sexuality. Hedley J declined to adopt this approach, questioning whether such a test could be 'workable' (§24–25), as did Mostyn J in Alan's case.

In *London Borough of Ealing v KS* (2008), a council argued that the capacity to consent to sex must include an understanding of specific risks to a person's mental health, of a pregnancy or failed relationship. They maintained that KS lacked capacity because she held false beliefs about the likelihood that any man who had sex with her would marry her, and thought she would be able to keep her child if she became pregnant. Roderic Wood J considered that this blurred the distinction between capacity and best interests (§142), and observed that similar 'false beliefs' might be held by many women in society, which went to the *wisdom* of sexual relations rather than the validity of consent (§144).

In *Re A (Capacity: Refusal of Contraception)* (2010) a council sought a declaration permitting contraceptives to be administered to a woman against her will, arguing that she needed to understand the long-range consequences of a pregnancy to refuse consent to contraception. Bodey J rejected this argument, saying that this set the bar too high and had shades of social engineering.

Ability to 'use or weigh' the information

The Court of Protection has generally downplayed the MCA's requirement to 'use and weigh' information in relation to sex. Early case law distinguished between the 'refined analysis' required to consent to medical treatment, and the test of capacity to consent to sex (*Council X v MM & Anor (No. 1)*, 2007). In *A Council v TZ* (2013) an expert psychiatrist argued that the capacity to consent to sex required an ability to evaluate 'a complex analysis of risks and benefits often in the abstract and hypothetical' (2013: §42). Baker J emphasized that for most people in society, choices about sexual relations were often emotional, instinctive and impulsive rather than rational: 'Human society would be very different if such choices were made the morning after rather than the night before' (§53). He warned of 'a danger that the imposition of a higher standard for capacity may discriminate against people with a mental impairment' (§55).

In *IM v LM* (2014) the Court of Appeal acknowledged that whilst *some* ability to use and weigh information in order to give a valid consent to sex was required by the MCA, this was 'unlikely to loom large in the evaluation of capacity to consent to sexual relations' (§81). Sir Brian Levenson held that tests of capacity to consent to sex 'should not become divorced from the actual decision-making process carried out in that regard on a daily basis by persons of full capacity' (§80).

The influence of person and situation-specific factors

One issue has dominated the case law on the capacity to consent to sex: to what extent might a person's ability to make a decision regarding sex be affected by who their sexual partner is, or the situation in which the decision is made? Until *IM v LM* the MCA case law was very unsettled on this point. Public authorities – concerned that a person may be in an abusive or harmful relationship – have persisted in arguing that a person who could pass a minimalist test of the capacity to consent to sex might yet lack mental capacity when it came to sex with a specific person. This approach was rejected in a number of cases. In *Council X v MM & Anor (No. 1)* Munby J questioned whether 'it can sensibly be said that she has capacity to consent to a particular sexual act with Y whilst at the same time lacking capacity to consent to precisely the same sexual act with Z' (§87). In Alan's case, Mostyn J asked 'Is the council supposed to vet every proposed sexual partner of Alan to gauge if Alan has the capacity to consent to sex with him or her?' (§35). In *TZ*, Baker J observed that 'To require the issue of capacity to be considered in respect of every person with whom TZ contemplated sexual relations would not only be impracticable but would also constitute a great intrusion into his private life' (§23).

However, in *R v C* (2009) the House of Lords endorsed a more situational and person-specific analysis for the purposes of the SOA 2003. The victim was a 28 year old woman 'with an established diagnosis of schizo-affective disorder, an emotionally unstable personality disorder, an IQ of less than 75, and a history of harmful use of alcohol' (§17). She met C shortly after her doctor had recommended her compulsory re-admission to hospital under the MHA, but before it had been carried out. She told him that she had recently been discharged from detention under the MHA and that people were after her. He offered to help her, so she went to his friend's house:

> He sold her mobile telephone and bicycle and gave her crack. She went to the bathroom but the defendant came in and asked her to give him a "blow job". Her evidence was that she was really panicky and afraid and wanted to get out of there. She was saying to herself "these crack heads … they do worse to you". She did not want to die so she just stayed there and just took it all.
>
> (§18)

The complainant knew what a blow job was (§26), but Lady Hale held that there was more to the capacity to consent to sex than simple understanding of the act *in general*, one must demonstrate *situational* understanding: 'it is difficult to think of an activity which is more person and situation specific than sexual relations' (§27).

It is easy to see why Lady Hale favoured a more situational understanding in this case. Feminist and disability rights scholars have argued that the validity of consent to sex must take into account wider situational and relational factors (Centre for Disability Law & Policy, 2012; Herring, 2012; McCarthy and Thompson, 2004). This situational approach was taken up only once by the Court of Protection, in *D County Council v LS* (2010). Yet the consequences of adopting this test in a civil law context are very different from the criminal law situation: rather than resulting in the punishment of sex offenders, the result may be the expansion of control and supervision over the potential victims, with far reaching consequences for their rights to privacy, relationships and – ultimately – liberty.

In *IM v LM* the Court of Appeal concluded that the invasion of privacy and the practical burden on public authorities of adopting a person- and situation-specific approach to capacity for the purposes of the MCA was too great, and endorsed the 'minimalist' approach. However, they maintained that the situational and person-specific analysis should be retained for criminal cases, where the focus was inevitably on the specific incident, with a specific person. This decision may yet be appealed to the Supreme Court.

Discussion

These cases illustrate many of the concerns of critics of the MCA. As Veitch, Freyenhagen and O'Shea predicted, the cases described here show that public authorities have indeed tried to 'smuggle in' evaluative commitments into the test of capacity to consent to sex, particularly around understanding the moral, emotional and social dimensions of sexual activity, although the Court of Protection has generally resisted these efforts. Far from being a neutral affair, the test of capacity itself has become a secondary battleground where lawyers and caregivers attempt to draw lines in the sand demarcating the boundaries of what sexual touching is permissible, and when others may lawfully intercede to prevent it. Meanwhile the requirement for understanding the health risks of sex looks likely to collapse into redundancy or have serious discriminatory and absurd effects.

The requirement to understand the nature of consent introduced by Hedley J is closely aligned with suggestions in the literature on sexuality and disability (Centre for Disability Law and Policy, 2012; Hollomotz, 2011; McCarthy and Thompson, 2004). It is unclear as yet precisely how a person must demonstrate this understanding. Must they be able to verbally articulate the principles of consent, or might it suffice – as Hollomotz (2011: 49) has suggested – 'that two individuals are content in each other's company, that they are able to communicate displeasure or alert a member of staff to help them in the event of an unwanted sexual approach and that they understand the sexual behaviour they are about to engage in'?

IM v LM leaves undisturbed the legal requirement to prevent sexual activity where a person is considered to lack the mental capacity to consent to it (§1). However, by endorsing a 'minimalist' conception of capacity to consent to sex, the Court of Appeal limited the circumstances in which public authorities and care providers can – and must – intercede to prevent sexual activity altogether. Because it is possible that a person might be found to have the capacity to consent to sex on the civil law test, yet lack the capacity to consent to sex with a particular individual or in particular circumstances under the SOA, this means that in theory public bodies and care providers may not be able to intercede to prevent sexual activity which could constitute a criminal offence. Yet the MCA offers other tools to control the sexuality of people with disabilities, even if they cannot be used to prevent sex altogether. For example, by contending that a person lacks the capacity to make decisions about contact with specific individuals, contact with those individuals might be restricted or supervised. Where there are concerns that a person cannot appraise the risks of new sexual partners, care plans may be devised to manage risks – including through careful monitoring of new partners by support staff (*A Local Authority v TZ (No. 2)*, 2014). However, where a person does have the capacity to consent to sex, public bodies may still be required to facilitate opportunities for sexual intimacy even within these restrictions (*Council X v MM*, 2007).

The SOA 2003 could still be used to intercede *after the event* where a person's consent to sex was invalid because of situational or relational factors. Yet the criminal justice system might tolerate some instances of sex which the MCA would not. The Crown Prosecution Service (2012) regards relationships of 'genuine affection' as a mitigating factor, and the Law Commission (2000: [4.74]) recommended that sexual activity between two people who *both* lacked capacity should not constitute an offence 'unless there is oppression or exploitation'. However, as Bartlett (2010: 141) comments, mitigation is not a defence: an offence would still be committed even if it were not prosecuted.

These cases reveal a deep and difficult tension between instincts to protect people who may be vulnerable to sexual exploitation, for whom the risks of emotional, social and health related harms arising from sexual activity may be greater, and a desire to respect their autonomy. They illustrate the stark reality that in striving to protect people from sexual offences, we have arrived at a position where the liberty of victims, not merely offenders, is at risk.

In the literature on disability and sexuality, there have been various attempts to frame what a valid consent to sex should look like. In contrast with the Court of Protection's minimalist approach, and more in accordance with the approach taken by Lady Hale in *R v C*, almost all of these have recommended taking into account situational and relational factors, although some have eschewed capacity based approaches. McCarthy and Thompson (2004) are sceptical about the value of tests of capacity to consent to sex, but do say that 'there needs to be reasonable degree of equality between the parties, so that both parties have sufficient power to make the choice to engage or not engage in sex, without fear of adverse consequences' (p.234). Herring (2012: 477) states 'There is no getting away from an assessment of the relationship the person is in and whether it is marked by the kind of values which enable sexual autonomy to be enjoyed'. The Centre for Disability Law and Policy (2012) endorsed McCarthy and Thompson's approach, but argued that the test for a legally valid consent in the context of sexual offences should be 'disability neutral', on the basis that to define an offence in terms of mental disorder or mental incapacity would be discriminatory and contrary to the CRPD. They suggest that one possible offence might be 'abuse of a position of power', and that consent should be given the same definition for everyone, as 'a consent freely and voluntarily given ... a consent is not freely and voluntarily given if it is obtained by force, threat, intimidation, deception or fraudulent means'. They do not discount the possibility that 'mental incapacity' might be a factor that would need to be taken into account in some cases, but their proposals would mean that where a person lacked mental capacity they would not *necessarily* be treated as incapable of giving a valid consent to sex. Palmer (2013) has argued the meaning of consent in general is contested and uncertain, and that a better concept than for defining sexual offences might be 'freedom to negotiate', an approach which would not assume 'that a person who is in some way "vulnerable" or dependent on others is never capable of actively choosing or negotiating their sexual encounters.'

These approaches have in their sights *exploitation* or oppression within a particular relationship, or at a particular point in time. They are focussed on the power dynamics between the individuals in the particular sexual encounter, rather than the person's disability *per se*, although without discounting that disability and dependence may be factors which impinge upon those dynamics. There are attractions to these approaches. They could create more space for people with intellectual and cognitive impairments to enjoy sexual relationships which are not oppressive or exploitative, whilst offering a flexible means of responding to those which are. But the very flexibility of these suggestions may be problematic: who is to decide what is exploitative, and what is oppressive?

Expanding the factors to be considered in connection with whether or not a sexual encounter was an offence, and framing them in a disability neutral way, might open up a broader discussion about vulnerability to sexual exploitation among disabled and non-disabled people alike. That could be a very important and worthwhile conversation. But it is not clear that these approaches are any less prone to subjective and arbitrary assessments than the test of 'mental capacity' was. Coming up with criteria which would 'permit the good sex, and outlaw the bad' is an extremely difficult enterprise (Bartlett, 2010). Might we have to concur with the Court of Appeal in *R v Bree* (2007), a case concerning whether a person could give a valid consent to sex when under the influence of alcohol, 'that there are some areas of human behaviour which are inapt for detailed legislative structures' (§35)?

Moreover, the recommendations from the literature on disability and sexuality do not clearly resolve the question of what should be done when a person is at risk of sexual exploitation – however it is defined. The criminal law's focus on perpetrators is clearly important, but what should public authorities and caregivers do when a person is actually known to be at a real risk of sexual exploitation? The approach under the MCA is to intervene in their 'best interests', in ways that potentially constitute enormous interferences with rights to liberty and private life. It is unlikely that this would be compatible with the CRPD, given its emphasis on autonomy and self-determination, but the CRPD also calls for people with disabilities to be given protection from violence, exploitation and abuse (Article 16).

One answer from the CRPD perspective might be that people should only receive protective measures that they consent to, or at least do not oppose, and that the consequences which may occur if those persons are then subject to exploitation are a fair price to be paid for ensuring that people with disabilities enjoy an equivalent 'dignity of risk' to others.[3] Another answer, suggested by Bartlett and Sandland (2013) is that we look at whether 'adult protection' legislation can itself be framed in a disability neutral way, to apply to disabled and non-disabled people who are at risk of exploitation and abuse. In fact, there are signs of a general adult protection jurisdiction emerging in England and Wales, which turns on situational vulnerability rather than 'capacity'. In a small number of cases, the High Court has claimed an 'inherent jurisdiction' to intervene where a person is considered to be at risk of abuse or neglect, and incapable of acting to protect themselves not because of 'mental incapacity' but because of the relationship of power between them and their abuser (for a review of the early case law, see Szerletics, 2011). Interestingly, efforts to put these judge-made powers to intercede in 'vulnerable situations' on a statutory basis met with considerable public opposition. The government withdrew the proposals, noting 'We believe it is highly significant that members of the public were far more strongly against the proposal compared to health and social care professionals' (Department of Health, 2013). It seems that the general public might endorse paternalistic interferences in the lives of people with intellectual and cognitive disabilities, but not where others might be exposed to exploitation or abuse for other reasons.

Flynn and Arstein-Kerslake (2014: 100) suggest that the 'duty of care' or 'defence of necessity' may be used to permit certain interventions under the CRPD, but 'these exceptions and defences need to be extremely limited and carefully defined, to prevent any return to a more regressive system'. As yet, nobody has closely examined precisely when such interventions might be permissible within the 'new paradigm' of the CRPD. Suggestions that there might be some scope for intervention under the 'new paradigm' take us back to the beginning of our journey: where should the line be drawn, what non-consensual interventions might be permissible to protect people against situations of abuse and exploitation? The CRPD poses a challenge – to draw that line equally for all persons, with and without disabilities. The critiques of 'mental capacity' considered here suggest that it was only ever an illusion that we could draw the line in an objective way, free of our subjective desires to secure particular ends, and free of potentially arbitrary and absurd outcomes.

Acknowledgements

With thanks to Phil Fennell for his helpful comments on a draft of this chapter.

Notes

1 By convention, High Court judges are referred to by their surname, followed by a 'J', and the surnames of Court of Appeal Judges – Lord or Lady Justices – are followed by 'LJ'.
2 Not his real name, but a name chosen by Mostyn J for the anonymised judgment.
3 For a discussion of the 'dignity of risk' in the CRPD literature, see Gooding (2012: 5).

Bibliography

39 Essex St Court of Protection Team (2013) Deprivations of liberty and prevention of offending, *Local Government Lawyer* (14 August 2013).

A Council v H [2012] EWHC 49 (COP)

A Council v TZ [2013] EWHC 2322 (COP)

A Local Authority v TZ (No. 2) [2014] EWHC 973 (COP)

A NHS Trust v DE [2013] EWHC 2562 (Fam)

Aintree University Hospitals NHS Foundation Trust v James [2013] UKSC 67

Aunos, M. and Feldman, M. A. (2002) Attitudes towards sexuality, sterilization and parenting rights of persons with intellectual disabilities, *Journal of Applied Research in Intellectual Disabilities*, 15, 285–296.

Bartlett, P. (2010) Sex, dementia, capacity and care homes, *Liverpool Law Review*, 31, 137.

Bartlett, P. and Sandland, R. (2013) *Mental Health Law: Policy and Practice*, 2nd ed., Oxford: Oxford University Press.

Brown, H. (1994) 'An ordinary sexual life?': a review of the normalisation principle as it applies to the sexual options of people with learning disabilities, *Disability & Society*, 9(2), 123–144.

Centre for Disability Law & Policy (2012) *Submission on Law Reform Commission.*

Committee on the Rights of Persons with Disabilities (2014) *General comment No 1 (2014) Article 12: Equal recognition before the law*, Geneva. (CRPD/C/GC/1).

Consultant Paper: Sexual Offences and Capacity to Consent (2011). NUI Galway.

Council X v MM & Anor (No. 1) [2007] EWHC 2003 (Fam)

CYC v PC [2012] MHLO 103 (COP)

D Borough Council v AB [2011] EWHC 101 (COP)

D County Council v LS [2010] EWHC 1544 (Fam)

Department of Health (2013) *Government Response to the Safeguarding Power of Entry Consultation*, London. Available at: https://www.gov.uk/government/consultations/consultation-on-a-new-adult-safeguarding-power (accessed 4 November 2014).

Dhanda, A. (2012) Universal legal capacity as a universal human right, in Dudley, M., Silove, D. and Gale, F., eds., *Mental Health and Human Rights: Vision, Praxis, and Courage*, Oxford: Oxford University Press.

Đorđević v Croatia (App No 41526/10) HEJUD [2012] ECHR 1640

Fennell, P. (1992) Balancing care and control: guardianship, community treatment orders and patient safeguard, *International Journal of Law and Psychiatry*, 15, 205–235.

Flynn, E. and Arstein-Kerslake, A. (2014) Legislating personhood: realising the right to support in exercising legal capacity, *International Journal of Law in Context*, 10(1), 81–104.

Freyenhagen, F. and O'Shea, T. (2013) Hidden substance: mental disorder as a challenge to normatively neutral accounts of autonomy, *International Journal of Law in Context*, 9(1), 53–70.

Gooding, P. (2012) Supported decision-making: a rights-based disability concept and its implications for mental health law, *Psychiatry, Psychology and Law*, 5(3), 431–451.

Herring, J. (2012) Mental disability and capacity to consent to sex: a Council v H [2012] EWHC 49 (COP), *Journal of Social Welfare and Family Law*, 34(4), 471–478.

Heyman, B. and Huckle, S. (1995) Sexuality as a perceived hazard in the lives of adults with learning difficulties, *Disability & Society*, 10(2), 139–156.

Hollomotz, A. (2011) *Learning Difficulties and Sexual Vulnerability: A Social Approach* London: Jessica Kingsley Publishers.

House of Lords Select Committee on the Mental Capacity Act 2005 (2013) Evidence Session No. 8. Tuesday 15 October 2013. Witnesses: Professor Amanda Howe, Dr

Julie Chalmers, Dr Dorothy Apakama, Professor Sue Bailey and Dr Tony Calland. Available at http://www.parliament.uk/documents/lords-committees/mental-capacity-act/mental-capacity-act-2005-vol1.pdf (accessed 4 November 23014).

IM v LM [2014] EWCA Civ 37

J Council v GU & Ors (Rev 1) [2012] EWHC 3531 (COP)

Jones, N. (2013) Good enough parents? Exploring attitudes of family centre workers supporting and assessing parents with learning difficulties, *Practice*, 25(3), 169–190.

Law Commission (1991) *Mentally Incapacitated Adults and Decision-Making: An Overview* (Law Com no 119) London: HMSO.

Law Commission (2000) *Consent in sex offences: A Report to the Home Office Sex Offences Review*, London: Law Commission. Available at: http://lawcommission.justice.gov.uk/docs/Consent_in_Sex_Offences.pdf (accessed 4 November 2014).

London Borough of Ealing v KS & Ors [2008] EWHC 636 (Fam)

Lord Chancellor's Office (2007) *Mental Capacity Act Code of Practice*.

McCarthy, M. (2011) Prescribing contraception to women with intellectual disabilities: general practitioners' attitudes and practices, *Sexuality and Disability*, 29, 339–349.

McCarthy, M. and Thompson, D. (2004) People with learning disabilities: sex, the law and consent, in Cowling, M. and Reynolds, P., eds., *Making Sense of Sexual Conduct*, Farnham: Ashgate Publishers.

Morgan, D. and Veitch, K. (2004) Being Ms B: B, autonomy and the nature of legal regulation, *Sydney Law Review*, 26, 107.

Palmer, T. P. (2013) *Sex and Sexual Violation in the Criminal Law: Findings from a Study into How People Distinguish Sex from Sexual Violation*, Bristol: University of Bristol and the Economic and Social Research Council.

PC & Anor v City of York Council [2013] EWCA Civ 478

Pitblado, A. (2013) The decision of the Court of Appeal in *PC v City of York*, *Elder Law Journal*, 3(4), 361–366.

R v Bree [2007] EWCA 256

R v C [2009] UKHL 42; [2009] 1 WLR 1786

Re A (Capacity: Refusal of Contraception) [2010] EWHC 1549 (Fam).

Richardson, G. (2013) Mental capacity in the shadow of suicide: what can the law do?, *International Journal of Law in Context*, 9(1), 87–105.

Samkange-Zeeb, F. N., Spallek, L. and Zeeb, H. (2011) Awareness and knowledge of sexually transmitted diseases (STDs) among school-going adolescents in Europe: a systematic review of published literature, *BMC Public Health*, 11, 727.

Sandland, R. (2013) Sex and capacity: the management of monsters, *Modern Law Review*, 76(6), 981–1009.

Series, L. (forthcoming) Legal capacity and participation in litigation: recent developments in the European Court of Human Rights, *European Yearbook of Disability Law*, Volume 5, Waddington, Quinn and Flynn (Eds). The Netherlands: Intersentia.

Shakespeare, T. (2013) *Disability Rights and Wrongs Revisited*, 2nd ed., London: Routledge.

Stefan, S. (1992–1993) Silencing the different voice: competence, feminist theory and law, *Miami Law Review*, 47, 763.

Szerletics, A. (2011) *Vulnerable Adults and the Inherent Jurisdiction of the High Court*, Colchester: Department of Philosophy, University of Essex.

The Select Committee on the Mental Capacity Act 2005 (2013) *Oral and written evidence – Volume 1 (A – K)*, House of Lords, UK Parliament.

Then, S.-N. (2013) Evolution and innovation in guardianship laws: assisted decision-making, *Sydney Law Review*, 35, 132.

United Nations, Convention on the Rights of Persons with Disabilities (adopted 13 December 2006, entered into force 3 May 2008) 2515 UNTS 3 (CRPD).

Veitch, K. (2006) Medical law and the power of life and death, *International Journal of Law in Context,* 2(2), 137–157.

Verlander v Rahman [2012] EWHC 1026 (QB)

Williams, V., Boyle, G., Jepson, M., Swift, P., Williamson, T. and Heslop, P. (2012) *Making Best Interests Decisions: People and Processes.* University of Bristol, University of Bradford and the Mental Health Foundation. Available at: http://www.mentalhealth.org.uk/publications/bids-report/ (accessed 4 November 2014).

X City Council v MB, NB and MAB [2006] EWHC 168 (Fam), [2006] 2 FLR 968

Y County Council & ZZ [2012] MHLO 179 (COP).

10

'MY SISTER WON'T LET ME'

Issues of control over one's own life
as experienced by older women with
intellectual disabilities

Iva Strnadová

Introduction

The aim of this book chapter and the research presented here is to provide
a deeper insight into the experiences of older women with intellectual
disabilities with empowerment and disempowerment, and to suggest ways
in which their autonomy can be increased and respected. While it might be
argued that a number of issues faced by women with intellectual disabilities
are similar to those faced by women with other types of impairment, 'the very
nature of intellectual impairment adds a complex layer of issues associated with
supporting independence, choice, autonomy and decision making' which are
rather unique to this population (Bigby 2012, 427). Furthermore the increased
longevity of people with intellectual disabilities is a relatively new phenomenon
(World Health Organisation 2000, 3). According to Perkins and Moran (2010)
the life expectancy of people with a mild level of intellectual disabilities and
general population has almost equalised. The increased longevity of people
with intellectual disabilities presents a number of new challenges for society, as
neither elderly care nor the disability sector are well prepared for this population.

Older women with intellectual disabilities are among the least understood
members of society. As highlighted by LeRoy *et al.* (2004, 429), 'their lives reflect
the political, philosophical, and practical changes that have occurred in the field
of disability services over the last 50 years. They are system exemplars – for
better or worse'. Many of these women experienced institutionalisation in their
early lives. They had restricted access to education, resulting in fewer chances
for subsequent employment, and therefore higher likelihood of dependence
on others and poverty. Biswas *et al.* (2005) have pointed out that women with
intellectual disabilities are of poorer health compared to women without

disability and men with and without disability, and their access to health services is rather sporadic. Social networks for these women are restricted to their carers, professional staff, and other people with intellectual disabilities (Forrester-Jones *et al.* 2006). These networks become even smaller as the women age (Robertson *et al.* 2001). The ongoing discrimination experienced by these women has been reported by a number of researchers (Julius *et al.*2003; Traustadottir & Johnson 2000). Having lived a life of segregation, and being repeatedly exposed to social and economical discrimination, it is not a surprise that a number of older women with intellectual disabilities experience disempowerment even in basic decisions about their lives and daily activities.

Martin (2006, 126), an author with intellectual disabilities, states that empowerment is about 'having a real say in decisions that affect our lives'. He further elaborated on this by stating that 'empowerment is not something you suddenly have one day' as 'it takes time to learn how to make decisions'. This is an especially important comment, given that people with intellectual disabilities commonly experience limited opportunities to practise self-determination (Nonnemacher & Bambara 2011). Even when given the opportunity, it cannot be expected that they will learn to be empowered overnight. For example if a woman with intellectual disabilities has lived most of her life in an institution or a group home, it cannot be expected that if given an opportunity to live on her own (possibly with support), she would be able immediately to act in a self-determined way and make choices about her day-to-day life. As with anything else, acquiring self-determined behaviour is a process, which needs time and opportunities to practise and learn. Wehmeyer (1996, 24) defines self-determination as 'acting as the primary causal agent in one's life and making choices and decisions regarding one's quality of life free from undue influence or interference'. In other words, self-determination is interrelated with empowerment.

Case studies

Here, the life experiences of older women with intellectual disability are examined in relation to self-determination and (dis)empowerment through the use of case studies from two research studies that examined the experiences of women with intellectual disability growing older. The aim of these research studies was to explore the perceived quality of life of older women with intellectual disabilities and the factors that influence their well-being, by listening to their life experiences. The main focus was on factors mediating the level of their autonomy (first study) and their self-reported satisfaction with life (second study). The results provide the basis for my argument that this group of citizens exercises limited control over their own lives, and thus continue to be disempowered.

Given that the women participating in both studies were from two different countries and continents, it is essential to discuss the changing context in the Czech Republic (a European post-communist country) and New South Wales (Australia), as experienced by these women over their life courses. People's experiences and opportunities are – among other things – influenced by the historical period, in which they live (Elder, 1994, 5). The lives of women participating in both studies were affected by the growth of disability movements, and by the paradigm shift away from being objects of social care towards being equal citizens having equal human rights on the same basis as others. Dew, Balandin and Llewelyn (2009) describe this shift as a transition from social stigmatisation, discrimination and institutionalisation to normalisation, deinstitutionalisation and antidiscrimination legislation, such as the ratification of the UN Convention on the Rights of Persons with Disabilities (United Nations, 2006). While this shift happened in both countries, the timing of these changes was different due to the different national political situations. The paradigm shift and deinstitutionalisation began in the 1970s in Australia. In the Czech Republic, 40 years of communist rule ended in 1989, and only then were the ideals of social inclusion, normalisation and deinstitutionalisation introduced on a more systemic level.

Our first study (Strnadová & Evans, 2012) focused on the subjective quality of life of older women with intellectual disabilities in New South Wales (Australia) and in the Czech Republic (Europe). In-depth interviews with 28 Australian women aged 40 to 78 years, and 27 Czech women aged 40 to 65 years were conducted. One year later another in-depth interview was conducted with most of these women, in order to verify the results of data analysis. Most of the participating women from both countries were single (41), some had a partner (9), one was married, two engaged and five women were divorced. In terms of living arrangements, most of the women in both countries lived in either a group home, retirement village or supported accommodation (26), and with relatives (20), while other participants lived alone (3), with their partner (3) or with their children (2).

The aim of this study was to develop a deeper insight and understanding about how older women with intellectual disabilities perceived the quality of their lives. Data analysis revealed that the core phenomenon influencing the perceived quality of life was the lack of control the participating women had on their lives (Strnadová & Evans, 2012). Besides participating in the two interviews, most of the women (18 from the Czech Republic and 24 from New South Wales) completed the Quality of Life Questionnaire (QOL.Q, Schalock & Keith, 1993). According to Schalock and Keith (2004) the validity of QOL.Q results might be influenced by differences in culture as some questions or items used in the scale might not represent the experience of life in different countries. This aspect was of a special interest to me as the expectation was that the subjectively perceived quality of life would be higher in women with intellectual disabilities in NSW, Australia, where the general quality of life is higher, and where there is a longer tradition of social inclusion for people with intellectual disabilities. In spite of this, the difference between the subjectively experienced quality of

TABLE 10.1 The demographics of the participants across the two studies

	Country	No. of participants	Age of participants	Marital status					Accommodation				
				Single	With partner	Engaged	Married	Divorced	Group home, etc.	Alone	Sibling, relative	Children	Partner
Study 1	NSW	28	40–78	20	5	1	1	3	9	2	12	2	2
	Czech Republic	27	40–65	21	4	1	0	2	17	1	8	0	1
Study 2	NSW	15	51–71	12	2	0	0	1	9	5	1	0	0

life of women from Sydney (Australia) and Prague (the Czech Republic) had no statistical significance $t(36) = 1.775$, $p > .05$ (Strnadová, 2009).

The second study examined the perceptions of the well-being of older women with intellectual disabilities (Strnadová *et al.* forthcoming). The research team consisted of four academic researchers and four researchers with intellectual disabilities who were older women themselves. Using an inclusive research approach provided another dimension for exploring the well-being and life experiences of this vulnerable population. Fifteen women aged 55 to 71 years, who lived in New South Wales (Australia), were interviewed. The demographics of this group of participants were similar to those of the participants in the first study. Most women were single (12), two had a partner and one was divorced. Some women lived in a group home (9), five women lived on their own and one lived with her sibling. Table 10.1 illustrates the demographics of the participants across the two studies and also across the countries where the studies took place. The core phenomenon resulting from the data analysis was changes in life as experienced by the older women. These changes related to their independence and the types of activities they were involved in. The interviewed women as well as some of the researchers with intellectual disabilities displayed many features of living a controlled life, which will be discussed in this chapter.

Though the aims and research questions were different for the two research studies, there were a number of similarities from the point of view of research methodology and data analysis. In both studies a semi-structured interview protocol was followed, and the women were interviewed at the place of their preference. The interviews were analysed using the grounded theory approach. The issues of living controlled lives and experiencing disempowerment became apparent in both studies, and will be explored further in this chapter.

Living controlled lives

The experience of disempowerment – which can be defined as deprivation of power, influence, and control over one's life – was very common for the women participating in both studies, and covered a wide spectrum, from not having many opportunities to make decisions about their daily activities at one end and the extreme of physical abuse at the other. Experiencing disempowerment was a life-long experience for a number of these women. In some instances, it was a result of the well-intentioned, but over-protective behaviour of people in their environment. For example, carers performed daily activities for these women, when they could have and would have liked to do them themselves, such as washing dishes, making a bed or shopping. As one of the women said:

> I go shopping with Mum, but she likes to be the one to get everything! I'm just the minder of the trolley. She likes to be the boss!
>
> (W11 in Strnadová & Evans, forthcoming)

This behaviour was at the very least, equally restrictive as the disability itself, resulting in some of the women developing a 'learned helplessness'. The handicapping behaviour of parents was also criticised by one of the participating women, who believed that parents should give their offspring as many opportunities for independence as possible:

> Their parents should make them [co-workers with intellectual disabilities] go shopping, their parents should make them pay a bill, because they're not going to be around all the time. Who's going to look after them if they're living on … (…) that's how come my mum made me go shopping. She made me make a bed. She made me do the cooking. She made me, even though she knew that I wasn't very good at other things, but at least I knew my way from A to B and back from B to A. At least I knew how to get on a bus and pay my fare, and that's another important thing. Instead of bringing them to work, get them on a bus. Make them get on a bus, even if it's only one way.
>
> (W13 in Strnadová & Evans, forthcoming)

Having a limited say about one's own life was not only an experience related to childhood and teenage years of the women, but also continued well into their adulthood and later years. The 'handicapping behaviour' was exercised by both families (often siblings) and staff members. In some cases, the decisions of participating women were either approved or not approved by their family members based on family values and beliefs. For example, one of the researchers with intellectual disabilities from the second study used an iPad not only for research purposes, but also to take photos. Her elder sister insisted that the iPad be taken from her, because she perceived some of the photos to be inappropriate. In this case, a morality judgement of an elder sister had a major impact on the life of this woman in her late fifties (Cumming *et al.* in press).

It was not only the family environment that created barriers to decision making. The staff of group homes, institutions, retirement villages and/or non-government organisations that supported the participants of the study also displayed the 'handicapping behaviour'. For example, a number of women in both studies referred to their limited choice in making decisions about where they live and how they spend their time. In the first study, one of the women from the Czech Republic referred to a process of being moved from an institution to a group home. During the whole process, none of the women who had lived in the institution for decades had been informed about this move, let alone consulted about their preferences. The woman confronted the principal of the institution to find out what was happening only after overhearing a discussion between staff members about the move. The initial decision was to move the women to diverse group homes within the country, depending on placements available. As this woman commented:

Each of us was meant to be at a different place, at different homes across the Republic. We cried a lot.

(Z11)

The participating woman and her co-habitants strongly and successfully advocated for keeping at least a few women together during these transitions as they had been in each other's social network for 37 years (Strnadová 2009). This woman described the impact of this huge transition in the following way:

we were taken back, all of us, not just me. Taken back, someone even died. It was too much for her and she could not cope. And another girl died shortly after this move, that she died because of nostalgia as she went there alone. That was a mistake because she didn't know anybody there, she was there alone. (…) I told them, send us at least in couples and not one by one. … So then they started to move us in two and three … And here they sent five of us.

(Z11)

The women living in group homes in both countries had very little say about who they lived with. This was also the experience of both participants and researchers with intellectual disabilities from the second study. One of the researchers with intellectual disabilities was the only woman living in a group home with five men with challenging behaviours. She was very unhappy about her life and her wish was to live with another woman. Despite her being vocal about this situation for a number of years, nothing has changed.

The experience of limited control over one's own life included the daily activities of these women. Women who lived in group homes had limited choices about how they spent their day, due to the availability of staff members. If they wished to visit a friend in another group home, they were restricted by whether a staff member would be available and willing to drive them there and bring them back. This experience is reflected in the following reflection of one of the participants:

Carers. One or two of them. If some of them have birthdays, or they decide to – they feel like taking us out, they do.

(W4 in Strnadová & Evans, forthcoming)

Living in a retirement village brought additional challenges to older women with intellectual disabilities. First of all, while they were placed in a retirement village in their early fifties, the other residents were in their late seventies and above. The feeling of aloofness was expressed by one of the women in the following way: 'Because there are two of us that are living in a retirement village, and it's not easy' (W10).

Among the issues relating to the age differences between general population and people with intellectual disabilities living in retirement villages was that the leisure activities offered in these villages were not suitable to people in their fifties. This ostracised people with intellectual disabilities even further. Furthermore the experience with support at aged care environments was different from the disability services. As one of the women emphasised:

> I've got people all around us, all the time. But we don't have – you know how a lot of people have carers come to them? We don't. We've got nursing staff on call if we want them. In our bathrooms and bedrooms, we've got nursing emergency call buttons.
>
> (W10)

One of the areas in which limited self-determination was most obvious was in the area of managing finances and making decisions on how to use them. Given the cognitive limitations of people with intellectual disabilities, this can be especially challenging for them and they might need assistance. This was the situation of most of the women participating in both studies. Some of the women commented on this aspect:

> Mum helps me. She looks after it for me, and if I need money I'll ask her and she'll give me some.
>
> (W27)

> My sister takes care of my money. If I want money, I ask her. She likes to keep my bankbook, because she's my carer.
>
> (W16)

Some of the women expressed their dissatisfaction with this arrangement and their wish to be able to decide how they would prefer to use their own finances. A few of the women insisted that they would be able to take care of their finances, one of them even describing her dependence on staff members in her group home in this matter as a humiliating experience:

> I simply don't want to be like a small girl, here you have 20 crowns for chocolate or something like that; that seems very infantile to me ... so I think that independence is the best thing ...
>
> (Z18 in Strnadová & Evans, forthcoming)

Others admitted that they would have difficulties managing finances. For example one of the women, when asked why she thought she was not handling her own finances, responded in the following way: 'Because I get confused ...' (AW8).

Only a few women displayed self-determined behaviour. These women were mostly living on their own or with their spouse. One of these women described vividly her continuing battles for her Disability Support Pension with regard to her employment options:

> I've been fighting Centrelink since October. They took my pension off me. I mean, who's going to employ me? I'm fifty-five. I've got osteoarthritis. Who'll employ me? No-one. I wrote to the Minister yesterday.
>
> (W24)

This woman also reflected on the vulnerability of her colleagues who have a more severe level of disability than she does:

> most of the people there are a lot more disabled than I am. My mind is very clear! But some of the people in here, if they got letters like I got from Centrelink, they wouldn't know – they would cry and cry and cry for hours, you know? I feel very sorry for them. They wouldn't have the same approach as me, you know?
>
> (W24)

An ability to battle a situation of disempowerment was displayed by some of the participating women in both studies who lived in abusive marriages. For example one of the women, who managed to end her abusive marriage, said:

> My marriage didn't work, because he used to bust me up all the time. (...) He wants me back, and he wants the kids and all that. (...) I don't answer, but I keep the letters just in case we have to ... I go to court (...) He's a violent person.
>
> (W8)

Another woman shared her experience with a husband with an alcohol abuse problem:

> He still rings up once a month to see how I'm going. (...) He had a drinking problem. Yeah, that's why I left him after eleven years. (...) I couldn't take it anymore.
>
> (W9)

The experience of abusive partners influenced some of the women in their planning for the future. One of the divorced women for example stated:

> I don't want to get married again. I've got a boyfriend, but at the moment I'm not thinking about getting married again. (...) I felt like I rushed the

first marriage, and I always think, "I don't want to rush this." Just take it slowly.

(W8)

Some women who displayed self-determined behaviour were in a position of a carer themselves, caring either for dying parents or an ill sibling. These women were forced by life circumstances to take control over their own lives and to take care of their family members in need. For example a woman caring for her sister described her situation in the following way:

> when Dad died I sold that, invested all my money, and went back home and looked after [my sister]. (…) … she's hard to handle, and now she's got a machine. She's got (…) sleep apnoea. (…) She puts the machine on. We had a bit of trouble with it at first, but it's good now.
>
> (W9)

Another woman was caring for her dying mother, which put a lot of strain on her:

> I live with my mum, but she's got cancer, so she's not going to live that long this year. There's two people that help me with cooking, and they bring me meals, but I mostly cook. Sometimes I go out and sometimes I order, but mostly I do the cooking just for myself, because Mum can't eat anymore …
>
> (W19)

Some of the women remained determined and in control of their lives despite their limited opportunities. This is reflected in the following statement:

> People with disabilities can do what normal people can do, as well. (…) I could be one of the actresses in a movie overseas, but if I wanted to do that I'd have to tell the truth and say I've got disabilities. Then they would know. They might not put me in, but they might put me in. So, I want to try to do that, you know? I want all people with disabilities to try as well, because some people have a mild disability, some people are worse than me, so it depends what I feel like doing, you know? Let all the people with disabilities know that they can do it as well. (…) I want them to do what their dreams are. I want my dreams to come true, that's the important (thing), that dreams can come true.
>
> (W21)

Discussion

The women participating in both studies were exposed to numerous environments and situations, in which they had minimal control over their lives.

The environments included their homes (either living with parents and siblings or living with partners), group homes, institutions or retirement villages.

Walmsley (1996) discussed the experience of some parents holding control over the lives of their adult children with intellectual disabilities. A number of women participating in both of the aforementioned studies had similar experiences. While some of them accepted their parents' over-protective behaviour, others tried to discuss with their parents and gain at least some control over their decisions. Yet others talked about their parents' life-long efforts to help them be as independent as possible, and referred to this as an example for other parents of people with intellectual disabilities, as they appreciated the level of independence and control over their life it allowed them to have.

The majority of women (35) participating in both studies lived in group homes or institutions, and had very limited social networks, consisting mostly of their co-habitants and staff members. This is consistent with the research of life experiences of 29 women with intellectual disabilities living in Ireland and the United States by LeRoy et al. (2004), according to which the participating women's network consisted on an average of 2–4 people, mostly paid staff. In Bigby's study (2008, 148), 62 per cent of adults with intellectual disabilities living in group homes 'had no-one outside the service system who knew them well or monitored their well-being'. The lack of social networks naturally means these adults have only a limited number of advocates in their lives, and thus provides a space for potential disempowerment. Many activities that the women wanted to participate in, such as visiting a friend, going out, etc., were dependent on staff availability and willingness to do so. This is also consistent with the study of LeRoy et al. (2004) who reported that given the women participating in their study did not drive and their use of public transport was rather limited, 'they remained at the mercy of families, friends or paid staff for travel opportunities' (p. 434). Similarly the expert group participants with intellectual disabilities in the McVilly et al. study (2006, 702) agreed that one of the major areas where they needed assistance with their friendships was 'getting to places where friends are', as well as going to movies, bowling or the local shopping centre to meet their friends. A number of them highlighted that their carers and/or staff did not always appreciate the importance of these friendships, and thus did not 'place sufficient priority on making time or transport available'. The women who participated in Welsby and Horsfall's study (2011) reported similar difficulties that they experienced when they tried to meet with their friends. The five participants in their study expressed that the difficulties with meeting friends was caused by a limited use of public transport (one of the women was not allowed to use public transport due to perceived risk of what might happen to her) and by their carers not being able to drive them. Furthermore, a number of these women, similarly to women participating in the two research studies presented here, also needed to ask for permission to go out with friends, which further contributed to their disempowerment. As argued by Welsby and Horsfall (2011, 805), while this exclusionary behaviour demonstrated by carers is being justified by concerns about safety of these women, 'these types of practices can heighten risk as they don't provide the necessary life experiences for people to learn the skills of character judgement, how to make and maintain friendships, manage money or use public transport'.

The limited choices in regards to moving from one setting to another, or about a roommate were a common experience of the participating women in both studies living in group homes or institutions. This is consistent with memories of self-advocates participating in the study by Nonnemacher and Bambara (2011).

Meininger (2001, 244) highlights the

> necessity of a right to autonomy in order to protect the weak from the unbridled and authoritarian self-realization of the strong. As in professional care relations the caregiver *per definitionem* is the stronger party, the right to autonomy and the respecting of that right must promote the view that this relation is guided by the priorities of the care-receiver rather than by those of the caregiver.

Older people with intellectual disabilities are often subjected to care by others, be it professionals or family members. While this care by others is not essentially a negative phenomenon, and is usually well intentioned, it can lead to over-protective behaviour. It is understandable that given the vulnerability of people with intellectual disabilities, parents and professionals try to do their best to protect these people. Drawing the line between support and creating dependence and 'learned helplessness' is a demanding task, yet so essential. People with intellectual disabilities are often aware of needing some support in their lives, as expressed by one of the self-advocates in Nonnemacher and Bambara (2011, 332) study: 'I want somebody to help me, yes, (...) Everybody needs help. I need help, you need help, everybody needs help'. It is a matter of how this support is provided; families and professionals should avoid imposing their own values and ideas, and instead provide support with respect to the person's preferences. This allows for independence and empowerment in everyday life situations.

The limited opportunities for self-determination experienced in retirement villages by a few participating women was not a surprising outcome. Wolfensberger (1985 as cited in Bigby, 2012) highlighted the contradicting philosophies of elderly care and disability services, with elderly care services 'providing "care" rather than "support", fostering "dependence" rather than "independence" and continuing "segregation" rather than "integration"'(Bigby 2012, 431). The fostering of dependence was well demonstrated by the following statement of one of the participating women living in a retirement village: 'No, the people in the complex – they have cleaners and stuff, and they come and do it for us' (W10). This woman was very independent and responsible for a number of cleaning-related tasks at her employment, yet not allowed to apply these skills at her own home. It would be an over-simplification just to blame aged care facilities for the disempowerment of older women with intellectual disabilities; however the suitability of these facilities for this population needs to be questioned on a case-by-case basis. We also need to consider the ways in which aged care services and disability services could collaborate more efficiently to support the ageing population of people with intellectual disabilities.

Regardless of whether they were living with carers or in group homes and retirement villages, the majority of the participating women did not manage their own finances, and received only a small amount of money on a regular basis to use according to their wishes. LeRoy *et al.* (2004) reported similar findings. Furthermore in LeRoy *et al.*'s study, as well as in both studies reported in this chapter, the participating women would have either preferred to have more money or to be in a control of their finances. As the self-advocates participating in Nonnemacher and Bambara's study (2011) stated, the inability to manage your own finances means that you lack control over your own life.

Some of the women participating in the two studies presented here displayed self-determined behaviour. These women were mostly living either independently or with their spouses. This is not a surprising outcome – Nonnemacher and Bambara (2011, 327) argue in their study that adults with intellectual disabilities living and/or working in independent settings displayed higher levels of self-determination than those living and/or working in 'more congregate settings'.

Conclusion

The results of both research studies revealed that in order for older women with intellectual disabilities to achieve a sense of self-determination and an ability to manage their everyday situations, they need to gain control over the decisions that affect their lives.

There are a number of ways in which older women with intellectual disabilities can be empowered. First of all, there is the crucial role of families in being supportive, but not over-protective, when preparing their children with intellectual disabilities for adulthood. This is, of course, easier said than done. Parents of people with intellectual disabilities are very focused on the vulnerability of their children, and often have problems 'letting go' of their children. This is highlighted by their concerns about what will happen to their offspring once they die. Yet supporting the independence and self-determination of their child with intellectual disabilities is crucial for that person's future success in life. One possible way to encourage this could be by providing opportunities for the ageing parents of adults with intellectual disabilities to meet and talk to young parents of children with a disability, to share their experiences and encourage the younger parents to support their children's independence from an early age.

The same applies to staff supporting older women with intellectual disabilities at group homes, elderly care facilities, and non-governmental organisations. The temptation to do things for people with intellectual disabilities, as 'it might be quicker/easier' might lead the staff members to do much more for their service users than necessary. Raising the awareness of paid staff about the importance of nurturing self-determination and empowerment of people with intellectual disabilities is of crucial importance.

Another issue that needs to be raised at this point is the high turnover in staff, as reported in a number of studies (LeRoy *et al.*, 2004). The positions of staff members working with people with intellectual disabilities are poorly paid, which impacts both the continuity and quality of support provided; changes in systemic and legislative levels are required if the situation is to be improved.

A factor that might affect the extent that staff members support the independence of people with intellectual disabilities is the need to find a way to balance the needs of a person with intellectual disabilities living in group settings with the needs of the other residents. While the establishment and maintenance of the social networks of the women in both studies were dependent on staff transporting them to see their friends, staff willingness was not always the main factor as to whether this occurred. Staff members need to uphold the congregate settings' schedules, which limits their flexibility to respond to the individual needs of their service users. Systemic changes are needed to revise the current 'flock-mentality structure' of many group homes and similar settings.

An issue common to women with intellectual disabilities living in diverse environments is managing their own finances. While having complete control over their own finances might not be an achievable outcome for all of these women, given their diverse levels of support needs, support provided in this area can certainly be handled with more dignity than their current experiences suggest. These older women should certainly not feel like they are children allowed to buy some sweets with their 'allowance'. To the greatest extent possible, they need to be partners in the decision-making process about their finances. This call for treating women with intellectual disabilities with dignity applies to every aspect of their lives across environments and people they live with, and it relates strongly to Lotan and Ells' (2010) call for professionals to 'adopt the ethical principle of "respect for persons" as their guiding value...'; to which I would add, not only professionals but also carers and any other relevant persons.

There are also questions to be asked and research to be conducted in the area of the consistency of approaches between schools and post-school settings. While schools – mainstream or special – focus on supporting independence, self-determination and increasing post-schooling options for people with intellectual disabilities, there remains the question of whether that support of independence continues in post-school settings. Are independence, self-determination and development of new skills the focus of people's families, group homes, day centres, or aged care facilities? What is the process of passing on information about individuals' preferences, strengths and support needs between the settings during transition times? These are just some of the issues that need to be investigated in order to improve support for women with intellectual disabilities in achieving self-determination and autonomy in the various environments they experience across their lifespan.

Acknowledgements

I would like to thank all the women with intellectual disabilities who participated in both studies for their willingness to share their life experiences. I would also like to thank Dr Tom Shakespeare and Dr Therese M. Cumming for providing their constructive peer-feedback on this chapter.

The first research study presented here received ethical approval from the University of Sydney Human Research Ethics Committee (Approval #04-2008/10575) within the project: 'Well-being of Women with Intellectual Disabilities: Voices of Women and their Families'; and the second research study was approved by the University of New South Wales Human Research Ethics Committee (Approval # HC11485) within the project: 'Investigating the Coping Skills of Ageing Women with Intellectual Disabilities: Developing a Strategy-Based Framework for Promoting Healthy Ageing'.

References

Bigby, C. (2008) Known well by no-one: Trends in the informal social networks of middle-aged and older people with intellectual disability five years after moving to the community, *Journal of Intellectual and Developmental Disability*, 33(2): 148–157.

Bigby, C. (2012) 'I hope he dies before me'. Unravelling the debates about ageing and people with intellectual disability, in N. Watson, A. Roulstone, & C. Thomas (eds), *Routledge Handbook of Disability Studies*, London: Routledge.

Biswas, M., Whalley, H., Foster, J., Friedman, E., & Deacon, R. (2005) Women with learning disability and uptake of screening: Audit of screening uptake before and after one to one counselling, *Journal of Public Health*, 27: 344–347.

Cumming, I., Strnadová, I., Knox, M., & Parmenter, T. (in press) Mobile technology in inclusive research: tools of empowerment? *Disability & Society* 29(7): 999–1012.

Dew, A., Balandin, S., & Llewellyn, G. (2009) Impact of historical time and social timing on the life course of adults with lifelong disability and their non-disabled siblings, *Journal of Policy and Practice in Intellectual Disabilities*, 6 (2): 103.

Elder, G.H. (1994) Time, human agency, and social change: perspectives on the life course, *Social Psychology Quarterly*, 57(1): 4–15.

Forrester-Jones, R., Carpenter, J., Coolen-Schrijner, P., Cambridge, P., Tate, A., Beecham, J., Hallam, A., Knapp, M., & Wooff, D. (2006) The social networks of people with intellectual disability living in the community 12 years after resettlement from long-stay hospitals, *Journal of Applied Research in Intellectual Disabilities*, 19: 285–295.

Julius, E., Wolfson, H., & Yalon-Chamovitz, S. (2003) Equally unequal: gender discrimination in the workplace among adults with mental retardation, *Work*, 20: 205–213.

LeRoy, B.W., Walsh, P.N., Kulik, N., & Rooney, M. (2004) Retreat and resilience: life experiences of older women with intellectual disabilities, *American Journal on Mental Retardation*, 109(5): 429–441.

Lotan, G. & Ells, C. (2010) Adults with intellectual and developmental disabilities and participation in decision making: ethical considerations for professional-client practice, *Intellectual and Developmental Disabilities*, 48(2): 112–125.

Martin, R. (2006) A real life – a real community: the empowerment and full participation of people with an intellectual disability in their community, *Journal of Intellectual and Developmental Disability*, 31(2): 125–127.

McVilly, K.R., Stancliffe, R.J., Parmenter, T.R., Burton-Smith, R.M. (2006) Self-advocates have the last say on friendship, *Disability & Society*, 21(7): 693–708.

Meininger, H.P. (2001) Autonomy and professional responsibility in care for persons with intellectual disabilities, *Nursing Philosophy*, (2): 240–250.

Nonnemacher, S.L. & Bambara, L.M. (2011) 'I'm supposed to be in charge': self-advocates' perspectives on their self-determination support needs, *Intellectual and Developmental Disabilities*, 49(5): 327–340.

Perkins, E.A. & Moran, J.A. (2010) Aging adults with intellectual disabilities, *Journal of the American Medical Association*, 304(1): 91–92.

Robertson, J., Emerson, E., Gregory, N., Hatton, C., Kessissoglou, S., Hallam, A., & Linehan, C. (2001) Social networks of people with mental retardation in residential settings, *Mental Retardation*, 39: 201–214.

Schalock, R. & Keith, K.D. (2004) *Quality of Life Questionnaire Manual: 1993 and 2004 revision*, Worthington, OH: IDS.

Strnadová, I. (2009) 'Kvalita života dospělých a stárnoucích žen s mentálním postižením' [In English: Quality of Life of Adult and Ageing Women with Intellectual Disabilities], Associate Professorship Thesis, Masarykova University in Brno.

Strnadová, I. & Evans, D. (2012) Subjective quality of life of women with intellectual disabilities: the role of perceived control over own life in self-determined behaviour, *Journal of Applied Research in Intellectual Disability*, 25(1): 71–79.

Strnadová, I. & Evans, D. (forthcoming) Older women with intellectual disabilities: overcoming barriers to autonomy, *Journal of Policy and Practice in Intellectual Disabilities*.

Strnadová, I., Cumming, T., Knox, M., Parmenter, T., & Lee, E. (forthcoming) 'And older women with disabilities, they have a future as well...'. Perspectives on life, well-being, and ageing by women with intellectual disabilities, *Journal of Intellectual Disabilities*.

Traustadottir, R. & Johnson, K. (2000) *Women with Intellectual Disabilities – Finding a Place in the World*, London: Kingsley.

United Nations (2006) *Convention on the Rights of Persons with a Disability*, available online at www.un.org/disabilities (accessed 28 December 2013).

Walmsley, J. (1996) Doing what mum wants me to do: looking at family relationships from the point of view of people with intellectual disabilities, *Journal of Applied Research in Intellectual Disabilities*, 9(4): 324–341.

Wehmeyer, M. (1996) Self-determination as an educational outcome: why is it important to children, youth and adults with disabilities?, in D. Sands & M. Wehmeyer, *Self-Determination Across the Life Span: Independence and Choice for People with Disabilities* (eds), Baltimore, MD: Brookes.

Welsby, J. & Horsfall, D. (2011) Everyday practices of exclusion/inclusion: women who have an intellectual disability speaking for themselves?, *Disability & Society*, 26(7): 795–807.

World Health Organisation (2000) *Ageing and Intellectual Disabilities – Improving Longevity and Promoting Healthy Ageing: Summative Report*, Geneva: World Health Organisation..

PART IV

Communication and representation

11

SOCIAL REPRESENTATIONS AND INCLUSIVE PRACTICES FOR DISABLED STUDENTS IN ITALIAN HIGHER EDUCATION

A mixed-method analysis of multiple perspectives

Fabio Ferrucci and Michela Cortini

Introduction

Following ratification of the UN Convention on the rights of disabled people (CRPD), many countries have undertaken to guarantee 'an inclusive education system *at all levels* and continuous learning throughout life' [our emphasis]. However, this undertaking does not seem to have reached higher education. In the European Union countries (EU 27), participation in post-compulsory education training courses decreases considerably, especially among disabled people. In 2002, in the 20–24 age range, the percentage of students involved in higher education was 43 per cent among those with no limitations; dropping to 36 per cent among students with some functional limitation and was further reduced to 23 per cent among those with serious functional limitation (NESSE, 2012). Despite special measures to assist the more disadvantaged social groups, including disabled students, they are still under-represented in universities (Brink, 2009; Boursicot and Roberts, 2009). Some progress has been made, but the gap is still significant. In 2009, in the 27 European Union countries, an average of 35.1 per cent of people without disabilities in the 30–34 age range had completed some form of higher education, whereas this figure fell to 21.4 per cent for disabled people. The situation varies from country to country (ANED, 2011).

There are a few comparative studies on the inclusion of disabled students at university level (Hurst, 1998; OECD, 2003, 2011, 2012; Ebersold 2008; ANED, 2011). Higher education is missing from the education chapter of the *World Report on Disability* (WHO-World Bank, 2011). From qualitative studies (Borland and James, 1999; Halloway, 2001) research has moved on to wider-ranging surveys (Jacklin *et al.*, 2007; Harrison *et al.*, 2009). Nevertheless, most of the existing empirical research takes place in the United States and the United

Kingdom, less frequently referring to other countries (Hadjiakakou and Hartas, 2008; Sachs and Schreuer, 2011).

The passage from anti-discriminatory to proactive policies has favoured the participation of disabled students in university courses (Equality Challenge Unit, 2013). However, access to university education is not always synonymous with success. Some empirical evidence supports the hypothesis that there is no significant difference in terms of academic performance between disabled students provided with adequate support and students without disability (Madriaga *et al.*, 2011). On the other hand, disabled students are more likely than other students to leave during the first year of the course, fail to complete the full course, take longer to complete the course, and are less likely to go on to postgraduate courses (OECD, 2011). It is therefore necessary to understand which factors influence the efficacy of inclusive practices.

Inclusive practices in higher education: a literature review

Following a social model approach (Oliver, 1996; Barnes *et al.*, 1999), empirical studies have focused on 'oppression' by university routines on the experience of disabled students (Beauchamps-Pryor, 2012). Halloway (2001) suggested that when disability is viewed as a problematic situation at individual level (as a medical approach would indicate), the organisational apparatus of universities is unprepared. Acquiring the necessary information to perform the typical actions of a university student (gaining access to buildings, attending lessons, using the library, taking exams) may require more time and may generate anxiety and stress for disabled students. Therefore, co-ordinated organisational change is required, following appropriate guidelines for universities.

Shevlin, Kenny, and McNeela (2004) believe that the positive behaviour of staff-members towards disabled students does not reflect specific training received from the university but rather personal sensitivity. This gives an episodic nature to inclusion, which 'does not have an effect on the common procedures in the higher education establishments' (Ibid.: 28). Some suggest that it is necessary to influence the behaviour of university personnel in order to favour the *empowerment* of disabled students (Vickerman and Blundell, 2010; Murray *et al.*, 2011), which must include not only administrative staff, but also influence how academic staff actually teach (Konur, 2006; Matthews, 2009).

Equality interventions do not necessarily empower. Madriaga *et al.* (2011: 915) argue that the classification and marginalisation of disabled students is caused by the 'predominant sense of normality' which is intrinsic to the same inclusive practices. The discretion with which students manage the assistance provided for them, and their hesitation in asking for non-essential support, reveals their intention to behave 'as normally as possible' (OECD, 2012), avoiding 'extra-visible' (Goode, 2007) and 'out of the ordinary' situations (Jacklin, 2011).

According to Riddell, Tinklin, and Wilson (2005) higher education institutions adopt two types of approach. The diagnostic approach considers diversity to be an exception and the presence of disabled students to be a constraint that impedes the normal functioning of universities. Interventions to provide support are considered to be a response to individual problems rather than being a question of fairness through which to offer equal opportunities for success. Alternatively, an educational approach considers measures implemented for disabled students to be a development factor for the university system. This approach is characterised by the 'inclusive ethos', generated when the acceptance of the disability and the attention paid to the accessibility of educational activities are an integral part of the institutional culture and are shared by all the persons involved.

The research summarised above converges on the idea that practices involved in inclusion, in reality, generate 'disablism', which is 'the social imposition of avoidable limitations on the aspirations and psycho-emotional well-being of people classified as "disabled" by those considered normal' (Thomas, 2010: 37). The relationship established between those who are 'socially constructed as being problematically different' and 'those who correspond to cultural criteria of incorporated normality' would be a 'disabling' relationship (Thomas, 2004: 28).

In order to have the same opportunities as others, disabled students must make their 'difference' known; that is to say they must be 'classified'. According to the data from research performed in some OECD countries, only a third of disabled students enrolled on courses make their condition known to have access to services (OECD, 2012). The remainder do not declare their own impairments either because they are afraid of being stigmatised (37.1 per cent); or because they do not consider themselves to be disabled (34 per cent); or, because they do not believe it is the right moment to do so (32.1 per cent). Inclusive practices in universities recreate the problem of 'phantom acceptance' for disabled students (Goffman, 1963). The management of this situation by students does not only depend on the presence of impairments, nor on social relationships considered to be oppressive. If it were so, in the first case everyone would make others aware of their own condition, while in the second nobody would do so.

The social model provides a biased perspective to understand the disabled students' experience. First, it interprets the complex network of relationships of disabled students reductively. Although, it highlights the 'dark side' of inclusive practices, it does not mention their successes. An impairment can constitute a serious impediment; however disabling effects may be attenuated by the relationships that the disabled students have with the people from whom they receive material and resources and draw motivation, which permit them to participate in university life. By defining disability as a form of social oppression, attention is almost inevitably focused on phenomena confirming this (Shakespeare, 2013: 77). The existing research neglects the informal relationships in which the disabled students themselves place great confidence. For example, the sense of belonging to the university community also depends on their relationships with family members and fellow students and on participation in group activities (study groups and sporting and artistic activities). A wide majority of students (56.8 per cent) consider relationships with family and friends to be the main factor in the success of their university experience (OECD, 2012), whereas teaching methods (28.1 per cent) and progress-checks (15.2 per cent) are mentioned less frequently.

Second, although social and cultural representations condition the inclusion/exclusion process, the social model removes the symbolic dimension away from relationships. The social psychologist Serge Moscovici suggests that the act of representation

> is a means to transfer whatever disturbs us and whatever is threatening our universe from the outside to within, from far away to nearby. The transfer is made by separating concepts and perceptions that are normally linked, and placing them in a context where the unusual becomes usual and where the unknown may be included in a recognisable category.
> (Moscovici, 1984; Italian translation 1989: 47)

Social representations also build and give form to reality, enabling communication and social interaction, marking the boundaries of and consolidating groups and they direct the processes of socialisation.

The network of relationships of disabled students are complex systems of actions in which the various actors move according to different goals, interests and representations, so that inclusive practices may coexist with practices leading to exclusion. Social practices and representations are interdependent. As practices can modify social representations, so, too, can representations modify practices (Abric, 1994; Mannoni, 1998).

In this study, we have adopted a relational concept of disability to avoid possible conflations between the separate dimensions that contribute to the phenomenon. The perspective of relational sociology (Donati, 2012) considers disability to be a problematic relationship for the acting subject, both internally, in that it involves the relationship between the organism and the personality, and externally, because it influences the intersubjective and structural relationships in which the acting subject is collocated (Ferrucci, 2004: 74). The relational paradigm shares many similarities with Shakespeare's definition of disability as 'a relationship between intrinsic factors (disablement, personality, motivation, etc.) and extrinsic factors (environmental, support systems, oppression, etc.)' (Shakespeare, 2013: 76).

Disabled students in Italian higher education: a pilot case study of action research at University of Molise

Italy is one of the European countries that has worked hardest towards inclusive education. The turning point on the road towards inclusion was reached with

Italian Law 104/1992, which guarantees disabled people the right to education in mainstream classrooms of every type and level of school and also in higher education. This law was later integrated with Italian Law 17/1999 specifically regarding universities. Almost all Italian universities have set up a service for disabled students which performs a range of functions – from orientation on arrival, services offered for teaching and from monitoring accessibility to teaching and training areas to coordinating accompaniment by fellow course members for disabled students, offering assistance for teaching and study activities (peer tutoring). Lastly, Italian Law 170/2010 recognises the right to flexible teaching methods for the students with specific learning, as well as adequate forms of evaluation, which are also applicable to university-level courses.

In Italian universities, the numbers of disabled students more than doubled from 4,813 in the academic year 2000–2001 to 13,744 in 2009–2010. Overall there was an increase from three disabled students per thousand at university to 7.8 per thousand. The increase is due both to the increase in the numbers of disabled students attending state schools and thus achieving the necessary qualification to attend university, and also to the range of services provided by Italian Law 17/1999.

In this context, the research undertaken at the University of Molise represents a pilot study with a double objective: to fill the gap on data about inclusion at university level and to provide an interdisciplinary methodological contribution congruent with the multi-dimensional nature of disability. In particular, the research aims to investigate inclusion processes by listening not only to the voices of disabled students, but also to other people involved, such as: students without disability; technical and administrative personnel; academic staff; tutors for the disabled students; and family members of disabled students. The research focuses on the critical issues encountered by disabled students during the academic trajectory, so as to be able to identify *best practices* in terms of supporting their right to education.

The University of Molise set up a Disability Office in 2002. The office is staffed by a team of two (one of whom is disabled) who belong to a non-profit association on disability issues with which the university collaborates. The activities of the office are co-ordinated by the delegate of the Rector of the University, assisted by six other teaching academic staff, one from each faculty. The Disability Office provides a welcome and support service, offering consultation and advice. Additionally, disabled students are assigned a peer tutor on request who facilitates attending classes and study activities. Furthermore, any individualised exam arrangements are agreed with the academic staff.

During the welcome phase, personnel supply general information about the university and university facilities. A form is completed at the first meeting which records personal details, the type of impairment and the type of assistance desired. Commonly, it is not the disabled student themselves who first establishes contact, but a family member or, less frequently, a friend. *Ad hoc* interventions often become necessary in order to agree 'reasonable accommodations', especially regarding exams. The type of assistance is agreed with the student themselves according to their specific requirements with mediation by the Disability Office. Generally, people with motor impairments request assistance with moving around, while those who have a sensory impairment prefer assistance with their studies (note-taking, one-to-one explanations, and studying together, for example).

The research and intervention was carried out between June 2011 and May 2012, as part of the 'You make the difference' project, financed by the Italian Ministry of Education and Universities. The project was used as an instrument to re-qualify the existing services provided by the Disability Office and to plan for new services with a greater degree of personalisation. The information collected and the results of the research presented here led to some discussion between participants in the research. The study led to improvements in operating systems, so they can meet the needs of disabled students better.

Methodology

Mixed-methods approach, or triangulation (Fielding and Fielding, 1986) refers to the idea of combining different perspectives, by using different researchers, different research paradigms or different data analysis tools. Our approach to triangulation is to offer a third way beyond qualitative and quantitative analysis (Bazeley, 2002). When we discuss textual material like our data, we have to say that the nature of data is qualitative *per se*. In other terms, we deal with words and linguistic representations and not with mere scores at a given test or questionnaire, nor with standardised responses on a Likert scale. The researcher can focus on the way by which discourses have been done, with the implicit belief that what does matter is the *how* something is said; in other words, what makes the difference are metaphors and specific word representations able to convey power. But the same textual material can also be approached making reference to the repetition of singular words and of word associations, assuming that what counts is *quantity*. In other words, even with a qualitative data set, such as transcripts of conversations or texts, it is still possible to choose between a qualitative approach and a quantitative one. In the present chapter we will explore a third possibility, analysing a dataset from two different perspectives: qualitative, anchored to discourse analysis; and quantitative, using content analysis.

The research design comprised focus groups with administrative and teaching academic staff as well as tutor students with disabilities, and in-depth interviews with disabled students. Such a mixed method reflects the nature of our research object, which is multi-composed by definition, and fulfils the aim of collecting the richest possible body of data, bearing in mind the ultimate goal of being action research. The rationale for adopting two highly qualitative data collection tools, instead of questionnaires, is rooted in the desire not to limit the natural expressions of thoughts and representations, being in search for an *emic* genuine point of view.

Specifically, we first conducted four interviews, with the head of the disability services of the University of Molise, with two disabled former students, with a parent of a disabled student and with a representative of the administrative staff. On the basis of the first results, we conducted and recorded four focus groups (with disabled students, teaching staff, administrative staff and tutors), performed in a non-directive interview style and each with 7–10 participants, and individual in-depth interviews with five students with different impairments. Then, we transcribed the audio material, analysed it via critical discursive analysis and ran a detailed textual analysis comparing different views about university experiences. The textual analysis was based on word occurrence and co-occurrence analysis, using the cosine coefficient as association index. Finally, on the same data set, we ran a specificity comparative linguistic analysis to analyse if there are differences between disabled students and others.

Given that this was an explorative study using a mixed-methods approach, we did not have a strong hypothesis: instead, we had a series of research questions. In particular, we were interested in the ways in which disabled students experienced the university setting, and in the social representations and behaviours of the different social actors involved in disabled students' services delivery.

Findings

A point that emerged at the beginning of every data collection session, when we asked participants to react to a free association task, is the difficulty in describing in brief terms what comes to mind in thinking about disability. There were very few images that come to mind for almost everybody, dominated by the image of the wheelchair. This highlights how common it is to reduce the disability world to just a few impairments, stereotyping disabled people.[1] If we keep in mind that the social representations are an important antecedent of our behaviour, we can understand all the risks involved in reducing disability to motor impairment. Through the development of our action research such a stereotype has decreased. Perhaps the first important result of our study lies in the new awareness which academic and administrative staff have developed concerning disability: that it is not only physical and often entails different forms of multiple impairments, along with psychological dimensions.

We have chosen the metaphor analysis, which identifies in metaphor clusters the big interpretative repertoires by which speakers construct sense. We have identified all the metaphors in our transcripts and then we have categorised them into clusters.

First of all, in the narratives of disabled students, there is an emerging category of university seen as *final destination* and *victory*.

> Example 1: I have got a very difficult story ... And for such a reason for me getting at the university has meant a victory, even if for me it has been what for a normal boy is a starting point, for me it has been a final goal.

In psychological terms, inverting what is naturally conceived as a starting point as if it was a final destination is very dangerous. This can block university motivation, since the whole personal satisfaction seems to be in accessing the university, with severe outcomes in terms of university drop-out. If a student is not committed to the final target represented by graduation and transition to employment, it will be more difficult for her/him to manage the daily duties of being a student.

Very often this idea of the success represented by the university access is linked to a sense of 'redemption', in comparison to secondary school experiences, which could have been very dissatisfying. If we took together these results, namely the university access as 'success' and as 'redemption', it shows the need for a deeper analysis of the disabled people's transition from school to university, along with analysis of the university vocational guidance services they receive.

> Example 2: actually it has been a battle against time, against everybody. I have had these difficulties, first of all motor difficulties, and just for such a reason it has weighed on me even more.

The second metaphor cluster refers to the idea of the university as a *battle*, something which is actually present also in university students without disability. What is to be noted is that in such a struggle there are new antagonists (example 2). Traditionally, the university experience is seen as a challenge to oneself. From example 2, on the other hand, although the idea of a challenge to oneself is present, in the metaphor of the battle against time, it is clear that the big struggle is against everybody; enemies are external. We may interpret this image in different ways, making reference to individual psychology. First of all, it is interesting that the enemy is externalised: we are not talking about personal limits, personal weaknesses, but rather a generic external enemy, collective in nature, everybody, on which it is possible to pour potential defeats.

There could be three different interpretations of this: 1) once more the creation of an external alibi; facing the fear of failure, it is more comfortable, in psychological terms, to visualise an external enemy, an external cause; 2) the difficulties a disabled student has to face during university are experienced as an enemy to be fought; difficulties which have to be added to the daily and ordinary efforts an able-bodied student has to face (think about the university students dropping out). This connects to the oppressiveness highlighted in example 2 'it has weighed on me even more', where the university experience is shown in all its difficulties, both internal to the student and external; 3) both the above mentioned interpretations are possible at a time.

> Example 3: it is a smart thing this faculty, but it seems that I do a little step forward and 10 ones backward, because I get carried away with despair.

From example 3, another verbatim extract from an interview with a disabled student, it suggests that the university experience is like a 'shrimp', where every step forward is followed by ten steps backward. It is interesting to note that the step forward is labelled as being a *little* step, as if once more to underline a minimal but very hard-earned aim. In psychological terms, the university life of disabled students is a path of despair, a word which suggests the emotional experience of a never-ending struggle.

Finally, always along the metaphor of the struggle, it is interesting to note the following example (example 4), full of words recalling the idea of a struggle fought to the limits (described by the repetition of 'strong', so able to transfer the idea of limits), which reveals a perennial feeling of hanging in the balance, between losing, connotatively described as 'giving in', and 'resisting'.

> Example 4: yes, because this deficit of mine, which was on the point of getting the better of me, since I was thinking about the possibility of giving in, but then, thanks to my friend, who did support me, I resisted, otherwise, I don't know, perhaps I could have given in, because especially at the beginning it has been definitely hard, hard.

We may wonder what allows them to resist. The answer emerges from the words of this female senior year student (example 4) who has won her battle (she did not stop at university enrolment but rather she achieved her bachelor's degree), where she states that she got it thanks to a friend of hers, stressing the importance of sharing the experience with a friend. Actually, university students are never alone; the number of colleagues may be even very high but the most important thing is finding a real friend among them, because making the grade alone is definitely difficult. To emphasise such a feeling, the disabled senior year student offers us the powerful image of 'getting the better of me', stating the difficulties are due to her deficit. It is interesting, to contrast this with the idea of disability as being something external to the individual. She could have said 'I got it, in spite of my disability'; but actually her narrative starts by stating 'this deficit of mine', first described as a personal characteristic, and then the narration externalises the disability, which was on the point of getting the better of her. We could wonder about the rationale for such an exclusion and for such ambivalence; it seems a distancing of the disability from the self, as if she would not recognise it as a part of herself; on the other hand this narrative can be interpreted as the effort to externalise a condition which could be used as an alibi for potential academic failure.

There is more to say about the role of social relationships among colleagues and friends during university. Example 4 may sound ambiguous in stressing an instrumental role played by disabled students' friends: they give very concrete help, and they are the supporters without whom disabled students are at risk of failure. But actually, the kind of support disabled students require is more psychological rather than material, and this is particularly evident when considering the non-verbal aspects of their communications concerning friendship and university colleagues. The real need is to have proper interactions, and not just receiving help, as it is clear in the following example, where a student wheelchair user regrets not having genuine opportunities to spend more leisure time with her university colleagues.

> Example 5: unfortunately I do not spend time with them out of the university, because of my logistic problems, since they organize evenings very far or where they go there are no disabled people facilities, there are always barriers so that we interact mostly by the Internet, ... of course with some of these I interact also out of the university but, generally speaking, the interaction is not so assiduous as I would like and I regret.

This shows that it is vital to extend the university mobility services (for example, the transfer from home to university buildings) also to non-teaching activities, in line with Thornton and Downs' (2010) proposal that disability services should be able to go beyond the medical model, to embrace the social model and, in particular, to support social relations of disabled students.

An additional cluster of images is that of 'inflated grades' during exams, along with the idea of 'pity':

> Example 6: at which point does my academic 'perfection' depend on my disability? Some 30 in place of 28? Some 28 in place of 25? If I were non-disabled? Hence my doubts, which cannot be solved, since they refer to teachers' individuality... anyway my aim has been always, in a conscious manner or not, to reduce such a conditioning. In other words, I have always faced exams with thorough preparation, in order to allow nobody to be in the situation of being forced to be moved to pity.

Personally, we have been particularly touched by the expression 'doubts, which cannot be solved', expressed with pain, a voice that repeats one of the disabled students interviewed by Riddell et al. (2007), who perceived staff displaying considerable anxiety in relation to assessment and, in particular, about conferring an unfair advantage on themselves in comparison with non-disabled counterparts who were having difficulty with the course. It would be interesting to analyse in more detail whether this perceived unfair advantage influences the perceptions which non-disabled student have of disabled students and especially the relationships among them. To sum up, from the point of view of disabled students it seems that the perceived advantage in terms of academic performance may be counterbalanced by a negative conditioning that influences the relationships with non-disabled peers.

We have combined the verbatim transcripts of the administrative and teaching staff, and have conducted both discursive and content analysis. The first thing which deserves attention is the 'problem' with the disabled students' families. During the focus group sessions the theme of the family arose several times, stressing that, very often, the university staff have to discuss with families and relatives rather than with the disabled students themselves and this is perceived as being a major restriction and real pity. Here the following example seems enlightening, which stresses the main cluster of metaphors, focused on the families that try to usurp their son's place.

> Example 7: We get the better of the families. ... I play the role of rottweiler ... I mean in order to manage the intrusiveness; sometimes it happens that they take their son's place.
>
> (FG disability services officer)

The difficulty in managing the disabled students' families pushes the disability services personnel to act in defence of the disabled students themselves, against the family that tries to take their place. In such a vein, the metaphor of Rottweiler is suggestive of the different reactions disabled students' families elicit, even in the people who are supposed to be at their service.

Before going into deeper analytical detail, it is important to note that we have prepared our text for analysis by doing what is known under the name of *lemmatization*, which gives a reorganisation of the T-LAB database. In particular, the idea is that of clustering together words that have the same root, like for example 'family' and 'familial'. Such an operation, of course, has been done only for the words considered interesting for the subsequent analyses, like 'university' or 'academic'. The output of the software T-Lab we have used (Figure 11.1) shows in the middle the most cited word, and all around the words that co-occur the most with it, according to an association index: the Cosine Coefficient; in graphical terms, the more two words co-occur, the closer they are.

One can 'dialog' with the software and ask to put in the middle a specific word of interest for the user in order to have a graphical representation of its associations (Lancia, 2012; Cortini and Tria, in press). In such a sense, T-Lab can assist the user following both an automatic analysis path as well as a customised one. By clicking on the words associated with the central one it is possible to get the phrase where the two words co-occur and this cue is particularly useful in terms of mix-method.

Regarding the automatic content analysis, it emerges that the most cited word for the academic staff is 'disability'. Behind the associations, calculated with the Cosine coefficient, there are the mental representations of disability of the administrative and teaching staff of the University of Molise. It would be interesting to focus on each of these associations, given that in order to feature in the radial diagram, two different words have been shown to be deeply linked to one another. However, constraints mean we are limited to stress two associations which seems to us most interesting.

FIGURE 11.1 Word association of the word most quoted by the academic staff: 'disabled-disability'

First of all there is a strong association with words like 'problems', 'requests', 'needs', recalling in strict terms the so-called social model of disability. And, in such a sense, it is interesting to find out, by the analysis of the real phrases where these association occur that by 'problems' and 'needs' the academic personnel make reference not only to the problems expressed by disabled students but also to their own problems in trying to respond to the others' needs. The second point of interest is the different words which personnel label disabled students, from 'boys', to 'students' to 'clients'. In particular, this latter term is very significant, since it implies a professional framework for the relationship between staff and students. Of course we are not saying that such a relation should be framed in a *personal* way but if we think about service seen as a best practice, perhaps the word 'client' does not fit very well with the idea of a truly personalised service.

If we examine the word associations for disabled students, the most cited word is 'university' (Figure 11.2). It is important to stress the deep expectancies disabled students pour into university, which emerge from the associations with words like 'important' or 'desiring'.

Another interesting theme is employability, evident in the associations with the word 'work'; in other terms, disabled students expect that university will help them in the transition to work. This is no different from what happens with

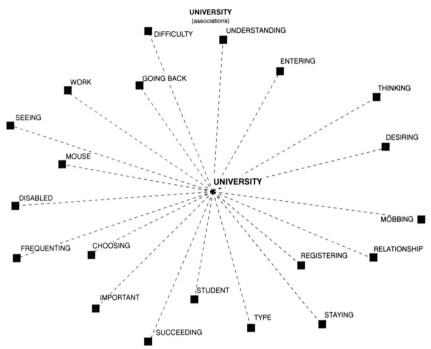

FIGURE 11.2 Word association of the most quoted word for disabled students: 'university'

non-disabled university students, especially during their senior year (Cortini *et al.*, 2011; Maiolo *et al.*, 2013).

The associations with words like 'Molise (Campobasso)', 'to choose' and 'to stay' seem to us significant in terms of vocational guidance. The disabled students very often first choose *where* to attend the university rather than *what* to study, as is evident in the following example, which represents one of the original sentences where 'university' and 'choice' co-occur.

> Example 8: And then the choice: I did stay in Campobasso and did enroll in law. Perhaps this has been one of the rare times during my life in which I have dared less in comparison to what I could do, and, I did feel not ready, as disabled, to leave the shell represented by my city.

In terms of the school-university transition, we know that generally speaking, choosing the city and then the university degree is a big risk, being an extrinsic choice, depending on contextual features rather than on personal preference. On the other hand, being realistic we have to accept that proximity is an important variable in university choice for disabled students but we do not think it should be the dominant one. If universities are chosen by geographical proximity, we need to question rights to education. The development of

FIGURE 11.3 Word associations of 'disability disabled student' for the disabled students

university e-learning and better university guidance for disabled students will enable access to choice by adopting an inner criterion rather than being forced to choose among the degrees offered by the nearest university. In such a vein, the metaphor of the shell represents a psychological defence that would deserve additional study.

When we ask the software for associations for 'disability' (Figure 11.3), it is remarkable to see the variety of supporting entities to whom disabled students make reference. Explicitly, they make reference to words like 'tutor', 'cooperative company', 'associations', to whom the academic staff have not made any reference. This difference seems to suggest that the university does not collaborate with other supports outside disability services, while, on the other hand, disabled students have clearly in mind who can assist them. In action-research terms, this result stresses the need to work closer together and to sustain a real network of agents able to optimise the university experience of disabled students. From another perspective, this result parallels how stereotyping means that different forms of disability have been reduced to the motor one. In a similar way, the different support and services a disabled student can receive have been reduced to those ones provided by the university itself.

It is enlightening to note the association with the word 'persons' and 'contact', stressing again that connecting with a particular person make the difference.

We have run linguistic specificity analysis, which is very useful since it compares two or more speakers or categories of speakers, in our case disabled students and academic staff. This analysis reveals that among the frequently-used words of academic staff there are 'problem', 'disabled student', 'disability', 'negative', 'training', 'to signal', echoing the results of the word association analysis and confirming the perspective of the social model according to which disability is the output of the university organisation. Nevertheless, when we move to the analysis of the frequently-used words of disabled students – with words like 'person', 'choice', 'difficult', 'help', 'relation', 'colleagues', 'friend' and 'to hope'– there is a realistic acceptance of difficulties but at the same time it is evident that disability should not prevent disabled people from achieving ('choice', 'to hope', for example). At university the disabled students are agents of social relationships that are not only negative conditionings but also positive opportunities.

Finally, we performed an exclusive linguistic specificity analysis that finds the words used by the first category of speaker but not by the other. The words used by personnel and not by disabled students are: 'facilitations', 'handicap', 'client', 'integration', 'constitution'. The words used only by the disabled students are: 'virtue', 'test', 'fear', 'to deserve', 'listening', 'friendship', 'transfers'. We should highlight 'to deserve' and 'facilitations', which are words that emerge when respondents talk about exams and assessment. On the one hand, for the academic teaching staff it is natural to assess disabled students with facilitations (not just extra time in examinations, but also enhanced marks). However, for disabled students it is vital to be evaluated in a fair way, to ensure that the mark they receive corresponds to their performance and not to their disability.

From research results to actions

Looking at our results in a holistic manner a series of possible actions emerges:

- *Monitoring attitudes towards disabled students*. It is a priority to monitor attitudes towards disability in general and, especially, towards disabled students. Attitude, as we have already stressed, is the best predictor of behaviour and its analysis would allow the possibility of planning policies and interventions in advance.
- *Implementing the vocational guidance services during the transition from school to university*. Our analysis shows that university choice is driven primarily by geographical proximity and this should challenge us to consider ways to empower the agency of disabled students, who have the right to a genuine choice of universities. We think that achieving this requires an integrative view of the transition from school to university, bringing together all the different actors; first of all the disabled students, their parents, their school teachers as well as vocational guidance counsellors.

- *Networking the different disability services.* Our results underline a scarce awareness of disability services offered by external organisations (for example, cooperatives, not for profit associations). In other words, the university is managing its relation with disabled students by focusing more on what it can provide, rather than on the disabled students and on what already exists and works well, even if it may appear invisible. In order to correct this inward-lookingness it should be useful to plan, every year, special training for all the academic personnel on the disability services, both internal and external, and to coordinate a series of activities that all these entities may do together.
- *Supporting disabled students by supporting disability tutors.* A possible support to be given to disabled students, without reducing the amount of facilitation, would be the possibility to be examined once a month, for every course. This would be of assistance to the peer tutors who help disabled students. Otherwise, they have to manage at the same time their own exams and those of the student they are tutoring. This challenge requires time management skills which young people of student age rarely possess.

Conclusions: a future research agenda

Our action research on university inclusion practices highlights how disability is a multi-dimensional phenomenon. It shares the methodological implications of the mixed-methods approach, so that 'the phenomenon of disability can only be understood analytically by bearing in mind the different levels, mechanisms and contexts' (Danermark and Gellerstedt, 2004: 350). Our relational approach shows the interdependence of social structure (geographical proximity and organisation of the university) with impairment and personal motivation of disabled students and with stereotyped representations of academic staff too. Disability is not solely a product of social organisation, nor simply of individual factors (impairment, personal motivation), and not only of culture. Disabling or enabling effect 'emerges' as a specific property of social relations, according to how the different dimensions interact. From this perspective, we can think about disabled students as agents of their academic career.

If we think about ways to extend our research, the first aim could be that of broadening the typology of research objects and of respondents; for example, we could also include parents and families of disabled students. In particular, the participation of disabled students' parents would allow us to deepen our understanding of the process by which disabled students choose university courses and plan transition to work. Here, the international literature suggests that behind the vocational choices of disabled people, there are actually their parents, who, by trying to protect their offspring, risk supplanting them. This adds to the instrumental dependence on one's parents a further, psychological dependence, that of not being able to understand and develop personal desires and goals. An additional research focus could be the relationships disabled students construct among themselves. We did focus on the relationships between disabled people and non-disabled people in the academic context. But the other side of the coin, deeply anchored to the idea of identity development, is what happens within the disabled students' community (Taylor and Palfreman-Kay, 2000). In particular, it would be interesting to study the role of the disability community in supporting personal autonomy and in all the processes that lead from academic access to academic success.

Note

1 In such a sense, it is important to stress that generally we adopt stereotypes to describe members of the outgroup, while we conceive members of our ingroup making reference to multiple and fine descriptors.

References

Abric, J.C. (ed.) (1994) *Pratiques sociales et representations*, Paris, Presses Universitaires de France.

ANED (Academic Network of European Disability experts) (2011) *Inclusive Education for Young Disabled People in Europe: Trend, Issues and Challenges*, Leeds: Human European Consultancy and Centre for Disability Studies, Leeds University.

Barnes, C., Mercer, G., and Shakespeare, T. (1999) *Exploring Disability. A Sociological Introduction*, Cambridge: Polity Press.

Bazeley, P. (2002) Issues in mixing qualitative and quantitative approaches to research. *AIDS, 21* (2), S91–S98.

Beauchamps-Pryor, K. (2012) From absent to active voice: Securing disability equality within higher education, *International Journal of Inclusive Education*, 16 (3), 283–295.

Borland, J. and James, S. (1999) The learning experience of students with disabilities in higher education: A case study of a UK University, *Disability & Society*, 14 (1), 85–101.

Boursicot, K. and Roberts, T. (2009) Widening participation in medical education: Challenging elitism and exclusion, *Higher Education Policy*, 22 (1), 19–36.

Brink, C. (2009) 'Standards will drop' and other fears about the equality agenda in higher education, *Journal of Higher Education Policy and Management, 21*(1), 1–19.

Cortini, M., Notarangelo, E., Cardellicchio, E. (2011) Obscure future? A pilot study on University students' career expectations. In Cortini, M., Tanucci, G., Morin, E., *Boundaryless Careers and Occupational Well-Being*, London: Palgrave Macmillan.

Cortini, M. and Tria, S. (in press) Triangulating qualitative and quantitative approaches for the analysis of textual materials: an Introduction to T-Lab, *Social Science Computer Review*, Published online before print 27 December 2013, doi: 10.1177/0894439313510108.

Danermark, B. and Gellerstedt, L.C. (2004) Social justice: Redistribution and recognition – a non-reductionist perspective on disability, *Disability & Society*, 19(4)< 339–353.

Donati, P. (2012) *Relational Sociology: A New Paradigm for the Social Sciences*, London and New York: Routledge.

Ebersold, S. (2008) Adapting higher education to the needs of disabled students: Development, challenges and prospects. In OECD (Organisation for Economic Cooperation and Development), *Higher Education to 2030*, Paris: OECD Publishing.

Equality Challenge Unit (2013) *Equality in higher education: statistical report 2013*. [Online]. Available from: http://www.ecu.ac.uk/publications/equality-in-higher-education-statistical-report-2013#sthash.zd3jjnBa.dpuf. [Accessed: 1 April 2014].

Ferrucci, F. (2004) *La disabilità come relazione sociale. Gli approcci sociologici tra natura e cultura*, Soveria, Mannelli: Rubbettino.

Fielding, N.G. and Fielding, J.L. (1986) *Linking Data: The Articulation Of Qualitative And Quantitative Methods In Social Research*, Beverly Hills CA: Sage.

Fuller, M., Bradley, A. and Healey, M. (2004) Incorporating disabled students with an inclusive higher education environment, *Disability & Society*, 19 (5), 455–468.

Gibson, S. (2012) Narrative account of university education: Socio-cultural perspective of students with disabilities, *Disability & Society*, 27(3), 353–369.

Goffman, E. (1963) *Stigma: Notes on the Management of Soiled Identity*, New York: Simon & Schuster.

Goode, J. (2007) 'Managing' disability: Early experiences of university students with disabilities, *Disability & Society*, 22 (1), 35–48.

Hadjiakakou, K. and Hartas, D. (2008) Higher education provision for students with disabilities in Cyprus, *Higher Education*, 55 (1), 103–119.

Halloway, S. (2001) The experience of higher education from the perspective of disabled students, *Disability & Society*, 18 (4) 597–615.

Harrison, M., Hemingway, L., Sheldon, A., Pawson, R. and Barnes, C. (2009) *Evaluation of Provision and Support for Disabled Students in Higher Education*, Report to HEFCE and HEFCW by the Centre for Disability Studies and School of Sociology and Social Policy at the University of Leeds.

Hurst, A. (ed.) (1998) *Higher Education and Disabilities: International Approach*, Aldershot: Ashgate.

Jacklin, A. (2011) To be or not to be 'a disabled student' in higher education: The case of a postgraduate 'non-declaring' (disabled) student, *Journal of Research in Special Education*, 11 (2), 99–106.

Jacklin, A., Robinson, C., O'Meara, L. and Harris, A. (2007) *Improving the Experiences of Disabled Students in Higher Education*, York: The Higher Education Academy.

Konur, O. (2006) Teaching disabled students in higher education. *Teaching in Higher Education*, 11 (3) 351–363.

Lancia, F. (2012) *T-Lab User Manual. Tool for Textual Analysis*. Available on www.tlab.it. [Accessed: 1 April 2014].

Leyser, Y. and Greenberger, L. (2008) College students with disabilities in teacher education: Faculty attitudes and practices, *European Journal of Special Needs Education*, 23 (3), 237–251.

Luna, C. (2009) But how can those students make it there? Examining the institutional discourse about what it means to be 'LD' at an Ivy League university, *International Journal of Inclusive Education*, 13 (2), 157–178.

Madriaga, M., Hanson, K., Helen, K. and Walker, A. (2011) Marking-out normalcy and disability in higher education, *British Journal of Sociology of Education*, 32 (6), 901–920.

Maiolo, M.E., Cortini, M., Zuffo, R. G. (2013) Education or employment? The challenging choice of today's youth, *Procedia – Social and Behavioral Sciences*, 84 (9) July 2013, 298–302.

Mannoni, P. (1998) *Les representation sociales*, Paris, Presses Universitaires de France.

Matthews, N. (2009) Teaching the 'invisible' disabled students in the classroom: disclosure, inclusion and the social model of disability, *Teaching in Higher Education*. 14 (3), 229–239.

Moscovici, S. (1984) The Phenomenon of Social Representations, in Farr, R. and Moscovici, S. (eds), *Social Representations*, Cambridge, Cambridge University Press.

Murray, C., Lombardi, A. and Wren, C.T. (2011) The effect of disability-focused training on the attitudes and perception of university staff, *Remedial and Special Education*, 32 (4), 290–300.

NESSE (Network of Experts on Social Sciences of Education and Training) (2012) *Education and Disability/Special Needs. Policies and Practices in Education, Training and Employment for Students with Disabilities and Special Educational Needs in the EU*, Brussels: European Union.

OECD (Organisation for Economic Cooperation and Development) (2003) *Disability in Higher Education*, Paris: OECD Publishing.

OECD (Organisation for Economic Cooperation and Development) (2011) *Inclusion of Students with Disabilities in Tertiary Education and Employment*, Paris: OECD Publishing.

OECD (Organisation for Economic Cooperation and Development) (2012) *Transitions to Tertiary Education and Work for Youth with Disabilities*, Paris: OECD Publishing.

Oliver, M. (1996) *Understanding Disability: From Theory to Practice*, London: Macmillan.

Riddell, S. (1998) Chipping away at the mountain: Disabled students' experience of higher education, *International Studies in Sociology of Education*, 8 (2), 203–222.

Riddell, S., Tinklin, T. and Wilson, A. (2005) *Disabled Students in Higher Education: Perspective on Widening Access and Changing Policy,* London and New York: Routledge.

Riddell, S., Weedon, E., Fuller, M., Healey, M., Hurst, A., Kelly, K. and Piggott, L. (2007) Managerialism and equalities: Tensions within widening access policy and practice for disabled students in UK universities, *Higher Education*, 54 (4), 615–628.

Sachs, D. and Schreuer, N. (2011) Inclusion of students with disabilities in higher education: Performance and participation in student's experiences, *Disability Studies Quarterly*. [Online] Database of Society for Disability Studies. 31 (2). Available from: http://dsq-sds.org/article/view/1593/1561. [Accessed: 1 April 2014].

Shakespeare, T. (2013) *Disability Rights and Wrongs Revisited*, 2nd edn. London and New York: Routledge.

Shevlin, M., Kenny, M. and McNeela, E. (2004) Participation in higher education for students with disabilities: An Irish perspective, *Disability & Society*, 19 (1), 15–30.

Taylor, G. and Palfreman-Kay, J. M. (2000) Helping each other: Relations between disabled and not disabled students on ACCESS programs, *Journal of Further and Higher Education*, 24 (1), 39–53.

Thomas, C. (2004) Rescuing a social relational understanding of disability, *Scandinavian Journal of Disability Research*, 6 (1) 22–33.

Thomas, C. (2007) *Sociologies of Disability and Illness: Contested Ideas in Disability Studies and Medical Sociology*, Basingstoke: Palgrave Macmillan.

Thomas, C. (2010) Medical sociology and disability theory, in Scambler, G. and Scambler, S. (eds), *New Direction in Sociology of Chronic and Disabling Conditions. Assault on the Lifeworld*, Basingstoke: Palgrave Macmillan.

Thornton, M. and Downs, S. (2010) Practice brief. Walking the walk: modeling social model and universal design in the disabilities office. *Journal of Postsecondary Education and Disability*, 23 (1) 74–80.

Vickerman, P. and Blundell, M. (2010) Hearing the voices of disabled students in higher education, *Disability & Society*, 25 (1), 21–32.

Watson, N. (2003) Daily Denials: The Routinisation of Oppression and Resistance, in Riddell, S. and Watson, N. (eds) *Disability, Culture and Identity*, London: Longman.

World Health Organisation and World Bank (2011) *World Report on Disability*. Geneva: World Health Organisation.

12

THE PROBLEM OF THE SUPERCRIP

Representation and misrepresentation of disability

Jan Grue

Scholars of disability have paid considerable attention to cultural representations and strategies of representation, perhaps particularly in the United States (Garland-Thomson 1996, Garland-Thomson 2009, Siebers 2010, Snyder and Mitchell 2000, Snyder and Mitchell 2006). This is partly because representations of disability and disabled people are "potentially allegorical in the sense that the act of characterization encourages readers or viewers to search for a larger concept, experience, or population" (Snyder and Mitchell 2000: 40).

That potential is a central premise for this chapter, which examines three recent variations of a familiar allegorical figure of disability, as represented in mass media and popular culture. I will primarily refer to this figure as the *supercrip*. The central feature of the supercrip is success at *overcoming*, at demonstrating ability beyond that which is commonly expected of disabled people. Such ability may be exhibited in many areas, but the most striking qualification for supercriphood, as well as the most problematic, is physical prowess.

The supercrip shares some features with what Tanya Titchkosky has called the abled-disabled (Titchkosky 2003), as well as with the *cyborg* (Haraway 1991, Reeve 2012) and the *techno-marvel* (Norden 1994). Supercrips and cyborgs have a mutual association with social fields such as sports and rehabilitation (Howe 2011), while cyborgs and techno-marvels share an affiliation with genres of fiction, particularly science fiction. The abled-disabled demonstrate the worth and value of disabled people in general, by serving as exemplary representatives of their group and/or community. I prefer supercrip, however, both because it is in common usage in disability studies (Hardin and Hardin 2004, Hartnett 2000, Kama 2004, Norden 1994) and because it preserves the sense that something exceptional is required of disabled people who wish to achieve recognition.

I will argue that a defining feature of supercrip narratives is their rationalization and legitimization of impairments as *positive attributes*. This happens when they are represented as causes of achievement and transformative experience. I will refer to this mechanism of rationalization and legitimization as a *topos* (pl *topoi*), after the Greek word for "place." The topos is a tool of traditional rhetoric (Aristotle, Tredennick and Forster 1960, Reinhardt 2003), argumentation theory (Braet 2004, Braet 2005, Toulmin 1958) and discourse analysis (Wodak and Meyer 2001, Wodak and Martin 2003). It is useful for my analytical purposes because it focuses attention on the double function of so-called commonplaces – to make sense of the unfamiliar and to reinforce the already-known.

The argumentative topos grounds claims and propositions in common or accepted knowledge, and may be phrased as a conditional. It performs the allegorical work suggested by Snyder and Mitchell by providing a link between the specific and the general. The cultural construction of supercrips depends, for example, on the Aristotelian common topos of *cause to effect*, which is usually instanced as the simultaneous mention of impairment and achievement. As Eleanor Roosevelt claimed in her autobiography: "Franklin's illness proved a blessing in disguise, for it gave him strength and courage he had not had before" (Roosevelt 1992 [1961]: 142).

The causal link may be understated, implicit, or even paradoxical, as in this example: "Oscar Pistorius has already inspired a generation with his 400m performance, despite being a double amputee" (Hendricks 2012). The causal direction of flow is essentially the same as in the Roosevelt example: Pistorius' inspirational status (the quote predates his being found guilty of culpable homicide) was a consequence, even if an indirect one, of the existence of his impairment.

We can extrapolate a formula:

$$(S)\text{upercriphood} = (A)\text{chievement} \times (I)\text{mpairment}$$

The greater the achievement and the greater the impairment, the more impressive the supercrip! I do not intend to implement this formula rigorously. Even in the age of New Public Management there is no intersubjectively valid, universal numeric indicator of human achievement. However, I will note that impairments are in fact often assigned numeric values – e.g. on a scale from 1.0 to 4.5, for Paralympic ranking purposes (Peers 2012).

A slightly trickier cod-mathematical question is that of *value polarity*. Achievement is a positive. Supercriphood appears to be positive to most people who are not actually disability scholars, disability activists, or … disabled themselves. Presumably, then, impairments are positive, because you cannot produce a positive quality from a positive and a negative. And in fact this appears to be the reasoning behind at least one attempt to represent disability in a positive light, i.e. the "affirmation model" of John Swain and Sally French, which they have summarized as follows:

> An affirmative model is being generated by disabled people through a rejection of the tragedy model. [...] Disabled individuals assert a positive identity, not only in being disabled, but also in being impaired. In affirming a positive identity of being impaired, disabled people are actively repudiating the dominant value of normality.
>
> (Swain and French 2000: 578)

The affirmation model of disability supposedly "encompasses" impairment, but it is unclear to me what this means. Swain and French are quite clear in presenting their reasons why being a part of a disability movement may be a basis for positive identity – these reasons include solidarity and shared experience as a way to reject identity threats.

When it comes to impairments, however, valorization appears to depend on achieved outcomes that are not intrinsic to or follow directly from the concept of impairment, certainly not in the way that solidarity and shared experience follow from progressive concepts of disability. And the fact of the matter is that impairment generally makes achievement harder.

For example, one Malaysian woman receives better health care and education because of her visual impairment (p. 574). Shakespeare *et al.* (1996) are invoked in order to claim that a rich, non-traditional sex life is made possible because of the need to circumvent the limitations of impairments (p. 575). Certainly, impairments represent many facets of human experience, and it would be unwise to categorically deny that the experience of impairment may entail positive qualities. My quarrel, rather, is with the supposition that the experience of impairment is valorized because good things sometimes happen to or are achieved by people with impairments. A better sex life, better education, or better health care can all be achieved by non-impaired people, and I've yet to see an argument that impairment necessarily has such consequences. Moreover, many forms of impairment make many forms of achievement very unlikely indeed, if not downright impossible. The Paralympic Games will never be open to any but the most physically fit disabled people, a criterion which excludes most chronic illnesses in favor of relatively stable impairments. This is the biggest flaw in the supercrip formula: it does not account for the fact that many impairments, were they to be assigned numbers, would have very different values over time.

Still, the affirmation model seems to need a positive conception of impairment, which at times threatens the basic integrity of the concept. One critique of Swain and French, which aims to develop their model, proposes a definition of impairment as "physical, sensory and intellectual difference to be expected and respected on its own terms in a diverse society" (Cameron 2008: 23). Such a definition dovetails with mystifying euphemisms like "differently abled" (whose usage frequency, according to the Google Ngram Viewer, appears to have peaked in 1996).

Taken to its logical extreme, this attitude may be referred to as a positive essentialist view of impairments, or impairment vitalism. I borrow this felicitous phrasing from a recent work (Overboe 2012), for its connotations. Vitalism usually connotes strength, physicality, and transcendence, and such vitalist connotations suffuse all three examples of impairment representations discussed in this chapter. Vitalist principles also seem to characterize the spirit of many affirmational slogans (e.g. "Lame is Sexy!") rather more aptly than more neutral phraseology might.

Effectively, there is a recurring dilemma when it comes to disability and representation: positive framings of the concept of impairment entail either a) logical inconsistency or b) a compensatory moral calculus. If impairments cannot be negative at all, if they merely entail "difference," then the concept is superfluous. If impairments *do* have negative aspects, however, then in order to maintain an overall positive impression, there must be compensations – as in Swain and French's examples.

The figure of the supercrip, as well as of the cyborg, therefore, thus embodies a compensatory argument that is deeply embedded in disability studies' attempts to dismantle negative representations of disability and disabled people. The (reconstructed) *topos* in question might be phrased as follows: "If a person with an impairment Z displays positive quality X or achieves positive accomplishment Y, then impairment Z is itself validated." This, of course, preserves the general premise that impairment Z must be validated, and is therefore intrinsically problematic.

Impairment as a problem – the rhetorical perspective

Disability has been analyzed as appearing always-already as a problem. It "typically generates the requirement for explanation and amelioration, but little else," according to the analysis of Titchkosky & Michalko (2012: 127). Unlike "natural" or "normal" bodies, which may be described neutrally, in terms of their capacities or features, bodies with impairments require explanation and action: An explanation of what went wrong, of how deviance from the norm came about, and action aimed at restoring normalcy in one way or another.

This is a matter of ontology, the exploration of which is becoming more central to disability studies (Hughes 2007), and which is intimately tied in with the matter of representation. It is one thing to say that *disability* is ontologically problematic, and to represent it as such. It is another and potentially quite scary thing to represent *disabled people* as intrinsically problematic, and scarier still to represent *people with impairments* as problematic. Even when the problem of impairment is represented as having a potential solution, it remains a problem – notwithstanding Swain and French's argument that the "non-tragic view of disability […] is not about 'the problem'" (p. 571).

In rhetorical terms, impairment remains an *exigence* – something that must be addressed and solved. In the work of Lloyd Bitzer (1968), a "rhetorical situation" was originally defined as a scene or situation originating with an exigence, something that cannot be passed over in silence. Rhetorical action, therefore, is the response to a problem that requires a solution. Notably, the most influential critique of Bitzer's position was made from a constructionist point of view (Vatz 1973). Causation does not run from exigence to rhetorical action; rather, it is rhetorical discourse that manufactures and sustains the social reality of the exigence. To pose a question is to act in a way that demands an answer (Austin 1962), but equally, answers presuppose the existence of questions (Grice 1975).

This is a potentially valuable contribution of rhetoric and discourse analysis to the study of disability and representation. In order to elicit the way that problems are framed – in order to reconstruct the presumed or presupposed exigencies, and see how the rhetorical situation is framed – we can look for *topoi*. Which conditionals and causal links are asserted or implied? How are specific representational examples linked to general knowledge?

One advantage of this discourse-centered approach is that it does not automatically begin with a familiar problem set. It forces a re-examination of assumptions about models and theories of disability, and their normative as well as epistemological status. The medical model of disability, for instance, can be linked to the set of topoi that treat disability as a *medically solvable problem*. Such topoi are not just found in the discourse of the medical professions. An organization of disabled people may in some contexts appear to be a forum for political activism, but it may also be a patients' rights organization – and use medical topoi – in other contexts (Grue 2011). There are times when impairments may productively be construed as problems, and other times when the problem frame is utterly inappropriate. The study of disability and representation should, among other things, address the difference between such times.

This in fact is one of the things disability studies does best. Look at the answers/representations in order to tease out the questions/problems that are already present in the culture. Disability has been described as a hidden history (Longmore 1987), though of course it has been hiding in plain sight. Just like normate bodies, extraordinary bodies are already prominent in the culture (Garland-Thomson 1996, Garland-Thomson 2009). Whether they are recognized as *disabled* bodies is another matter. Disability studies claims extraordinary bodies for disability; it also tries to show that these bodies are represented in ways that influence perceptions of disability and disabled people. The problem frame is only one option among many.

Disability studies can, a little facetiously, be conceived as an imperialist project: it tries to claim vast amounts of territory. If this (somewhat questionable) metaphor holds, the closest model is the British Empire: with humble origins and limited resources, it can only succeed in its ambition by exploiting the contradictions and conflicting interests of local populations. Explorers originating in disability studies may also range quite far from home.

This suggests the trajectory of the remainder of this chapter. I wish to look at some prominent and widely disseminated representations of people with impairments in popular culture today, in order to provide a *reduction ad absurdum* of the problem frame and the compensatory achievement stance. I also wish to stress the emphasis, in my examples as in the culture at large, on the kind of *physical* achievement that is essentially incompatible with the majority of chronic illnesses. People with impairments can, it seems become supercrips and icons of achievement by distancing themselves from people with unstable chronic illnesses. This, in turn, undermines the whole notion of disability and disablement as a complex interaction between bodies, environments and social structures.

My examples are representations of a) ordinary people with impairments, whose compensatory achievement lies within the realm of everyday experience, b) exceptional people with impairments, the representation of whom focuses on remarkable achievements, and ultimately c) fictional people, whose impairments serve only to provide motivation and legitimacy for their fantastical compensatory achievements. They are, in order:

- Participants on *Beyond Boundaries*, a TV series originally developed for the BBC, since exported to multiple countries.
- Paralympic athletes, notably the sprinter Aimee Mullins.
- Hollywood superheroes, in some of their recent iterations.

All three examples draw on the topos of cause and effect – there is a strong link between impairment and achievement. They also share the problem frame, and represent "having an impairment" as a highly *solvable* problem. Through the twin forces of willpower and technological intervention, impairments are framed as obstacles that can be, and should be, overcome. Thus, they also reproduce the supercrip/cyborg figure.

My examples are of course not chosen at random. Rather, they constitute *exemplars*, in Thomas Kuhn's sense of the word – "concrete problem-solutions" (Kuhn 2012 [1970]: 186). Their relevance to disability studies must be inferred. Disabled people have impairments, and inferences made about people with impairments may be transferred to disabled people. Sometimes the people in the examples are explicitly identified as disabled, sometimes they are not, but they all belong to the set of people who have extraordinary bodies – bodies with impairments.

If representations of bodies with impairments are to be interesting to disability researchers, interest should be generated on multiple levels – on the level of critical appraisal of social and cultural phenomena, but also on the level of pragmatic usefulness. My last goal, stated before I proceed to actual analysis, is to develop a critique that provides insight into the kind of disability construal that might conceivably have socio-political purpose.

First example: *Ingen grenser* (Norwegian edition of *Beyond Boundaries*)

Beyond Boundaries is a reality TV series in which a group of people with physical impairments go on an expedition through challenging terrain, supervised and led by an experienced outdoorsman (a man, at least, both in the British original and the Norwegian edition). The BBC has so far broadcast three series, taking place in Nicaragua, Africa, and the Ecuadorean Andes.

Beyond Boundaries was a popular format in Sweden and in Mexico, as well as on Flemish television, but it became a national phenomenon in Norway with the title *Ingen grenser* (literally: *No Boundaries* – for clarity I will keep the Norwegian title from here on). The second series, the most successful so far, reached a market share of 67 percent at its highest, with 1.4 million viewers – in a country of approximately 5 million people.

The success of the program probably has something to do with its appeal to national character. While the UK original program was tinged with colonialist imagery, the Norwegian program appeals to popular sentiment through images of familiar, national landscapes. The expeditions in the first and second series were conducted across Northern and Central Norway respectively, and the expedition leader in both cases was Lars Monsen, a "wilderness expert" with national standing (somewhat comparable to the UK's Bear Grylls). The use and enjoyment of unsullied nature is a Norwegian national pastime and source of pride, and the goal of the second expedition, Snøhetta mountain, is a national icon.

The second series in particular spawned much media coverage, with many participants becoming minor celebrities. The breakout star was Birgit Skarstein, in her early twenties and a recent paraplegic after botched surgery. She spoke with the prime minister by phone, participated on the country's largest chat show, and is at the time of writing a rising Paralympic athlete. All participants, however, have also been the subjects of multiple media stories that track their progress after being on the program.

Ingen grenser emphasized group solidarity, cooperation, and notably *willpower*. The following voiceover was played at the start of every episode:

> Lars Monsen on a trip through the wilderness with eleven participants with very different resources for carrying out an expedition. The participants have different physical impairments. They have to want more, give more, and cooperate more than everyone thinks possible. [...] Together they will show that nothing can prevent them from carrying out a grueling expedition. Together they will show that abilities and optimism have ... *no limits*.

The qualities of wanting more and giving more play themselves out in various physical challenges. The distance is traversed partly on horseback, partly by canoe, but mostly by foot and over fairly rough terrain. The participants have been supplied with two cross-country wheelchairs, which are solidly constructed but have to be operated manually. Three of the participants need to use them at various stages, and the duties of pushing and pulling have to be taken up by the stronger and more mobile participants. There is therefore a need both for cooperative efforts, and for each participant not to tax him- or herself beyond the point of exhaustion. The quality and capacities of the equipment is not a matter of discussion or arbitration, but are part of the given framework of the expedition. Some leeway is given on occasion – how far to go, when to pitch camp – but the participants are constrained in terms of the overall trajectory and goals.

Ingen grenser was, at the time of broadcast, accused by disability rights advocates and others of playing to voyeurism and reproducing freakshow dynamics with its audience, the central argument being that the display of people with extraordinary bodies performing physical feats is inherently tied to the history of freakshows and freakery.

In my view, this is not necessarily the case. Historically, freakshows were displays that contested and played with boundaries between humanity and alterity (Orning 2012). They were unsettling and disturbing, and intentionally so. When they disappeared, in a historical development that coincided with the expansion of modern medicine, they did not take the display of extraordinary bodies with them. What disappeared was a particular way of looking at such bodies, as well as a social and commercial framework for doing so. There is ample freakery in modern reality television, but *Ingen grenser* does not fit the format. It is a profoundly normalizing program, which emphasizes the latent ability of people with extraordinary bodies to do ordinary things – if they have sufficient willpower.

By way of contrast, emphasis on willpower, physical mastery, and normalization, connects *Ingen grenser* to the historical and contemporary discourse of rehabilitation, in which the central problem to be solved is the problem of disciplining one's body to the point where one can be admitted (or readmitted) to everyday life. That discourse arose as freakery waned – particularly in the wake of the First and Second World War. In rehabilitation discourse, abnormality is neither entertainment nor commercial opportunity. Rather, the *process* of normalizing abnormality – the problem of disciplining the body – constitutes grounds for moral instruction and moral approval.

Ingen grenser, with its month-long trek across rough terrain, is both a television program and a strenuous exercise program. Its goals and constraints, which were developed ahead of time by professionals, not participants, are enforced by the same agents. Participants that do not display a sufficient degree of enthusiasm or effort are, at various times, encouraged and admonished. Their lack of willpower is a problem that is both equal to and entwined with their impairments.

This framework of benevolent paternalism allows for two subject positions for the participants: enthusiastic or recalcitrant. To exceed one's previously assumed limitations (the "boundaries" of the title) is to be morally laudable; to fail to do so is a moral failure. Early press on the program's third Norwegian series introduced a new host/expedition leader, who "cried when participants refused help."

There is no more call for a reality series featuring disabled people to represent that group in a statistically accurate way than there is for *Big Brother* to accurately represent the British population in general. Nevertheless, some observations can be made about the participants on *Ingen grenser*. There were eleven participants on the second series, all of whom had physical impairments. Some had sensory impairments, but most had mobility impairments. Some of these had mobility impairments resulting from cancer, but were in remission at the time of filming. Although the distinction between impairments and chronic illnesses is not easily made, all participants had impairments that were fairly stable or very stable in terms of predictability and secondary effects.

Such a selection of people with impairments is a clear precondition for a program such as *Ingen grenser*. Too many wheelchair users or people with unpredictable chronic illnesses, and there is no month-long trek through the wilderness. Too many such people, in fact, and there would be no way to move beyond bodily boundaries. Instead, a balance is struck in which impairments are manageable, and disability is a solvable problem. As in the discourse of rehabilitation, disability can be overcome, though it cannot be transcended. For that, we go to the second example.

Second example: the Paralympic athlete as inspirational figure

Significant global media coverage of the Paralympics began with the Sydney Games in 2000 (Cashman and Darcy 2008); the 2012 Games in London were probably the most widely disseminated Games in history. As host nation, the UK broadcast 150 hours of live coverage.

The iconography used to portray the event is that of physical achievement despite (clearly visible) physical limitation. The Paralympics, as a "complex of elite disability sport" (Purdue and Howe 2012: 22) represents something of a paradox. The performance must be at a level that will interest a generic, presumably able-bodied audience, while there is an expectation that the Paralympic athletes will serve as credible role models for other people with impairments (Joukowsky *et al.* 2002). This paradox points to another flaw in the supercrip equation. There are, in fact, strict limits to how much a supercrip can and should achieve. The disabled athlete cannot be *too* impressive, or must risk accusations of transcending the category of disability entirely, and thus of cheating.

The paradox has been explicated by the double amputee, former Paralympic sprinter Aimee Mullins, who has questioned, through argument and performance, the assumptions that support the Paralympics as a separate arena for competition. Her argument focuses on the dividing line between "natural" and "cyborg" bodies, i.e. the point at which a compensatory prosthesis becomes interpreted as a performance aid, and at which the rationale for requiring an athlete to compete in the Paralympics rather than the Olympics is not the presumption of disadvantage, but of advantage.

Mullins, who has explored the topics of prosthetics and technological development via the TED conference format, has also pointed out the limitations placed on technological optimism by economic realities. Her "14 pairs of legs" are her possessions not only because they have been built, but because they have been bought. To her, the problem is systemic.

Such points do not survive the transition to meme-hood. Originally coined by Richard Dawkins as the cognitive equivalent of a gene, i.e. a maximally effective mechanism for transmitting of information, in current usage "memes" refer to images with captions, usually encapsulating a claim or an attitude, and heavy in pop-cultural references. One such meme is "What's your excuse?", variations on which feature that phrase superimposed on images of double amputees running – including images of Mullins. Much like the promotional imagery for the 2012 Paralympic Games in London, which feature wheelchair users and amputees hovering in mid-air, "What's your excuse?" shows Mullins in mid-stride, on a beach in a black bikini, blocking out the sun so that her body is surrounded with a halo effect. Her status as a star athlete, including any mention of support systems, is transmuted into iconic transcendence.

"What is your excuse?" is also, of course, a potentially hostile question. Variations of the text include the phrase "What the fuck is stopping you?" Variations in the imagery, which extensively feature well-muscled people with impairments, are also directed at obesity, here interpreted as the direct result of a deficit in willpower.

The Paralympic athlete is a questionable figure in more than one sense. He or she may literally be questioned by examining boards that certify degrees of disability in order that competition be fair, but may also be positioned as being of questionable morality if his or her achievement is too great, if the achievement appears insufficiently effortful. There must be a problem of the right order. The world of iconic imagery demands transcendence, while real-world institutions demand the very bodily features that make transcendence impossible. The only place where these contradictions can be resolved is in fiction, which provides the third example.

Third example: Hollywood superheroes

Superhero fiction constitutes one of the most important, if not the most important genre in popular cinema during the last few decades. Drawing on the sources of audience familiarity (through comic books), spectacle (through sophisticated special effects) and ample potential for long-term brand and franchise building (through sequels based on the comic books' open-ended narratives), Hollywood studios and their conglomerate owners have increasingly turned to superheroes, along with fantasy-themed movies, to maintain profits in a beleaguered entertainment market.

A mainstay in superhero fiction is the notion of heroism paired with extraordinary ability as a compensation for trauma, injury or even impairment. To give some examples, Bruce Wayne embarks on a training program to become the masked crime-fighting Batman because of his parents' murder, and Matt

Murdock develops superhuman echo-location abilities after being blinded by radioactive material.

The superhero Iron Man emerges from injury done to his alter ego, Tony Stark. In the 2008 film, the energy source that powers Iron Man's cybernetic exoskeleton also powers a magnet that prevents shards of metal from reaching Stark's heart and killing him. Stark's egoism and vanity are tempered by his heroic calling; his impairment makes him vulnerable and dependent on a technological device, but also turns him into a force for moral good.

Superhero cinema takes impairment vitalism to its logical conclusion. There is no injury without benefit, and no impairment without corresponding ability. The mutants of the X-Men universe, the 2000 film of which arguably inaugurated the current onslaught of films, are probably the clearest expression of this logic. Professor X, the mentor and guide of the "good" mutants, is a paraplegic with telepathic powers. His second-in-command, Cyclops, shoots energy bolts from his eyes, thus requiring special goggles in order to interact normally with the people around him. (Without his goggles, he must always keep his eyes closed, and so is blind.) The fan favorite Wolverine has a metal skeleton, grafted onto his bones through painful surgery. The list, not surprisingly, goes on.

The mutant superheroes are not disabled by economic arrangements and lack of labor power. They are stigmatized, ostracized, and legally discriminated against; particularly in the 2000, 2003, and 2006 films, "mutation" is developed as a metaphor for difference in sexuality and sexual orientation. The alternative metaphorical reading of mutation as ethnic difference has also been proposed; readings of mutation as impairment have been fewer and less developed.

In a superhero universe, impairments are, perhaps unsurprisingly, entirely subservient to narrative requirements. The 2012 film *The Dark Knight Rises* has Batman placed in an underground prison with a broken back and worn-out knees. He recovers partly through intensive training, but mostly through sheer force of will, ultimately to defeat his enemies. Crucially, the body does not bear limitations of its own. In an early scene, we are informed that Batman's knee has practically no healthy cartilage remaining, but by the end he moves gracefully and seemingly without pain. The damaged body is only the visual expression of a mind plagued with doubt – the lack of self-confidence and absolute willpower that defines Batman's true, archetypal character.

This narrative schema, in which injury is inevitably followed by overcoming, has little to do with medicine and much to do with martial discipline. The superhero's injured or impaired body exemplifies the narrative prosthesis of Snyder and Mitchell. It provides a reason for the audience to care. Even Superman, the most god-like of all superheroes, must have at least the potential for bodily weakness, provided *ex machina* by the substance kryptonite. Once the reason to care has been established, however, it can be dispensed with. What really matters are the subsequent feats of heroism.

Retracing our steps: who gets left behind by the cyborgs, techno-marvels and supercrips?

Through the three examples, I've traced an exponential and quite speculative curve. Superheroes are not, in fact, disabled. But representations of superheroes provide a funhouse mirror for the assumptions made about bodies with impairments that are made in coverage of the Paralympics and in reality television where disability is an explicit and central feature. Such representations are worth examining because disability, though often perceived as a special category, one that does not touch on other forms of bodily experience, could be and should be a prism for such experience in the most general, most fundamentally human sense.

We should be worried when representations of what is effectively bodily impairment lose touch with reality. We should be even more worried when representations of bodily impairment focuses on *limitations* to the detriment of *frailty*. While impairments and illnesses are sometimes mentioned alongside each other, as though they were very different categories, they belong on a continuum.

To reiterate, the assumption I am most critical of is that being a disabled person *ought to be* the source of extraordinary willpower and achievement – a moral imperative which results in impossible demands on people with impairments as well as people with chronic illnesses.

It is perhaps not surprising that this assumption is made in the context of superheroism or the Paralympic Games. It is not terribly surprising that it is made in the context of a reality TV program. All three examples represent narrative genres, which depend on implicit and explicit relations of cause and effect. What is slightly more surprising is the extent to which that assumption underlies affirmation models of disability, and influences notions of positive disability identity.

Although far from being dominant modes of thought about disability, affirmation and identity paradigms are important. They are particularly important because they have to do with the self-perception of disabled people – most of whom, in a statistical and demographic sense, probably do not identify themselves as disabled. It is a recurring topic in academic and activist circles that "coming out" as disabled is a difficult process. Most people would probably prefer just to be a little ill, or having a bit of trouble, and not actively identifying as *a disabled person*. Disability connotes stigma. That is probably inevitable. Ableism can be fought, but the *defeat* of ableism is as much of a utopian project as the elimination of racism or sexism.

In the meantime, the representation of disability and disabled people as a basis for identification is a topic that is potentially even more troublesome than in the context of race and gender, even as it engages with both those topics. The emphasis placed on inherent, essentialist *strength* by activists in any identity category usually risks embracing ableism. Moreover, that risk applies equally to disability advocates.

There is an *aporia* here. Talking about impairments and injuries in positive ways tends to result in a displacement of qualities. It is never the injury or impairment itself that is positive, but its potential for achievement that is presumably unlocked by the traumatic experience. Sociologists of health and illness have long employed this perspective (Frank 2007, Frank 2010). Once this attitude is vulgarized, it becomes a moral imperative to treat illness as an instructive and transformative experience (Ehrenreich 2010).

Is there an antidote? Possibly, expectations could be reversed. Franklin Delano Roosevelt (in)famously concealed his impairment in public life, and so was not represented as disabled until fairly recently (Gallagher 1985). Although an extreme example, the reframing of the FDR story shows the potential of disability studies as a critical discipline. Paul Longmore's hidden history of disability holds relevance for our understanding of contemporary phenomena. To point out, repeatedly, that "this is disability" is not always effective, but the claim nevertheless has to be made. This, too, is *to do* with disability, because it is connected to bodies, bodily experience and bodily reality.

Superhero stories exist in a fantastical space – not only bodies, but everything down to and including the laws of physics may be altered. The laws of narrative still apply, however, and are in many cases susceptible to lobbyist groups. The study of representations of disability may not be – should not be – an act of lobbyism in itself, though it may produce an occasional white paper.

Acknowledgement

A version of this chapter forms part of *Disability and Discourse Analysis* (2015) and thanks are due to Ashgate Publishers for giving permission to reprint earlier material.

References

Aristotle, Hugh Tredennick and E. S. Forster (1960) *Posterior Analytics / Aristotle,* [Translated] by Hugh Tredennick. Topica/Aristotle; [Translated] by E. S. Forster. Cambridge, MA, London, Harvard University Press/Heinemann.

Austin, J. L. (1962) *How to Do Things with Words,* Cambridge, MA: Harvard University Press.

Bitzer, Lloyd (1968) The rhetorical situation, *Philosophy and Rhetoric* 1(1):1–14.

Braet, A. C. (2004) The oldest typology of Argumentation Schemes, *Argumentation* 18(1):127–48.

Braet, A. C. (2005) The common topic in Aristotle's Rhetoric: precursor of the Argumentation Scheme. *Argumentation* 19(1): 65–83.

Cameron, Colin (2008) Further towards an Affirmation Model, in *Disability Studies: Emerging Insights and Perspectives,* edited by T. Campbell, F. Fontes, L. Hemingway, A. Soorenian and C. Till. Leeds: The Disability Press: 12–27

Cashman, Richmard and Simon Darcy (2008) *Benchmark Games.* Petersham: Walla Walla Press.

Ehrenreich, Barbara (2010) *Smile or Die: How Positive Thinking Fooled America and the World,* London: Granta Books.

Frank, A.W. (2007) Five dramas of illness, *Perspectives in Biology and Medicine* 50(3):379–94.

Frank, A.W. (2010) *The Wounded Storyteller: Body, Illness, and Ethics*, Chicago, IL: University of Chicago Press.

Gallagher, Hugh Gregory (1985) *FDR's Splendid Deception*, New York: Dodd, Mead.

Garland-Thomson, Rosemarie (1996) *Freakery: Cultural Spectacles of the Extraordinary Body*, New York, NY: New York University Press.

Garland-Thomson, Rosemarie (2009) *Staring: How We Look*, Oxford/New York: Oxford University Press.

Grice, H.P. (1975) Logic and conversation, in *Syntax and Semantics, Vol. 3*, P. A. M. Cole (editor) New York: Academic Press.

Grue, Jan (2011) Interdependent discourses of disability: a critical analysis of the social/medical model dichotomy, Ph.D., Faculty of Humanities, University of Oslo, Oslo.

Haraway, Donna (1991) A Cyborg manifesto: science, technology, and socialist-feminism in the late twentieth Century, in Haraway, Donna and Ulrike Teubner *Simians, Cyborgs and Women: The Reinvention of Nature*. New York: Routledge: 149–81.

Hardin, Marie and Brent Hardin (2004) The "supercrip" in sport media: wheelchair athletes discuss hegemony's disabled hero, *Sociology of Sport Online* 7(1): 1–16.

Hartnett, Alison (2000) Escaping the 'Evil Avenger' and the 'Supercrip': images of disability in popular television, *Irish Communication Review*, 8: 21–29.

Hendricks, Maggie (2012) Inspirational moments: Oscar Pistorius in the best picture you'll see, Yahoo Sports (http://sports.yahoo.com/blogs/fourth-place-medal/oscar-pistorius-best-picture-ll-see-2012-olympics-115020678--oly.html, consulted 27 September 2014).

Howe, P. David (2011) Cyborg and supercrip: the Paralympics technology and the (dis) empowerment of disabled athletes, *Sociology* 45, 5: 868–882.

Hughes, Bill (2007) Being disabled: towards a critical social ontology for disability studies, *Disability & Society* 22(7): 673–684.

Joukowsky, Artemis A.W., Larry Rothstein and US Paralympics (2002) *Raising the Bar: New Horizons in Disability Sport*, New York: Umbrage Editions.

Kama, Amit (2004) Supercrips versus the pitiful handicapped: reception of disabling images by disabled audience members, *Communications* 29, 4: 447–66.

Kuhn, Thomas S. (2012) [1970] *The Structure of Scientific Revolutions*, Chicago, IL: University of Chicago Press.

Longmore, Paul K. (1987) Uncovering the hidden history of people with disabilities, *Reviews in American History*, 15: 355–364.

Norden, Martin F. (1994) *The Cinema of Isolation, a History of Disablity in the Movies*, New Brunswick, NJ: Rutgers University Press.

Orning, Sara (2012) Fleshly embodiments: early modern monsters, Victorian freaks, and twentieth-century affective spectatorship. PhD, Literature, University of California Santa Cruz.

Overboe, James (2012) Theory, impairment and impersonal singularities: Deleuze, Guattari and Agamben, in B. Hughes, D. Goodley and L.J. Davis (editors) *Disability and Social Theory: New Developments and Directions*, Basingstoke: Palgrave Macmillan.

Peers, Danielle (2012) Interrogating disability: the (de)composition of a recovering Paralympian, *Qualitative Research in Sport, Exercise and Health* 4(2): 175–88.

Purdue, David E.J. and P. David Howe (2012) Empower, inspire, achieve: (Dis) empowerment and the Paralympic Games, *Disability & Society* 27(7): 903–916.

Reeve, Donna (2012) Cyborgs, cripples and icrip: reflections on the contribution of Haraway to disability studies, in B. Hughes, D. Goodley and L.J. Davis (editors)

Disability and Social Theory: New Developments and Directions, Basingstoke: Palgrave Macmillan.

Reinhardt, Tobias, ed. (2003) *Topica/Marcus Tullius Cicero,* Edited with a Translation, Introduction, and Commentary by Tobias Reinhardt, Oxford: Oxford University Press.

Roosevelt, Eleanor (1992) [1961] *The Autobiography of Eleanor Roosevelt.* New York: Da Capo Press.

Shakespeare, Tom, Kath Gillespie-Sells and Dominic Davies (1996) *The Sexual Politics of Disability: Untold Desires*, London: Continuum.

Siebers, Tobin (2010) *Disability Aesthetics*, Ann Arbor, MI: University of Michigan Press.

Snyder, Sharon L. and David T. Mitchell (2000) *Narrative Prosthesis: Disability and the Dependencies of Discourse*, Ann Arbor, MI: University of Michigan Press.

Snyder, Sharon L. and David T. Mitchell (2006) *Cultural Locations of Disability*. Chicago, IL: University of Chicago Press.

Swain, John and Sally French (2000) Towards an affirmation model of disability, *Disability & Society* 15(4): 569–582.

Titchkosky, Tanya (2003) Governing embodiment: technologies of constituting citizens with disabilities, *Canadian Journal of Sociology/Cahiers canadiens de sociologie*, 29(4): 517–42.

Titchkosky, Tanya and Rod Michalko (2012) The body as the problem of individuality: a phenomenological disability studies approach, in B. Hughes, D. Goodley and L. J. Davis (editors), *Disability and Social Theory: New Developments and Directions*, Basingstoke: Palgrave Macmillan: 127–142.

Toulmin, Stephen (1958) *The Uses of Argument*, New York: Cambridge University Press.

Vatz, Richard (1973) The myth of the rhetorical situation, *Philosophy and Rhetoric* 6(3): 154–161.

Wodak, Ruth and Michael Meyer, eds. (2001) *Methods of Critical Discourse Analysis*, London: Sage.

Wodak, Ruth and J. R. Martin (2003) *Re/Reading the Past: Critical and Functional Perspectives on Time and Value*, Amsterdam: John Benjamins.

Films

Daredevil (2003) Mark Steven Johnson. Marvel Enterprises.
Iron Man (2008) D: Jon Favreau. Marvel Enterprises.
The Dark Knight Rises (2012) D: Christopher Nolan. Warner Brothers.
X-Men (2000) D: Bryan Singer. Twentieth Century Fox.
X2 (2003) D: Bryan Singer. Twentieth Century Fox.
X-Men III (2006) D: Brett Ratner. Twentieth Century Fox.

13

USER, CLIENT OR CONSUMER?

Construction of roles in video interpreting services

Hilde Haualand

Video interpreting[1] enables a flow of information between people through a chain of technological and human resources. Video interpreting always includes a (qualified) sign language interpreter, who relays a conversation between a Deaf person using sign language and a hearing non-signer by way of a videophone, a studio and eventually a regular telephone if the parties communicating are at different locations. These entities are also part of an entanglement of legal regulations, political motivations and financial resources that are shaped by as well as shape the organisation of the video interpreting services and the definitions, understandings and roles of the technologies and the involved persons.

Video interpreting services have been established in several countries over the past decade, and are increasing in popularity among persons who use sign language. Three quotes from three different Deaf persons in different countries testify to the sense of effectiveness the video interpreting services can provide, and the quite similar experience of using the service across these countries:

> If I need to call, that is great. When you sign, it takes a short time, and then it is done. It is smooth communication and that is nice.
>
> (Tom, 30, United States)

Kari from Norway compares her use with hearing people who talk on the phone:

> The video interpreting service works fine. It is the same as what hearing people do when they talk on the phone, it is easy.
>
> (Kari, 35, Norway)

Inga from Sweden gave a similar account of her experience:

> It is like an ordinary telephone, and I can sign just like I want. With the interpreter, one gets so much more information about the other person, like when the person slows down or pauses to think. I know a lot more about what happens at the other end. It feels as if I blend in with the videophone, and it is efficient.
>
> (Inga, 60, Sweden)

These similar accounts of how videophones and video interpreting services function at their best contrast with striking differences between the three countries in terminology, financial mechanisms, regulations and dispersion of the service. Inga from Sweden can call the national video interpreting service because the Swedish government has a policy that telecommunication services should be accessible for disabled people. When Tom in the United States uses the video relay service in the United States he is a telecommunication consumer accessing his civil right (access to functionally equivalent telecommunication services). Kari can use the video interpreting service because she is entitled to receive sign language interpreter services. These differences also reflect different political and legal approaches to disability in the three countries. Video interpreting services offer a micro-level case to show the workings of macro-level politics. The differences described in this chapter will be used as a springboard for discussing how video interpreting and videophones construct and enable the different roles Deaf people may take or be ascribed with, depending on how video interpreting services are organised. While videophones and video interpreting services have the potential to increase Deaf people's access to telecommunication and other communication situations, the organisation and definitions of the service impacts both the degree of accessibility and inclusion (Haualand, 2014).

The empirical material will be used to show how videophones and video interpreting services construct Deaf users a) as consumers with a civil right, and b) as clients of interpreter services, c) experts at the technological frontier, d) as users of an assistive technology, and e) as a group of people in need of inclusion through increased accessibility. Three of these constructions are from Sweden, one is from the United States and one from Norway. The initial quotes testify to a similarity in experience of communication flow in various systems, which may lead an observer to assume that the distribution of roles and responsibilities through the videophones and networks that constitute the services have no significance, so long as the video interpreting service itself 'works'. However, the various categorisations and roles show that video interpreting services are not mere intermediaries between two persons talking with each other on the phone; the services are also mediators of politics with multiple outcomes. The categorisations are not exhaustive, but serve to illustrate how the political motivations and organisation of the video interpreter service have a significant role in defining and demarcating the possible scopes of action for the people who are involved in providing or using the service. At the same time, they show how the different systems for videophone distribution and video interpreting service provision restrict as well as unleash potential attributes of videophones and the roles and responsibilities of actors that are involved. In the United States and Norway, which have quite narrow definitions of the video interpreting service (as a telecommunication or interpreter service respectively), the range of different categories are less obvious than in Sweden where the video interpreting service has a broader political foundation than in the other two countries.

The quotes in this chapter are excerpts from three of around 30 semi-structured interviews with Deaf people in the United States, Sweden and Norway, where topics included use of communication technologies in general and videophones in particular.[2] These interviews were part of multi-site fieldwork in the same three countries conducted around 2006–2007 and 2009–2010, where the main bulk of data is from participant observation in/of various conferences and workshops (and reports from these); archive, website and document searches and analyses; as well as observation of their own and other people's use of the relevant technologies and the video interpreting services in each country. In the analysis of this material, a wide, but not necessarily personally observed, socio-political context is incorporated, which is also consistent with what Moore (2005) has observed as typical for contemporary anthropologists who study ongoing processes of change. Rather than first trying to understand the perspectives of those who use the video interpreting services (whether these are sign language/Deaf people, designers, providers, non-signers or interpreters), the analysis is

> inspired by the praxiographic approach (Mol, 2002) that is less interested in the human perspectives, experiences or interpretations of a certain culture and more focused on the socio-material enactment of practice. It is about the specific ways in which the phenomenon studied exists in the world, about the ways in which it is entangled.
>
> (Sørensen, 2010, 44)

In this chapter, three workshops that took place over a period of six weeks in the autumn of 2009 serve as a springboard to show how Deaf people are ascribed with different roles. The descriptions are connected to interviews and observations during fieldwork made before and after these events.

The United States

In the United States, the bulk of the discourse related to video interpreting service is about video relay service (VRS), which is defined as a telecommunication service to secure what is defined as a civil right; the right to functionally equivalent telecommunication services for all, including disabled people. All citizens have the right to use whatever telecommunication equipment they have (including videophones) to access various telecommunication services, at any time. The service is stipulated in the Americans with Disabilities Act and the Telecommunication Act, and the service has been growing rapidly since the late 1990s. The provision of video interpreting services is organised as an open market, where the service providers must follow the Federal Communications Commission (FCC) regulations for reimbursement. These regulations also include specification for maximum waiting times (no more than a couple of minutes) and a requirement that the services must run 24/7. The service providers compete to provide the most user-friendly videophones and the best qualified interpreters to capture as many customers as possible, in order to receive income from the telecommunication relay service fund financed by the telecommunication carriers.

The Federal Communications Commission (FCC) frequently announces workshops and hearings in their premises in the governmental blocks of south-western Washington, DC. One of many steps towards achieving functional equivalence was the replacement in 2009 of IP addresses that functioned as videophone numbers, with ten-digit numbers. The prequel to the workshop on 'Ten-Digit Numbering and E911 Requirements for VRS and IP Relay' held at the FCC in September 2009, was that some resistance had been recorded by consumers to register for a ten-digit number[3] and choose a default video relay service provider. The event was an open discussion between parties that expressed slightly different interests, but shared a common basic understanding that video interpreting is about functional equivalent telecommunication services. They all had a common interest in identifying consumer behaviour in order to implement best practices to change this behaviour.

The construction of a consumer

The participants in the panel at the FCC workshop in September 2009 were mostly what could be termed consumers, and represented different lobby and special interests groups. The service providers were relegated to the audience. The consumer representatives identified obstacles and suggested possible strategies to make the service provider's clients register for a ten-digit number. The Deaf videophone owners were constructed as the consumers, and authority was distributed to them in at least two visible ways at this workshop. First, the workshop was organised in a way that made the consumers speak to the service providers about the various considerations the providers had to take into consideration in order to make all their consumers register. There were few, if any incidents of requests or recommendations from the service providers to the consumer representatives at this workshop. This is not to say that the service providers never send messages or appeals to their clients or consumers, but what this particular workshop made evident, was that spaces for feedback and requests from the consumer to the service providers are a frequent feature of the video relay service market in the United States. This is related to the second aspect of distributed authority towards the consumers; the service providers are dependent for their success on making their consumers register, since unregistered consumers also are lost clients, and hence also lost income. The behaviour of consumers (in this and other matters as well) directly influences the service providers' revenue from the telecommunication relay services fund, and the service providers rely on their cooperation as well as satisfaction with their services in order to survive.

The mutual relationship between the consumer representatives and service providers at the workshop was also visible in how Cynthia talked about the service. She was interviewed in 2006 and 2009, and during both of the interviews, her relationship and manoeuvres vis-à-vis the VRS providers were discussed. Until 2006, the videophones from different providers were rarely compatible with each other or with video interpreting services from other companies than the one who provided a particular videophone model. It was not unusual to have videophones from more than one provider installed.

> I have two videophones, one from CSD[4] and one from Sorenson, and I use both. When I know who has which, then I know which equipment to use. In this area, most people have Sorenson, but I also have friends who use CSD. And as for interpreters, I prefer fast service. Sorenson still has waiting time. So if I am bored with the wait time at Sorenson, I switch to CSD and get an interpreter immediately.
>
> (Cynthia, 30, United States)

She had several options in a market where she was defined as a consumer with a right and opportunity to make personal choices. She did choose several videophones and service providers and ended up with a collection of technical gadgets in her home in order to maximise choice and flexibility. When Cynthia was interviewed again in 2009, all videophones were compatible with each other and the various service providers, so this was not a topic to discuss anymore. The implementation of ten-digit numbers was the new main topic of conversation about VRS at the time I revisited Washington, DC, and I asked her what she thought of the ten-digit number process. She said she was not sure if she had registered but assumed she had, since the service continued to work well for her. Cynthia had not experienced any technical or organisational rupture with the implementation of the ten-digit number, and no longer needed to use a particular videophone model to call another videophone owner depending on which service provider they used. Unlike in 2006, Cynthia no longer had to focus on how the service worked and barely noticed the changes. It may seem that the videophone had been 'blackboxed', defined by Latour as

> the way scientific and technical work is made invisible by its own success. When a machine runs efficiently, when a matter of fact is settled, one need

focus only on its inputs and outputs and not on its internal complexity. Thus, paradoxically, the more science and technology succeed, the more opaque and obscure they become.

(Latour, 2000, 304)

This is what Bob, another Deaf American, revealed:

Relays have become much better. Yes, in general. Faster and clearer. And I become more independent. Don't have to depend on other people.

(Bob, 35, the United States)

When Bob says he does not 'have to depend on other people' when the relay services improve, it is a contradiction. In order to use the relay services he is dependent on technologies he is able to use and people who work to provide these services, but these now operate so successfully that they have become opaque, and Bob no longer 'sees' the chain of resources involved. His statement testifies to Moser's comment, that when a body's relationship with a network of human and technological resources is unproblematic, 'the distributedness, the networks and even the bodies tend to move into the background and become invisible' (Moser, 2003, 158). Bob and Cynthia have become consumers who take access to the products and services they use for granted, without really thinking about how it works or why they are able to use the video relay services at all.

Norway

The Norwegian video interpreting service is organised as an extension of the national sign language interpreter service under the National Insurance Agency (NAV), and the telecommunication sector is not involved. Anyone entitled to sign language interpreter services as stipulated in the National Insurance Act may use the service, but only if they have access to compatible equipment for video interpreting. The video interpreter service is considerably younger than the US service, and has not reached the same level of dispersion.

NAV also hosted a workshop in the autumn of 2009. The workshop was primarily directed at interpreter service managers and other administrators working in the regional centres for assistive technology to provide videophones and other assistive technologies. It was an information meeting for a group of people who were not yet fully familiar with the video interpreting service and the regulations stipulating provision of videophones. Contrary to similar meetings in the United States (and Sweden), this meeting was not between a group of actors already familiar with the service who needed to update themselves or discuss anticipated changes. Rather, it was a meeting where representatives from the video interpreting services management group confirmed the National Insurance Agency (NAV) as an obligatory passage point (cf. Callon, 1986), both as the major stakeholder, and for distribution of the videophones and service provision.

Users of sign language interpreter services

The National Insurance Agency is responsible for procuring and assigning the equipment for video interpreting and providing an extended interpreting service through the videophones. The videophone is defined as 'equipment for video interpreting' and the service is organised as a supplement to the regular interpreter service. Since the service was established as a means to improve access to the labour market and enhance inclusion of Deaf people at work (NAV, 2013), the distribution of dedicated videophones is limited to work-places.[5] The service runs from eight in the morning until eight in the evening on weekdays, and is closed during the night and at weekends.

At the workshop in 2009, the management group emphasised how the regional offices could use the video interpreting service as a tool to increase the efficiency of interpreter services in their region. Video interpreting could replace a community interpreter for many types of assignments, and a model showed how there was a potential for large time and cost savings for each assignment undertaken using a videophone rather than a physically present/ community interpreter. As a consequence of this more efficient way to provide interpreter services, especially for short assignments, it was anticipated that the Deaf clients would experience increased access to interpreter services, and indirectly enhance their work-place capacities since communication with their colleagues would be more efficient. Unlike the United States, it is not functionally equivalent telecommunication services that intend to enhance capacity or agency for Deaf people, but increased access to interpreters. The focus is thus on how videophones can connect the interpreter to the Deaf person. Telecommunication access is barely mentioned, except when telephone calls are mentioned as an example of the kind of interpreting assignments suitable for the video interpreting service.

Per, a Deaf Norwegian, talks about the video interpreting service in this manner when he compares the video interpreting service with a physically present interpreter:

> I can use the service to talk with a colleague, or understand what my boss says at a briefing. But sometimes I also make a phone call, and then I use the videophone. So it is an important and great tool for helping a Deaf person in a hearing work-place. Without it, there would have been more barriers, but it does not solve everything. The best solution would be a physically present interpreter, but it is ok, absolutely ok.
>
> (Per, 35, Norway)

Per evaluates it the same way as it was presented to him by the regional NAV office which provided his videophone. He also defines the videophone as a technical object that increases access to the interpreter service, and does not see the videophone primarily as a telecommunication tool, which is the definition of the videophone in the United States. His experience is still not that of 'blending in' or 'independence', and he says the barriers would be less with an interpreter physically present.

Solveig also has a videophone at her work-place. As with Per, her story is a testimony about how 'technical objects contain and produce a specific geography of responsibilities' (Akrich, 1992, 207), but also reveals the dependence any object or actor has on a network of humans and non-humans in order to function or act. The videophones cannot be taken for granted, and the service cannot be reached anytime, as in the United States. To use the service, Deaf people must qualify (be employed and approved by the government to use sign language interpreters in the work-place), and call during the regular business hours of the interpreter service.

> Well, when I have contact, the interpreting has been fine. But it is the technology that fails me, with its demands on understanding the system and my dependence on other people to repair it for me. I think it would have been easier if I could fix it myself. I am dependent on the computer technician, the interpreter service and others. If I was able to call someone to help me, it would have been okay, but when the videophone doesn't work, I can't call – and it becomes a vicious circle.
>
> (Solveig, 45, Norway)

The technical problems she describes occur in the United States and Sweden as well, but Solveig's experience is of having little capacity to act or solve the problems. NAV has delegated the responsibility to maintain her equipment to a local computer technician, who may know more or less about how the videophones work, and may even not be accessible at all times. She is acutely aware of her dependence on the technicians and the interpreters. The network is not seamless, and when one consequence of the rupture is that she cannot even use the videophone, the lack of access or dependence on other people becomes very tangible. This is a contrast to Bob's statement that he did not have to depend on other people. Both Solveig in Norway and Bob in the United States are relying on technologies and other people, but these have been blackboxed to Bob, while they are highly visible to Solveig.

Further, the videophone in Norway has been defined as a tool to access an interpreter, not as a communication tool per se. The right to have a videophone installed at work is related to Solveig's right to receive interpreter services – a right that is not fundamentally violated if the videophone does not work. She may still access a physically present sign language interpreter. In a study of a baby watch system which allowed parents to follow their premature babies via video communication technology, Oudshoorn et al. (2005) showed how the designers of the technology imposed their images of the other user groups in the development of the service. Stereotypical images 'functioned as an important element in shaping the technological decisions' (Oudshoorn et al., 2005, 94), and the nurses at the hospital had most of the power to decide when and how the baby watch system could be used. In a similar way, the right to decide how and when the videophones and the service can be used is retained within NAV. In Solveig's case, the competency and responsibility is not delegated to her, but to the interpreters and technicians at NAV and the management at her workplace. Rather than delegating authority outwards, from the interpreters to the Deaf people, the capacity to act remains within the interpreter studios and the technical department of the National Insurance Agency. The video interpreting service is a service to increase access to interpreters, and the system is constructed in a way that maintains the Deaf end users as persons who use sign language interpreter services. This aspect is also present in Sweden, but as will be shown, the system for videophone and video interpreting service provision is more multi-faceted there, and has aspects of technology, interpreting and accessibility.

Sweden

In Sweden, the political emphasis is on securing increased accessibility for deaf and hearing impaired people through telecommunication technologies. The video interpreting service is considered a governmental responsibility, and the public authority responsible for the telecommunication sector is also responsible for procuring and regulating the service. The service is operated by a public regional sign language interpreter agency that serves the whole country. Regional medical-rehabilitative authorities provide the videophones. Deaf people receive a videophone at no cost, but only after an application has been signed by a physician or employer and approved by the regional authority. The video interpreting service in Sweden has been operating since the late 1990s and has gained much popularity in the target population.

Compared to Norway and the United States the Swedish system appears more complex. with more stakeholders and responsible government sectors who are entangled in a network that make them mutually dependent on each other (Haualand, 2014). The actors in this network meet physically about once a year at the annual meeting hosted by one of the major videophone stakeholders. The meeting in October 2009 was one of these annual seminars, aimed at the regional officers in charge, and providers of alternative telephony (including both text- and videophones), and text- and/or videophone developers and manufacturers (who had the regional authorities as their primary market in Sweden). The hot topic of the meeting was implementation of an EU Directive on public procurements (European Union, 2004) and new text- and videophone procurement procedures for the regional authorities. As a consequence of the anticipated change in procurement practice, most of the discussion was related to new videophone procurement and distribution processes. However, much time was also given to product presentations of both video- and text telephones and discussion on the latest technological developments. Representations of the users and use of the videophones permeated the discussions. These representations were however different from each other, and rather than constructing one idea about the end user (as a telecommunication consumer like in the United States or as a user of interpreter services in Norway), there were at least three different representations of the end users. First, the Deaf users were conceived as experts in the field of digital video communication. They are directly involved in the development and design of the videophones that are developed both for use in and export from Sweden. Another view of the Deaf end users was founded on a medical-rehabilitative view, presupposing 'special' or 'alternative' communication needs in a group of disabled people. Only one or two representatives from the national video interpreting service were present at the seminar, but the continuous reference to the video interpreting service made by the other participants staged a third perspective on video interpreting; increasing accessibility. These three perspectives can also be viewed as different ways of engaging with a videophone, none of which is more valid than the other, but nevertheless implies different ways the actors evaluate videophones and the other actors (Thevenot, 2002). Thus, they also represented different paths of humans and technologies that distribute agency, but as is shown, the flow of agency was not unidirectional.

Deaf as expert

At the seminar in October 2009 hosted by the Swedish Institute of Assistive Technology, there was no formal representation from consumer associations or institutions, but a few Deaf technicians and advisors were there by virtue of professional involvement. This group also had first-hand knowledge and user experience with the videophones and distribution practices that were discussed at the meeting. During a demonstration by a major video conference system provider, a Deaf advisor commented to his hearing colleague that the picture quality was good enough only when people spoke. A hand wave demonstrated that the picture was distorted in a way that is annoying and disturbs a conversation in sign language. His hearing colleague responded that the videophone should be tested for picture quality before making any conclusions. The Deaf advisor gave his hearing colleague a more detailed explanation to make him see the delay in the picture. The colleague then noticed the small interruptions in the transmission that would not interfere with a sound based conversation where the video is only supportive, but is seriously disruptive for a conversation in sign language. The Deaf advisor's expertise or visual authority was no longer questioned.[6]

The mixed role as a delegate from a public authority or as an engineer, and a videophone/video interpreting service user was not unique to this conference. There are at least two companies in Sweden that specialise in developing and manufacturing videophones targeted at sign language users, and several of the engineers in these companies are Deaf or have Deaf family members. The two companies target their activities and products at customers in Sweden and beyond, are involved in international telecommunication standardisation and development projects and deliver videophone communication solutions to several countries, including Norway and the United States. During a visit to one of these companies a few months after the seminar, the engineers were working with the procurement documents from a regional authority in an area of Sweden with a large population. The specifications in the documents for user interfaces, interoperability with other videophones, cost issues and text standards were discussed in different constellations of co-workers, who continuously made references to discussions with panels of expert users, competitors and their own products, video interpreting, generic softphones (computer software for making telephone calls), various protocols for transmitting digital information, as well as internal resource management. There was a very visible process of designing the next version of their videophone, and they worked to make their product fit in a vast infrastructure of digital standards, public documents and specifications, and familiar software interfaces. In a meeting between a Deaf engineer and one of the expert users on their user panel, the dialogue was peppered with references to existing software and the digital infrastructure. Through participation in discussions on international standardisation, Swedish engineers are also involved in attempts to improve digital infrastructure to ensure that the high demands Deaf people have for digital video compression and information submission becomes the general standard. Videophones are thus not only constructed as a 'telephone' for sign language. The videophone also places sign languages in the innovation frontier, and makes sign languages and their users a reference standard for all digital video communication. The primary users of sign language (Deaf people), are identified both as experts in the development of these videophones as well as the primary users of the results of the innovation process. It seems however, that the role of the Deaf expert that is established through the innovation process is accompanied by the quite different role of Deaf people defined as people who need the assistance of technology.

Assisted by technology

The largest group at the seminar was advisors from regional medical-rehabilitation centres and public employment offices, responsible for providing videophones for home and work-place uses respectively. With the implementation of the EU Directive, the regional authorities become a target market group for developers and manufacturers of videophones. The regional authorities procure videophones to distribute them to Deaf people who apply for, and have the right to receive videophones as an assistive technology. The criteria for being granted a videophone in Sweden is a medical diagnosis and a statement explaining why a videophone is necessary. This legal regulation makes the provision of videophones a health issue.

Inga, a Swedish Deaf woman, has years of experience with videophones and video interpreting services at work. Through her work and her involvement with the local Deaf club, Inga also has a consultative position in her local Deaf community. She has both personal and professional experience with the system for provision of videophones, and explained the application procedure and her opinion about it.

> Often, those applying for a videophone must be interviewed on why they want a videophone. I think it is crazy. Everyone should just get one, but no – you have to motivate and explain why you need one. It should be a matter of course, but it is almost like a visit to the doctor where you are examined, and then you have to wait for an answer, and it may take a year before your application is considered, a decision is made and you get the videophone.
>
> (Inga, 60, Sweden)

In the quotation at the beginning of this chapter, Inga stated that the videophone is a communication technology with which she can use a language experienced as natural to her. She does not see videophones as a medical technology, which is how she feels the distribution system defines the videophones. Her experience with the 'medicalisation' of videophones when Deaf people request a videophone at home seems to collide with the competency and agency associated with the videophone in her office. Her relationship to the videophone resembles the relationship the above-mentioned engineers establish: the videophone is an advanced technology which creates the possibility to use what is a natural language to her for distant communication. This reveals that the videophone is not an object with one single definition, but it exists in multiple practices. Inga is accustomed to view her videophone as an effective communication tool giving her the competency to act. At the same time, she cannot ignore the practice of the regional authority, which requires her to consent to a medical examination if she wants a dedicated videophone installed at home without having to cover the large cost herself. By comparing the application procedure to a medical examination, she reveals an experience of medicalisation of what she perceives as an ordinary need (to make phone calls).

The accessibility tool

In Sweden, videophones are not only a medical technology, or a telephone for sign language users, they are (like in Norway) also a tool for using video interpreting services. The political motivation behind the video interpreting service in Sweden is to increase disabled people's accessibility to telecommunication services. The video interpreting service is procured by the telecommunication authority and operated and marketed by a regional sign language interpreter agency. The regional agency's subsidiary Bildtelefoni.net is currently the only provider of video interpreting services, and provides services to Deaf people all over Sweden.

In Inga's interview she emphasised the efficiency of the video interpreting service, in particular when compared to the text relay service; however there are still problems, which hold back a full sense of independence. Johan's experience for example is quite typical.

> I am a bit annoyed by the hours of operation. If I need to call in the morning I have to wait until they open at eight. It is closed if I need to call for a taxi after a party in the evening. And sometimes there are long queues before noon, busy signals and difficulty in getting through. Lots of work time is lost that way.
>
> (Johan, 30, Sweden)

The videophone could be defined in several ways, and in Sweden these definitions retain and confirm Deaf people's status as both users of medical technology and cutting-edge users of visual communication technologies. In a third definition, the videophone is also an accessibility tool to include a group which is excluded from the general telecommunication network. The 'accessibility tool' definition is closely related to the definitions brought forth by the engineers (advanced technology) and the regional authorities (medical technology). Provision of videophones and video interpreting services distributes agency to Deaf people by enabling distant communication in sign language. At the same time, organising a service with limited operating hours and capacity reinforces the restrictions Inga experienced when she first applied for a new videophone: that the flow of agency cannot be taken for granted. Inga and Johan are repeatedly made aware of their dependence on a system that works. The service is not rendered completely seamless to Swedish users, and they still find themselves in a position where they are explicitly faced with their reliance on the capacity of and access to the video interpreting service.

The Swedish network appeared as a composition of different definitions of the videophones, the video interpreting service and Deaf people, and the Deaf users of videophones relate to several of these at the same time. The flow of agency is not directed univocally to the Deaf users (as in the United States), and they alternate between several roles: a competent technology operator; a person with a medical condition; and as people who experience exclusion and needs measures to increase their access to society. This multiplicity is also a testimony to a plurality of actors. The system appears as more complex than the systems for video interpreting in the United States and in Norway. In the United States, the sign language interpreters have few if any roles other than being mere operators in what is considered a telecommunication business, while the Norwegian system is all about providing sign language interpreting services – even though more than two-thirds of the assignments are interpretation of telephone calls (NAV, 2010).

Constructing categories – demarcating roles

Though quite new, the video interpreting services described in this chapter do not represent or provide a whole new set of roles and responsibilities for the users in the three countries. They are invented as well as implemented in structures that give the users certain roles. Videophones delegate responsibilities and competencies to the users, whether these are interpreters, Deaf people or technicians, but as has been shown, there is also a process of reductionism involved. The process of reductionism has been particularly strong in the United States and Norway, where one definition dominates the distribution of videophones and video interpreting service provision. However, the multiple and parallel definitions in Sweden show that the video interpreting service and the videophone need not be confined or reduced to being either a telecommunication tool, an accessibility tool or a tool to access interpreters. The technology and the service have the potential to be all of these, and more. The different aspects of video interpreting also show that the same technology has different uses and definitions among various groups and people within a society, and over time. Surely, the reductionism which is embedded in the process of inventing and organising the technology and the related service is demarcated, as well as institutionally embedded in different political systems? As such, they also contribute to a stabilisation and naturalisation of these political systems (Haualand, 2011; Jasanoff, 2004). Hence, establishing video interpreting services also demarcate and 'naturalise' the roles and positions of the actors that are involved whether these are the interpreters, the engineers or the Deaf end users.

Videophones and the video interpreting services may indeed open up new communication possibilities for sign language using Deaf people, and increase accessibility and participation. However, in the organisation of these services there are also processes that simplify and demarcate the potential uses of the service, and certain aspects may be silenced. The initial quotes testified to a similarity in experiences of the video interpreting service across the diverse systems for providing and defining this service and its users. Kari, Inga and Tom are part of networks of humans (themselves and the interpreters to name a few) and non-humans (the videophone, the studio, the digital infrastructure and more), but the potential of this network to extend their capabilities varies. All the people interviewed do indeed engage in a sequence of actions with material entities and actors with different roles. These roles are not new, since they did not come with the videophones, but were both confirmed and slightly adjusted with the new technology and service. The Americans' roles and rights as telecommunication consumers are reiterated by the efficiency with which they can reach the service. The Norwegians live in a country where the right to sign language interpreters is among the most extensive in the world, and the videophone is a further expansion of this right. The Swedes participate in a service using a technology which appears to be at the vanguard of modern telecommunication, but is still defined as a medical technology via the distribution process. None of these Deaf people uses the video interpreting service in complete isolation. When they engage in the chain of video interpreting, they are also part of networks that differ from country to country. Hence, they perform different roles when they engage in using video interpreting services, despite the similarity in their experience of flow, ease and blending in with the technology and the service at the moment they use it.

Notes

1 International discourse related to video interpreting services often use video relay Service with the abbreviation VRS as a common name for the services provided in a growing number of countries worldwide. In this chapter, the concept 'video interpreting' (or 'video interpreting services') is used as the general term, unless it has been important to emphasise that a particular national system is discussed. The reason for this is the prevailing position VRS has in the United States, and its specific reference to a telecommunications service. In the United States, there is a sharp demarcation between VRS and video remote interpreting (where the signer and non-signer are at the same site), and the visibility of the latter is diminutive compared to discussions about video relay services. The telecommunication aspect is one of several possible definitions or ways to organise the service (Haualand, 2011, 2014), therefore the more 'neutral' concept 'video interpreting' is used here.

2 The interviews were videotaped and later translated to English from American, Swedish or Norwegian Sign Language.

3 Until 2009, videophones did not have regular telephone numbers, and could only be 'called' via IP-addresses. The implementation of ten-digit numbers for videophones in the United States was a step towards ensuring functional equivalence, since a ten-digit number would make videophones less 'different' from other telephones, and make it less discouraging to call a videophone (via the video relay service) from a regular telephone.

4 Sorenson and Communication Services for the Deaf (CSD) are two major video relay service providers.

5 Private persons may download an application with a licence to call the video interpreting service from a computer, tablet or smartphone.

6 This could also be an indication that Deaf people have a slightly enhanced visual capacity, as also has been indicated by cognitive scientists (Bavelier, 2002; Bavelier *et al.*, 2006; Emmorey *et al.*, 1993).

References

Akrich, M. (1992). The De-Scription of Technical Objects. In W. E. Bijker & J. Law (Eds.), *Shaping technology/building society: studies in sociotechnical change*. Cambridge, Mass.: MIT Press.

Bavelier, D. (2002). Changes in the Spatial Distribution of Visual Attention after Early Deafness. *Journal of Cognitive Neuroscience, 14*(5), 687–701.

Bavelier, D., Dye, M. W. G., & Hauser, P. C. (2006). Do deaf individuals see better? *Trends in Cognitive Sciences, 10*(11), 512–518.

Callon, M. (1986). Some Elements of a Sociology of Translation: Domestication of the Scallops and the Fishermen of St Brieuc Bay *Power, Action and Belief*. London, Boston and Henley: Routledge & Kegan Paul.

Emmorey, K., Kosslyn, S. M., & Bellugi, U. (1993). Visual Imagery and Visual-spatial Language: Enhanced Imagery Abilities in Deaf and Hearing ASL Signers. *Cognition, 46,* 139–181.

European Union. (2004). *Directive 2004/17/EC of the European Parliament and of the Council of 31 March 2004 coordinating the procurement procedures of entities operating in the water, energy, transport and postal services sectors.*

Haualand, H. (2011). Interpreted Ideals and Relayed Rights – Video Interpreting Services as Objects of Politics. *Disability Studies Quarterly, 31*(4) http://dsq-sds.org/article/view/1721/1769.

Haualand, H. (2014). Video Interpreting Services: Calls for Inclusion or Redialling Exclusion? *Ethnos, 79*(2), 287–305.

Jasanoff, S. (2004). Ordering Knowledge, Ordering Society. In S. Jasanoff (Ed.), *States of Knowledge. The Co-production of Science and Social Order.* London: Routledge.

Latour, B. (2000). *Pandora's hope: essays on the reality of science studies.* Cambridge, MA: Harvard University Press.

Moore, S. F. (2005). Comparisons: Possible and Impossible. *Annual Review of Anthropology, 34*(1), 1–11. doi: 10.1146/annurev.anthro.34.081804.120535.

Moser, I. (2003). *Road traffic accidents: the ordering of subjects, bodies and disability.* Oslo: University of Oslo.

NAV. (2010). Sum anrop. In J. Hansen (Ed.), (E-mail ed.). Oslo NAV.

NAV. (2013). Bildetolktjenesten. 2013, from http://www.nav.no/helse/hjelpemidler/tolketjenesten/183114.cms (accessed April 2014).

Oudshoorn, N., Brouns, M., & van Oost, E. (2005). Diversity and Distributed Agency in the Design and Use of Medical Video-Communication Technologies. *Inside the politics of technology: agency and normativity in the co-production of technology and society.* Amsterdam: Amsterdam University Press.

Sørensen, E. (2010). Producing Multi-sited Comparability. In T. Scheffer & J. Niewöhner (Eds.), *Thick comparisons – reviving the ethnographic aspiration.* Leiden and Boston: Brill.

Thevenot, L. (2002). Which Road to Follow? The Moral Complexity of 'Equipped' Humanity. In J. Law & A. Mol (Eds.), *Complexities: social studies of knowledge practices.* Durham, NC. Duke University Press.

14

READING OTHER MINDS

Ethical considerations on the representation of intellectual disability in fiction

Howard Sklar

> Every day he watched the "cool" kids torture the crap out of the fat, the
> ugly, the smart, the poor, the dark, the black, the unpopular, the African,
> the Indian, the Arab, the immigrant, the strange, the feminino, the gay –
> and in every one of these clashes he saw himself.
>
> (Díaz 2008: 274–75)

In fiction, authors often attempt to represent the minds of characters who are
significantly different from themselves, and in some cases different from most
people. On the one hand, this imaginative act allows us to extend ourselves
beyond our own experiences – to "see ourselves," as Junot Díaz suggests
above, in the struggles and loves and realities of others. Yet, even though this
extension of our imaginations through literature may or may not contribute
to our capacity to empathize with others (see, for instance, Hakemulder 2000;
Keen 2006, 2007; Sklar 2009, 2013c), the process of identification whereby
an author *creates* an Other also raises some important questions. How much
can a writer claim to understand or know of the experiences of another? If, as
Lundeen (2001: 92) suggests, "in literature, as in life, there are shared borders
of identity that we are compelled to recognize but cannot cross," how are we
to approach these "borders," and what would it mean for fiction generally if
authors were never to "cross" them? In this chapter, I will consider some of
the ethical implications of representing others in fiction by looking at several
narratives that attempt to portray the experiences of people with intellectual
disabilities. In examining these works, I will focus particularly on some of the
techniques that have been used to represent the minds of such characters. I
suggest that, whether through extreme flights of narrative experimentation or
excessive dependence on traditional or stereotypical tropes in characterization,

non-disabled authors apparently have felt entitled to represent this population with impunity, and often in ways that demean, diminish or misrepresent the lives of actual people with intellectual disabilities. In this sense, I argue, the representation of intellectual disability in fiction provides a paradigmatic case of the border crossing against which Lundeen warns – and that, indeed, most authors face in the act of creating fictional others.

On terminology and personhood

Before turning to the discussion of fictional characters, it is important to clarify my use of the term "intellectual disability." Nearly everyone who works in the area of Disability Studies recognizes the implications of the use of particular terms for the perception of people with intellectual disabilities by society, to say nothing of the effects of these designations on their own self-perception. Some of these terms – *intellectual disability, cognitive impairment, developmental disability,* and the now generally disfavored *mental retardation* – are clinically descriptive in the sense that they convey a set of diagnostic features related to the cognitive or mental functioning of the individual, but can also stigmatize and set apart the people to whom they are attached. For this reason, in part, Goodley *et al.* (2004) adopt the more general label *learning difficulties*, arguing that "it is the term preferred by many in the self-advocacy movement" (58; see also Koenig 2011: 3, 6). While I recognize the advantages of less stigmatizing terms in this context (see Goodley 2007; Goodley and Rapley 2001: 229), I have opted for *intellectual disability* and *people with intellectual disabilities* here and elsewhere (for instance, Sklar 2011, 2012, 2013a, 2013b), because this term more specifically delimits the range of disabilities in question while avoiding some of the negative connotations associated with the term *mental retardation*. Having said this, I hasten to emphasize that I approach all of these terms with considerable reservation, as well as a full awareness of the difficulties with, and inadequacies of, nearly all of the terminology surrounding this issue.[1]

Moreover, these misgivings are directly relevant to the question at hand. As I will suggest, many representations of intellectually disabled characters rely significantly on the use of stereotypes, tropes, and figurative language that tend to diminish readers' understanding of the lives of people with intellectual disabilities. In this sense, such portrayals essentially serve the same function as labels, providing a blanket perception of the individual that, as Shakespeare (2006: 71) notes, "means that the person's individuality – not only their personality, but also other aspects of their identity such as gender, sexuality and ethnicity – can be ignored, as the impairment label becomes the most prominent and relevant feature of their lives." In the case of people with intellectual disabilities, I claim, the prominence and accessibility of narratives – in both written and cinematic fiction – may turn seemingly innocuous stories into convenient and familiar labels, or archetypes, that allow readers and viewers to come to distorted understandings of the "types" of lives that these characters represent.

Some representative intellectually disabled characters

In recent years, I have examined a number of characters who might be labeled "intellectually disabled": Lennie Small, in Steinbeck's *Of Mice and Men* ([1937] 2006); Benjy Compson, in Faulkner's *The Sound and the Fury* ([1929] 1995); Charlie Gordon, in Daniel Keyes's *Flowers for Algernon* ([1966] 1994); Forrest Gump, in Winston Groom's novel *Forrest Gump* (1986); Mattis, in Norwegian author Tarjei Vesaas's *Fuglane* ([1957] 2005), or *The Birds* (1969); Chauncey Gardner, in Jerzy Kosinski's *Being There* ([1970] 1980), Maggie, in Toni Morrison's short story "Recitatif" (1997); Isaac, in Bernard Malamud's story "Idiots First" (1966); and Spiros Antonapoulos, in Carson McCullers's *The Heart is a Lonely Hunter* ([1940] 2008), among others. As this very partial list suggests, there is no shortage of intellectually disabled characters in fiction.

It would clearly be impossible to provide a complete survey of these representations here. I would however like to highlight some of the most important features in several of these works, in order to demonstrate my broader point – that authors take great liberties in representing the minds of such characters. In keeping with the title of my chapter, I will focus primarily on the class of narratives that purport to show the thoughts, or thought processes, of the protagonists, although I will have occasion later to consider how other narratives, viewing the characters as it were from the outside, also reveal the mental characteristics of their protagonists.

Perhaps the most extreme example of mental representation is that of Faulkner's Benjy in *The Sound and the Fury*, but we also find a clear example in the character of Charlie in Daniel Keyes's *Flower for Algernon*. Both narratives present a type of internal "voice," although the specific nature of that voice is different in each case. Indeed, as I suggested in my introduction, it is precisely the *assumption* of this "insider's perspective" on the part of the writer that makes these representations problematic. In the case of actual autobiographies and life histories, especially when subjects are actively involved in creating the form and content of the narrative, these can provide a genuine representation of the experience of the individual (see particularly Koenig 2011, Bogdan and Taylor 1994; also Couser 2001, Sklar 2012). However, in the case of fictional representations, with the possible exception of semi-autobiographical narratives, the author by definition is *not* the other whom he wishes to represent, and this makes the effort to portray the emotions and thoughts of another speculative, at best.

In *The Sound and the Fury*, this tension between the author's experience and that of the protagonist is particularly evident, since we are primarily dealing not with the *literal* voice of an intellectually disabled man as he verbally relates his experiences, but with an internal fictional "voice" that conveys his thought processes. Narrative theorists have applied a variety of terms to characterize Benjy's narrative voice. Cohn (1978) refers to this voice as "interior monologue," in the sense that we are made privy to the inner speech of the character. Palmer (2004: 24), on the other hand, prefers to describe it as "uninterrupted, unmediated free direct thought," in that we have direct access to the character's thoughts without the intervention of another narrator or narrative "tags" such as "Benjy thought." However it's defined or termed, Benjy's thoughts skip – as Cohn suggests, in "radically dechronologized" fashion (1978: 182) – from one remembrance to the next. The narrative is frequently difficult to follow, due to the fact that Benjy's thoughts break off in mid-event and move suddenly to the remembrance of another event. A single example will serve to convey the general features of this type of monologue:

> "Hello, Benjy." Caddy said. She opened the gate and came in and stooped down. Caddy smelled like leaves. "Did you come to meet me." she said. "Did you come to meet Caddy. What did you let him get his hands so cold for, Versh."
>
> "I told him to keep them in his pockets." Versh said. "Holding on to that ahun [iron] gate."
>
> "Did you come to meet Caddy." she said, rubbing my hands. "What is it. What are you trying to tell Caddy." Caddy smelled like trees and like when she says we were asleep.
>
> *What are you moaning about, Luster said. You can watch them again when we get to the branch. Here. Here's you a jimson weed. He gave me the flower. We went through the fence, into the lot.*
>
> "What is it." Caddy said "What are you trying to tell Caddy.
>
> (Faulkner [1929] 1995: 4, emphasis original)

In this passage, the italicized portion shifts the focus from Benjy's recollection of an encounter with his sister, Caddy, to a separate incident in which Luster, the son of the Compson family's maid, comments on Benjy's behavior. These shifts occur throughout the narrative and complicate readers' ability to locate the events in place and time.

In addition to this scattered, dechronologized form of narration, there are a number of ways in which Benjy's "voice" seems intended to imply his intellectual difference. Returning again to the passage just cited, we find Caddy, who is perhaps the most sensitive to his needs, trying to find out what Benjy wants: "Did you come to meet Caddy." And then: "What is it. What are you trying to tell Caddy." Caddy's questions suggest Benjy's apparent inability to articulate what he wants or needs or feels in this instance. Yet, Benjy apparently doesn't register them as questions, as the absence of question marks and the repeated use of "Caddy *said*" (never "Caddy *asked*") indicate. Indeed, we are left wondering the extent to which Benjy actually understands the conversations and events that he records, since he never expresses his opinion or tells what he feels in response to the things that he perceives.

Complicating our efforts to sort out the nature of Benjy's thoughts and perceptions is the constructed, aesthetic quality of the narrative itself. As Scholes and Kellogg (1966) suggest, Faulkner here "retreats from a purely mimetic concept of characterization" by introducing a more poetic verbal pattern into the monologue. What results is a kind of super stream of consciousness in which the character's limited mind accounts for an excessive distortion of normal thought patterns, which communicates all the more effectively on a level well above anything the character himself may be supposed capable of achieving.

(199–200)

This distinction between Benjy's presumed cognitive abilities and the heightened "level" of the narration may be significant in identifying Faulkner's artistry, but it also obscures the very natural inclination on the part of readers to associate Benjy with real-life counterparts – to imagine a human presence behind the fictional artifice. In this sense, while the narrative may possess tendencies that signal a "retreat" from a traditionally realistic form of representation, our inclination is to regard Benjy as a human being, rather than simply a character. Yet, the narrative frustrates this inclination, as suggested earlier, in that Benjy never rises even to the level of a complete character; indeed, he remains an alien being, at best, and a non-entity perhaps for many.

By contrast, Charlie Gordon in *Flowers for Algernon* is more self-aware, and certainly more intellectually capable. *Flowers* is comprised of short journal entries, or "progress reports," that Charlie has been asked to write in order to record the results of an experimental neurological operation that, if successful, will make him highly intelligent. Charlie's development through the course of the novel, and particularly his ability, as his intelligence increases, to analyze his own previous intellectual disability and to explain his experiences to his testers (and to us as readers) provides a fairly significant and moving example of character disclosure, and particularly of insight into the experiences of an intellectually disabled man. More troubling, though, are the stereotypical tropes with which we are introduced to the character in the first few journal entries. Our first exposure to this voice, at the beginning of the novel, gives an immediate sense of Charlie and his capabilities:

progris riport 1 martch 3

Dr Strauss says I shoud rite down what I think and remembir and evrey thing that happins to me from now on. I dont no why but he says its importint so they will see if they can use me. I hope they use me because Miss Kinnian says mabye they can make me smart. I want to be smart. My name is Charlie Gordon I werk in Donners bakery where Mr Donner gives me 11 dollars a week and bred or cake if I want. I am 32 yeres old and next munth is my brithday.

I tolld dr Strauss and perfesser Nemur I cant rite good but he says it dont matter he says I shud rite just like I talk and like I rite compushishens in Miss Kinnians class at the beekmin collidge center for retarded adults where I go to lern 3 times a week on my time off.

(Keyes [1966] 1994: 1)

The author, Daniel Keyes, uses broad strokes here – misspellings, the lack of awareness of the ways in which the experimenters are evaluating him – to portray Charlie's intellectual disability. On some level, as is often the case with intellectually disabled characters, readers are meant to feel "sad" for Charlie, as well as share his eagerness for the procedure that will deliver him from his pitiable state. In this sense, the novel follows a familiar tendency to view disabled figures according to what Carlson refers to as the "personal tragedy model," in the sense that their disability is seen as "objectively bad, and thus something to be pitied, a personal tragedy for both the individual and her family, something to be prevented and, if possible, cured" (Carlson 2010: 5; see also Goodley and Rapley 2001: 230). Indeed, late in the novel, Charlie looks at his reflection in the mirror and sees an intellectually disabled "other self," not in the form of recollections but as a distinct and separate individual, and it is in this instance that we gain a clear sense of how the hyper-intelligent Charlie sees his "less-developed" self:

> I don't know how I knew it was Charlie and not me. Something about the dull, questioning look in his face. His eyes, wide and frightened, as if at one word from me he would turn and run deep into the dimension of the mirrored world. But he didn't run. He just stared back at me, mouth open, jaw hanging loosely.
>
> (Keyes [1966] 1994: 175)

The "dullness" of the "look in his face," as well as the "loosely" hanging mouth, are staples of the stereotypical representation of people with intellectual disabilities.[2]

We see similar tendencies in *The Sound and the Fury*, when, in a later section, a character describes Benjy as

> a big man who appeared to have been shaped of some substance whose particles would not or did not cohere to one another or to the frame which supported it. His skin was dead-looking and hairless; dropsical too, he moved with a shambling gait like a trained bear. His hair was pale and fine. It had been brushed smoothly down upon his brow like that of children in daguerreotypes. His eyes were clear, of the pale sweet blue of cornflowers, his thick mouth hung open, drooling a little.
>
> ([1929] 1995: 233)

Here again we find a number of tropes typical of the representation of people with intellectual disabilities: the "thick mouth" that "hangs open"; the association with animals – here, a bear – and with children. Yet, even though Benjy is merely "*like* a trained bear" or his brow is "*like* that of children," there can be little doubt that, for the narrator, he is Other in both appearance and nature, from the "dead-looking" skin to the fact that he "appeared to have been shaped" in ways that are distinctly unlike other human beings. Significantly, we find a similar account in the description of Lennie in *Of Mice and Men*, who, we are told, is

> a huge man, shapeless of face, with large, pale eyes, with wide, sloping shoulders; and he walked heavily, dragging his feet a little, the way a bear drags his paws. His arms did not swing at his sides, but hung loosely.
>
> (Steinbeck [1937] 2006: 2)

As Halliwell notes, these associations with animals and children contribute significantly to our perceptions of the character's intellectual difference: "Lennie's 'shapeless' features and 'heavy' walk mark him out as an idiot figure, with his large size, his proximity to animals (bear) … reinforcing his lack of freewill and rationality" (Halliwell 2004: 144).

In each of these novels, then, despite their general sensitivity to the lives of the characters that they portray, we find descriptive features that suggest distortion, shapelessness, a decided lack of what we would normally define as *human*. Zunshine (2006) has argued that, as readers, we make use of the real-life cognitive skill called Theory of Mind, which involves, in part, "ascrib[ing] to a person a certain mental state on the basis of her observable action (e.g., we see her reaching for a glass of water and assume that she is thirsty" (6). In terms of the application of this skill to fiction, she suggests, "We all learn, whether consciously or not, that the default interpretation of behavior reflects a character's state of mind, and every fictional story that we read reinforces our tendency to make that kind of interpretation first," (3–4). Consequently, I claim that the physical features of the characters that I have discussed above imply the minds that reflect those qualities, whether the disclosure of these minds is overt, as in the cases of Benjy and Charlie, or suggestive, as in the case of Lennie.

Archetypes of intellectual disability: a survey of characters

What we find is that most of these characters fall into specific categories, in that they possess general, indeed stereotypical, mostly unflattering qualities according to which people with intellectual disabilities are sometimes identified in the popular imagination.[3] Of the characters mentioned at the beginning of this essay, we find:

- The Animal (Lennie, Benjy)
- The Wise Fool (Chauncey Gardner, Forrest Gump)
- The Uncontrollable Monster (Lennie)
- The Big Oaf (Lennie)
- The Cipher (Benjy, Isaac)
- The Blank Slate (Benjy, Forrest Gump)
- The Slovenly Dullard (Antanoupolos)
- The Genial Simpleton (Charlie).

We can see that these characters in some sense fall into what Frye ([1957] 1971) defines as archetypes, or "associative clusters" (102), in that the features that are used in each of the representations serve as shortcuts for readers to identify characters in particular ways. These archetypal figures, in turn, each possess characteristics that are reflective of particular types of *minds*. Thus, there is not one "idiot figure," to use Halliwell's (2004) term, but several different types that may or may not have characteristics in common. Moreover, few of these descriptors can be said to be positive, although the very fact that Lennie and Benjy fall into several archetypal categories suggests that they are more complex, more human, in terms of their modes of representation than others that serve more symbolic or suggestive functions within their respective narratives.

In terms of function, such "archetypal" figures can be seen as a form of *narrative prosthesis*: According to Mitchell and Snyder (2000: 49), many disabled characters in fiction serve as "a crutch upon which literary narratives lean for their representational power, disruptive potential, and analytical insight." In other words, the specific features of these characters derive less from the impulse to reveal human experience than to serve the larger aims – symbolic, aesthetic, satirical, social, political, etc. – of the narratives of which they are constituent parts. Halliwell (2004: 14) somewhat resists this view, claiming that with many such characters there is "an inner lack of coherence," with the relatively felicitous result that "idiot figures are often 'open' characters in process rather than fixed functions." He points especially to "modernist and postmodernist writing in which characters are rarely stable entities: sometimes fragmentary, sometimes incomplete, and sometimes discontinuous." Yet, even though such characters may lack the continuity of their more realistic counterparts, I suggest that it is virtually impossible for us *not* to respond even to "fragmentary" postmodernist characters as though they were essentially "like people," since the features by which we identify them most closely resemble those of human beings. It is precisely for this reason, moreover, that the decidedly *non-human* characteristics that we find associated with intellectually disabled characters are so problematic. Indeed, it would be difficult for readers to dissociate their impressions of Benjy and Lennie generally from the very animalistic and childlike features described above. Even Charlie Gordon, who very decidedly *develops* in the course of *Flowers*, does so by *growing out of intellectual disability*. His disability, then, remains something fixed, something he looks back on, something relatively static, however complex his characterization may be.

By contrast, one of the most revealing aspects of the characterization of Mattis in Vesaas's *The Birds* is that he doesn't truly fit any of the archetypes (or any others that we might devise). Indeed, while he occasionally shows signs of several of these categories, he never is *reduced* to any of them. For instance, at one point in the novel, Mattis's sister, Hege, expresses concern about something that she fears Mattis will do. Mattis replies, "You don't need to worry, Hege, I know what I can and can't do" (1969: 214 [(1957) 2005: 198]). Shortly after this, he adds, "Do you suppose I haven't been *thinking*?" and the narrator tells us –

or perhaps Mattis's thoughts tell us – "The word they normally avoided for Mattis's sake – and here he was using it himself, carefully and deliberately" (1969: 215 [(1957) 2005: 199]). The presumption is that Mattis cannot tell the difference between what he "can and can't do" – and perhaps in this case he cannot. Yet his defiance also suggests all of the other ways that that presumption extends into the rest of his life, into all of the things that he endeavors to do. Mattis is known as "Simple Simon" in the village – "*Mattis Tust*" in Norwegian – and he is locked in this role in a way that largely determines his sense of his own identity – that in fact turns him into a living archetype. Thus, at one point in the novel he thinks, "Everyone was clever except him" (1969: 97 [(1957) 2005: 91]). In the last pages of the novel, Mattis tries to face this identity, thinking, "*One person's like this, another's like that.* . . . That was as near as he dared come to thinking about it" (1969: 222, emphasis original [(1957) 2005: 205]). In this way, as I have pointed out at length elsewhere (Sklar 2013b), the author treads a fine line between trying to imagine the experiential world of Mattis and recognizing the limitations of his own authorial agency.

These boundaries are directly explored in *Flowers for Algernon*. As Charlie develops greater intelligence and begins to look analytically at his previous life as an intellectually disabled man, he realizes that there is no one else who can tell his story, no one else who has lived in both worlds. Charlie's observation about his own, unique status thus raises the question: Who is most equipped to tell the stories of people with intellectually disabilities? Of course, in Charlie's case, the words are not those of an intellectually disabled man, but of the novelist. Who, then, is Daniel Keyes, and by what authority does he speak for Charlie?

Narrative ethics and the representation of intellectual disability

The issue of authors *speaking for* people with intellectual disabilities lies at the heart of my investigation. One of the emphases in my research has been to look at how *actual* intellectually disabled individuals tell their own stories – in keeping with one of the central aims of the Disability Rights movement generally: "to determine and relate their own stories" (Gilson *et al.*, 1997: 16; cited in Shakespeare 2006: 68). While an examination of autobiographical narratives is beyond the scope of this chapter, I wish to emphasize several points that relate closely to the issue at hand.

Already in 1986, Levine and Langness (1986) observe of their own research into the life stories of people with intellectual disabilities: "It is only through their voices, and the careful examination of what they say and do in everyday life that we can fully interpret their behavior independently of the label of retardation" (191). In other words, by relying on the voices of people with intellectual disabilities scholars of disability can become familiar with experiences that abstract labels or diagnostic categories do not fully illuminate. Since that time, this emphasis on fidelity to the actual voices of "people who have lived it"

(Bogdan and Taylor 1994: 30) has remained a guiding principle among many ethnographers.[4] Similarly, Savarese (a neurologist) and Zunshine (a cognitive literary scholar) have pointed to "the difference between the privileged outsider view and the newly empowered insider one" (Savarese and Zunshine 2014: 18), and have encouraged the use of "neurodiverse teams" (19) in considering the lives (in the case of their own research) of autistic individuals. Ultimately, they advocate what Savarese terms "neurocosmopolitanism ..., the idea of a trans-neurocommunity, the feeling of being respectfully at home with all manner of neurologies" (20).

This ability to feel "at home" in other neurologies, clearly, is one of the benefits of reading the life stories of people with intellectual disabilities,[5] and it is this supposed capacity to provide the "inside view" that makes fictional representations of intellectually disabled characters compelling, especially from a neurocosmopolitan sensibility. From this perspective, we would certainly be justified in asking if the intellectually disabled characters that we find in fiction would be recognized as "true" by people who, however different they may be from each other, share some or many of the attributes of intellectual disability, or who have formally received that diagnosis. Or are they simply narrative prosthetic "crutches" that bear little resemblance to the lives of real people?

Or, perhaps more problematically, do such narratives – however well-intentioned and sympathetic to the characters they portray – primarily convey essentialist notions of the experiences of people with intellectual disabilities? Zunshine (2014: 21) warns of this possibility, when she suggests that the "mindreading" by which Theory of Mind frequently is understood "might as well [be]... called ... mind misreading," in that,

> more often than not it actually *limits* our perception and interpretation and lures us into insidious cognitive traps. For instance, it is vulnerable to essentialist thinking (e.g., just consider how easy it is for us to slide into believing that the capacity for complex mental states is what makes us "essentially" human), and as such can be used as an effective "trope of dehumanization" (Vermeule 2002: 87).
>
> (Zunshine, 2014: 21)

Similarly, most of the qualities associated with intellectually disabled characters emphasize and even exaggerate traits that imply an almost (and sometimes decidedly) insurmountable gap between them and the rest of humanity. As a result, fictional accounts of the lives of people with intellectual disabilities – rather than serving as empathetic bridges between readers and the actual experiences of these individuals – can instead become barriers to genuine "neurocosmopolitan" understanding.

Of course, fictional characters are not "real people." They are literary creations designed primarily to serve the aesthetic needs of the narratives in which appear. For this reason, the suggestion that many of the characters described in this chapter "misrepresent" the lives of actual people with intellectual disabilities may be highly problematic for literary scholars. To criticize a work of narrative fiction for misrepresenting people with intellectual disabilities, however, is not to say that all characters need to possess certain characteristics, or to be "positive," or to be simplified so that everyone can "get it." Rather, I am suggesting that they be made more *complicated* by ensuring that they are as dynamic and varied as the broad range of experiences of actual intellectually disabled people. "Accuracy," indeed, means here "true" to the types of experiences that people with intellectual disabilities experience, whether or not they have actually gone through them themselves, and however distant from the experience of the character their own experiences may be.

Perhaps it is unreasonable to expect ordinary readers to notice or to bother with such matters. But it is certainly fair, I suggest, to expect literary scholars and students of literature to examine some of the assumptions that have led them to overlook, ignore, or forgive on "aesthetic" grounds the features of fictional narratives that have consistently skewed readers' perceptions of people with intellectual disabilities. I also believe that it is entirely reasonable for readers to expect that novelists not cross these "borders of identity," as Lundeen (2001: 92) calls them, without great care, and that the results of that border crossing be subject to examination regarding the accuracy of the work.

Notes

1 See Burke (2008), Carlson (2010) and Koenig (2011) for overviews of the difficulties inherent in some of these terms. In addition, Biasini *et al.* (2009) provide a historical review of the term *mental retardation* in particular. Bogdan and Taylor (1994: 3–25, 205–25) and Edgerton (1993: 216–34) also engage in critical (and sometimes conflicting) assessments of the label *mentally retarded*, and of the process of labeling generally. For related discussions of *disability* itself, see Harris (2010), Gilman (2002: 271), Goodley and Rapley (2001), Carlson (2010: 86–101), and Shakespeare (2006).
2 For a thorough analysis of this representation, see Sklar (2013a).
3 Kriegel (1987) develops a similar argument – albeit with a different and more limited set of "categories" – in identifying the features present in representations of what he calls "The Cripple in Literature."
4 See, for instance, Sklar (2012: 125–36), for an overview of approaches to the life stories of people with intellectual disabilities.
5 The advantages of the "insider view" are sometimes offset, however, by the difficulty sometimes in knowing whose voice has been represented through sometimes heavily edited autobiographical narratives. On this issue, see for instance Sklar (2012), Couser (2001), and Coogan (2007).

References

Biasini, Fred J., Lisa Grupe, Lisa Huffman, and Norman W. Bray (2009) Mental retardation: a symptom and a syndrome, in Sandra D. Netherton, Deborah Holmes, and C. Eugene Walker, eds. *Child and Adolescent Psychological Disorders: A Comprehensive Textbook*. Oxford: Oxford University Press. Accessed online at: http://www.ibis-birthdefects.org/ start/mentalSyndrome.htm.

Bogdan, Robert and Steven J. Taylor (1994) *The Social Meaning of Mental Retardation: Two Life Stories*, New York, Teachers College Press.

Burke, Lucy (2008) Introduction: thinking about cognitive impairment, *Journal of Literary Disability* 2.1: i–iv.

Carlson, Licia (2010) *The Faces of Intellectual Disability: Philosophical Reflections*, Bloomington, IN, Indiana University Press.

Cohn, Dorrit (1978) *Transparent Minds: Narrative Modes for Presenting Consciousness in Fiction*, Princeton, NJ, Princeton University Press.

Coogan, Tom (2007) Me, thyself and I: dependency and the issues of authenticity and authority in Christy Brown's *My Left Foot* and Ruth Sienkiewicz-Mercer and Steven B. Kaplan's *I Raise My Eyes to Say Yes*, *Journal of Literary Disability* 1.2: 42–54.

Couser, G. Thomas (2001) Making, taking, and faking lives: ethical problems in collaborative Life Writing, in Davis and Womack: 209–26.

Couser, G. Thomas (2002) Signifying bodies: life writing and disability studies. In Snyder et al.: 109–17.

Davis, Todd F. and Kenneth Womack, eds. (2001) *Mapping the Ethical Turn: A Reader in Ethics, Culture, and Literary Theory*, Charlottesville, VA, University Press of Virginia.

Díaz, Junot (2008) *The Brief Wondrous Life of Oscar Wao*, New York, Riverhead Books.

Edgerton, Robert B. (1993) *The Cloak of Competence: Revised and Updated*, Berkeley, CA, University of California Press.

Faulkner, William ([1929] 1995) *The Sound and the Fury*, London, Vintage.

Frye, Northrup ([1957] 1971) *Anatomy of Criticism: Four Essays*, Princeton, NJ, Princeton University Press.

Gartner, Alan and Tom Joe (1987) *Images of the Disabled, Disabling Images*, New York, Praeger.

Gilman, Sander L. (2002) 'The fat detective: obesity and disability,' in Sharon L. Snyder, Brenda Jo Brueggemann and Rosemarie Garland-Thomson (eds) *Disability Studies: Enabling the Humanities*, New York, MLA.

Gilson, Stephen French, Anthony Tusler, and Carol Gill (1997) Ethnographic research in disability identity: self-determination and community, *Journal of Vocational Rehabilitation* 9: 7–17.

Goodley, Dan (2007) 'Learning difficulties,' the social model of disability and impairment: challenging epistemologies, *Disability & Society* 16.2: 207–231.

Goodley, Dan, Rebecca Lawthom, Peter Clough, and Michele Moore (2004) *Researching Life Stories: Method, Theory and Analyses in a Biographical Age*, London, Routledge Falmer.

Goodley, Dan and Mark Rapley (2001) How do you understand 'learning difficulties'? Towards a social theory of impairment, *Mental Retardation* 39.3: 229–32.

Groom, Winston (1986) *Forrest Gump*, New York, NY, Washington Square Press.

Hakemulder, Jèmeljan (2000) *The Moral Laboratory: Experiments Examining the Effects of Reading Literature on Social Perception and Moral Self-Concept*, Amsterdam and Philadelphia, PA, John Benjamins.

Halliwell, Martin (2004) *Images of Idiocy: The Idiot Figure in Modern Fiction and Film*, Farnham, Ashgate.

Harris, James C. (2010) Developmental perspective on the emergence of moral personhood, in Kittay and Carlson: 55–73.

Kaufman, Sandra Z. (1986) Life history in progress: a retarded daughter educates her mother, in Langness and Levine: 33–45.

Keen, Suzanne (2006) A theory of narrative empathy, *Narrative* 14 (3): 207–36.

Keen, Suzanne (2007) *Empathy and the Novel*, Oxford and New York, NY, Oxford University Press.

Keyes, Daniel ([1966] 1994) *Flowers for Algernon*, London, Gollancz.

Kittay, Eva Feder and Licia Carlson (2010) *Cognitive Disability and Its Challenge to Moral Philosophy*. Chichester, Wiley-Blackwell.

Koenig, Oliver (2011) Any added value? Co-constructing life stories of and with people with intellectual disabilities, *British Journal of Learning Disabilities* 28: 213–221.

Kriegel, Leonard (1987) The crippled in literature, in Gartner and Joe: 31–46.

Kosinski, Jerzy ([1970] 1980) *Being There*, New York, NY, Bantam.

Langness, L. L. and Harold G. Levine, eds. (1986) *Culture and Retardation: Life Histories of Mildly Mentally Retarded Persons in American Society*. Dordrecht, D. Reidel.

Levine, H. G. and L. L. Langness (1986) Conclusions: themes in an anthropology of mild mental retardation. In Langness and Levine: 191–206.

Lundeen, Kathleen (2001) Who has the right to feel? The ethics of literary empathy. In Davis and Womack: 83–92.

Malamud, Bernard (1966) Idiots first, in Malamud, *Idiots First*, New York, NY, Dell.

McCullers, Carson ([1940] 2008) *The Heart is a Lonely Hunter*, New York, Penguin.

Mitchell, David T. (2002) Narrative prosthesis and the materiality of metaphor. In Snyder *et al.*: 15–30.

Mitchell, David T. and Sharon L. Snyder (2000) *Narrative Prosthesis: Disability and the Dependencies of Discourse*, Ann Arbor, MI, University of Michigan Press.

Morrison, Toni (1997) Recitatif. In Hazel Rochman and Darlene Z. McCampbell (eds.), *Leaving Home*, New York, HarperCollins.

Palmer, A. (2004) *Fictional Minds*, Lincoln and London, University of Nebraska Press.

Prendergast, Catherine (2001) On the rhetorics of mental disability. In James Wilson and Cynthia Lewiecki-Wilson (eds.) *Embodied Rhetorics: Disability in Language and Culture*, Carbondale, IL, Southern Illinois University Press: 45–60.

Savarese, Ralph James and Lisa Zunshine (2014) The critic as neurocosmopolite; or, what cognitive approaches to literature can learn from disability studies: Lisa Zunshine in conversation with Ralph James Savarese. *Narrative* 22.1: 17–44.

Scholes, Robert and Robert Kellogg (1966) *The Nature of Narrative*, Oxford, Oxford University Press.

Scholes, Robert and Robert Kellogg (1994) Cultural representation of disabled people: dustbins for disavowal? *Disability & Society* 9.3: 283–299.

Shakespeare, Tom (2006) *Disability Rights and Wrongs*, London, Routledge.

Sklar, Howard (2009) Narrative structuring of sympathetic response: theoretical and empirical approaches to Toni Cade Bambara's 'The Hammer Man.' *Poetics Today* 30.3: 561–607.

Sklar, Howard (2011) 'What the hell happened to Maggie?': stereotype, sympathy, and disability in Toni Morrison's 'Recitatif'. *Journal of Literary and Cultural Disability Studies* 5.2: 137–154. Special issue, 'Representing Disability and Emotion.'

Sklar, Howard (2012) Narrative empowerment through comics storytelling: facilitating the life stories of the intellectually disabled. *Storyworlds: A Journal of Narrative Studies* 4: 123–149.

Sklar, Howard (2013a) The many voices of Charlie Gordon: on the representation of Intellectual Disability in Daniel Keyes's *Flowers for Algernon*, in Kathryn Allan, ed. *Disability in Science Fiction: Representations of Technology as Cure*, New York, NY Palgrave Macmillan.

Sklar, Howard (2013b) 'Anything but a simpleton': the ethics of representing intellectual disability in Tarjei Vesaas's *The Birds*. In Jeremy Hawthorn and Jakob Lothe (eds.), *Narrative Ethics*. New York: Rodopi, Value Inquiry Book Series.

Sklar, Howard (2013c) *The Art of Sympathy in Fiction: Forms of Ethical and Emotional Persuasion*. Amsterdam and Philadelphia: John Benjamins (Linguistic Approaches to Literature series).

Snyder, Sharon L., Brenda Jo Brueggemann, and Rosemarie Garland–Thomson, eds. (2002) *Disability Studies: Enabling the Humanities*, New York, NY, Modern Language Association.

Steinbeck, John ([1937] 2006) *Of Mice and Men*, London, Penguin.

Vermeule, Blakey (2002) Satirical mind blindness. *Classical and Modern Literature* 22.2: 85–101.

Vesaas, Tarjei. (1969) *The Birds*. Translated by Torbjørn Støverud and Michael Barnes, New York, William Morrow.

Vesaas, Tarjei. ([1957] 2005) *Fuglane* [*The Birds*], Oslo, Gyldendal Norsk Forlag.

Whittemore, Robert D., L. L. Langness, and Paul Koegel (1986) The life history approach to mental retardation, in Langness and Levine: 1–18.

Zunshine, Lisa (2006) *Why We Read Fiction: Theory of Mind and the Novel*, Columbus, OH, The Ohio State University Press.

INDEX